WORLDVIEW APOLOGETICS

A Christian Worldview Apologetic Engagement
With Advaita Vedanta Hinduism

Pradeep Tilak

I dedicate this book to my wife, Sunita.

PREFACE

This book is an introduction to Christian Worldview Apologetics. It applies Worldview principles to engage Advaita Vedanta Hinduism with the biblical responses of Christianity. The Christian Worldview focus is as much theological as philosophical.

Chapter 1 introduces the biblical mandate for apologetics, reviewing the historical and contemporary apologetic scene. It highlights diverse methodological principles in Worldview apologetics, laying the groundwork for the method employed.

Chapter 2 introduces Vedanta Hinduism through the teachings of Sankara, Ramanuja, and Madhva. This is a primer for those unfamiliar with Advaita.

Chapter 3 examines Christian rapprochement and antithesis with Vedanta Hinduism. The apologist applies Worldview apologetics in understanding the access points and biblical dividing lines when these two worldviews confront one another.

Chapter 4 commences the apologetic engagement with proof. The Advaitin presents the monistic worldview and the ultimate reality, otherwise known as Brahman. The foundational Christian worldview is represented with the scriptures, God, man, and his salvation in Jesus Christ.

Chapter 5 addresses the offense part of apologetics. The adherents of each worldview contrast their viewpoints against the viewpoint of the other system. Vedanta's monism, impersonal reality, inclusivity, and rationality are contrasted with Christianity's historic self-revelation of God to man.

Chapter 6 handles apologetic defense through the lens of experience, epistemology, and correspondence with reality. The Hindu worldview has transcending experience, supra-rational epistemology, and deep coherence. The Christian admits a transitory universe, which has no existence as a contingent creation, apart from God.

Chapter 7 reviews Worldview apologetic practice under metaphysics, epistemology, and ethics. These deal with the ontology of reality in its manifestations and our understanding of the truth. It concludes with how we live out this knowledge today.

Chapter 8 addresses the personal, rather than technical tone of apologetics. Kierkegaard's engagement of the stubborn will helps us understand the radical nature of convictions. After presenting the Gospel worldview, the Vedanta position is shown to be impossible from those very paths that the Hindu trusts.

Chapter 9 culminates the study of Gospel-centered apologetics. The Gospel forms the core of the apologetic encounter, in content and methodology. This book opens the venue for more sound arguments to be built around the Gospel and to tear down false worldviews.

Chapter 10 makes final recommendations on practical Christian apologetics to Hindus. A biblically self-aware approach is commended to honor God in the defense of the faith.

This book is the fruit of my 2013 dissertation at Southern Seminary. It is the culmination of over a decade of spiritual and intellectual wrestling with the Christian truth set in the context of evangelism to Hindus, particularly those of the pantheistic persuasion. My prayer is that it would serve Christians to be faithful to God and loving toward man in apologetics.

Shrewsbury, Massachusetts.   Pradeep Tilak
August 17, 2015.

Table of Contents

3. CHRISTIAN APOLOGETICS TO VEDANTA

4. PROOF: PRESENTING THE CASE

5. OFFENSE: HIGHLIGHTING THE STRENGTHS

6. DEFENSE: RESPONDING TO CHARGES

8. PERSONAL APOLOGETICS

9. GOSPEL-CENTERED APOLOGETICS

10. THE PAST, THE PRESENT, AND THE FUTURE

CHAPTER 1

THE CONTEXT OF WORLDVIEW APOLOGETICS

Worldview apologetics is well situated on the lofty and majestic context of Christian apologetics. Currently there are a vast array of Christian apologetic methods and foci. These approaches provide both a defense against the intellectual attacks on Christianity while going on the offensive against false world systems. To explore the context of Worldview apologetics,[1] it helps to first delve into the broader biblical mandate for apologetics which grounds the enterprise. The contextual study will array broadly the principles and key methodological aspects of apologetics, before their specific elements are reused in the targeted context of Worldview apologetics.[2] The strengths and weaknesses of each method will be viewed primarily through the lens of Classical, Evidential, Reformed, and Fideistic apologetics.

While the content of apologetics largely frames the above methodologies, the ethical delivery of apologetics introduces additional criteria to evaluate apologetic encounters. The dangers facing the apologist will be examined in terms of faithfulness to God, to one's own integrity, and toward unbelievers. This will set up the gauge for success or failure in the intellectual, moral, and emotional honesty of the apologist.

Apologetics is sometimes seen as a purely philosophical activity, but Christian apologetics is a vital component of both theology and philosophy. Worldview apologetics can be broadly defined as the defense of the Christian worldview. Positively, it presents and defends biblical theology toward unbelief with evidence and reason. Negatively, it contrasts unbelieving worldviews as a whole against the gospel framework, critiquing foundational errors of unbelief that are untenable.[3] This effort is leveraged by Bryan Sims whose evangelical apologetic follows the flow of redemptive history to develop a biblical worldview expanding upon the Transcendental and Abduction approaches. He argues for

---

[1]A worldview is "how one views or interprets reality. The German word is *Weltanschauung*, meaning a 'world and life view,' or 'a paradigm.' It is the framework through which or by which one makes sense of the data of life. A worldview makes a world of difference in one's view of God, origins, evil, human nature, values, and destiny." Norman L. Geisler, *Baker Encyclopedia of Christian Apologetics* (Grand Rapids: Baker Books, 1999), 785.

[2]Francis J. Beckwith, William Lane Craig, and J. P. Moreland, *To Everyone an Answer: A Case for the Christian Worldview* (Downers Grove, IL: IVP, 2004), 9, 14-17.

[3]Steven B. Cowan, "Introduction," in *Five Views on Apologetics*, ed. Stanley N. Gundry and Steven B. Cowan (Grand Rapids: Zondervan, 2000), 8. Colin Grant, "Why Should Theology Be Unnatural?" *Modern Theology* 23 (2007): 103. Grant demands that theology challenge today's philosophy.

a biblical worldview analysis that follows the fundamental turning points of salvation and human history: creation-fall-redemption (CFR). These turning points or epochs are essential because of the universality of their scope, existential significance, and narrative nature. In addition, the CFR schema, with its universal and existential dimension, supplies evangelical apologists with abundant connecting points with dialogue partners.[4]

The Worldview apologetic in this book attempts a comprehensive application from a broad range of apologetic strategies within a biblical framework that is in the spirit of Sims' dissertation. To this end, it helps to first review the Christian theological mandate before looking into the philosophical outworking of that biblical charge.

Biblical Mandate

The Christian mandate for apologetics comes from various texts of Scripture.[5] 1 Peter 3:15 requires Christians to be prepared to make a defense ἀπολογία, from which the term apologetics is derived. This pericope is examined for the mandate:

> Now who is there to harm you if you are zealous for what is good? But even if you should suffer for righteousness' sake, you will be blessed. Have no fear of them, nor be troubled, but *in your hearts honor Christ the Lord as holy, always being prepared to make a defense to anyone who asks you for a reason for the hope that is in you*; yet do it with gentleness and respect, having a good conscience, so that, when you are slandered, those who revile your good behavior in Christ may be put to shame. For it is better to suffer for doing good, if that should be God's will, than for doing evil.[6]

Apologetics is typically a Christian response to an inquirer of the reason for our hope. In the milieu of these verses, the following apologetic aspects stand out:

The apologetic mandate is surrounded by verses on suffering. Suffering is also the overall theme of the book.[7] Peter makes it clear that the believer must not suffer for doing wrong, but rather must be zealous for doing good. In his exemplary life of goodness to the unbeliever in word and deed, the believer can expect suffering, including

---

[4]Bryan Billard Sims, "Evangelical Worldview Analysis: A Critical Assessment and Proposal" (Ph.D. diss., Southern Baptist Theological Seminary, 2006), 20. Sims' dissertation utilizes specific input to develop the Worldview apologetic in the CFR framework. This book broadens that approach, expanding the Transcendental approach to a fully Reformed, presuppositional method, while leveraging every apologetic method, including elements of Abduction by inferring the best explanation. Sims develops the works of epistemologist Robert Audi and philosopher of science Imre Lakatos. The breadth of Sims' approach is thus defended: "Each element of the CFR matrix possesses tremendous evidential potential in terms of commending the Christian worldview" (ibid., 20). Sims notes that his "apologetic approach might be appropriately dubbed 'presuppositional evidentialism,' but . . . the best strategy is [to call it] 'worldview apologetics'" (ibid., 23). See also William A. Dembski and Jay Wesley Richards, eds., *Unapologetic Apologetics: Meeting the Challenges of Theological Studies* (Downers Grove, IL: InterVarsity Press, 2001), 15: "Apologetics must never be divorced from the offense of the gospel."

[5]Some key apologetic texts include: 1 Pet 3:15, 2 Cor 10:5, Phil 1:7, 16, Jude 3, Titus 1:9, and 2 Tim 2:24-25. It can be argued that the entire Scripture, as God's revelation to man, provides reasons for the Christian hope as an extended apologetic. It primarily answers the questions of the believer and instrumentally responds to the unbeliever through what is commonly called apologetics.

[6]1 Pet 3:13-17.

[7]Travis B. Williams, "Suffering from a Critical Oversight: The Persecutions of 1 Peter within Modern Scholarship," *Currents in Biblical Research* 10 (2012): 284.

slander and persecution, on account of the gospel. This suffering is a blessing from God and not viewed as a failure of apologetics. Misunderstanding and willful misrepresentation of unbelievers does not hinder the Christian apologist. However, any apologist doing evil directly hinders the task. This urges the Worldview apologist to self-examine his apologetic methods since sinful actions will not just result in his personal suffering, but also impact the effectiveness of his apologetic to unbelievers.

Apologetics is also to be done without fear of those who cause suffering.[8] Christians can be calm inwardly when assaulted from the outside by questions and more. This assurance is accomplished by honoring Christ the Lord as holy. This honor theme is central to Worldview apologetics – by exalting Christ as Lord, one no longer fears any assaults, but maintains a high view of God and his holiness right in its midst. By trusting in God one has great confidence in him. This poise enables the apologist to not fear the unbelievers' arguments or to lose his peace in the heat of the debate. The fear of man and of defeat is thus replaced by a godly fear which prepares one to rightly defend the faith.

This central text on apologetics requires Christians to make a defense or give a reason for their hope.[9] The Christian response substantiates the hope that all Christians have. Alvin Plantinga presents some persuasive defensive arguments using the concept of basic beliefs. The response must engage the unbelievers' questions with sound arguments and present the gospel truth in clear terms, explaining why the Christian belief is true.[10] Worldview-wise, the Christian viewpoint is primarily presented in cogent terms, which the unbeliever should be able to follow reasonably, even if he would not commit to it.

1 Peter 3:15 also speaks of the gentleness and respect that must characterize these apologetic encounters.[11] In cases where the unbeliever has the power to harm, like in Peter's time, this mandate becomes even more urgent. The Christian's conscience must be clear, since the discussion could possibly result in the unbeliever misrepresenting and slandering him. However the conduct of the Christian ought to put to shame and discredit such malicious actions, since the truth proclaimed by a well-lived Christian life should speak just as loudly as the verity of the words that actually defend the faith.

Worldview apologetics involves a fundamental value system that undergirds the thought and actions in all aspects of life. The Christian worldview centers on the gospel of Jesus Christ. This worldview's effectiveness increases to the extent that it touches and explains diverse aspects of life – from the micro to the macro, from the

---

[8]Ibid., 283. The reason to fear on a human plane was very real in the time of Peter.

[9]Michael Sudduth, "Reformed Epistemology and Christian Apologetics," *Religious Studies* 39 (2003): 302-04.

[10]Simon Blackburn, *Oxford Dictionary of Philosophy* (Oxford: Oxford University Press, 2005), 81. Truth is used here in line with the Correspondence Theory of Truth. This definition is used with variations by philosophers from Aristotle and Aquinas to Bertrand Russell and William P. Alston. True statements correspond to facts, and truth is the equation of the intellect and the object, herein referring to realist metaphysical verities concerning God and propositions from the Bible. See also Charles Taliaferro, *Contemporary Philosophy of Religion* (Malden, MA: Blackwell Publishers, 2009), 2. For a brief historical reference see Norman Geisler and William C. Roach, *Defending Inerrancy: Affirming the Accuracy of Scripture for a New Generation* (Grand Rapids: Baker Books, 2011), 233-37. For an overview see Alan G. Padgett and Patrick R. Keifert, eds., *But is it All True? The Bible and the Question of Truth* (Grand Rapids: William B. Eerdmans Publishing Company, 2006) along with J. P. Moreland and William Lane Craig, *Philosophical Foundations of a Christian Worldview* (Downers Grove: IL, InterVarsity, 2003), 130-52.

[11]"Christian Witness in a Multi-Religious World: Recommendations for Conduct: World Council of Churches Pontifical Council for Interreligious Dialogue World," *International Bulletin of Missionary Research* 35 (2011): 194.

material to the immaterial. The Christian worldview claims such universal implications by virtue of its truth claims over all of life. Thus a robust Worldview apologetic will center on the core of the gospel foundation and have a wide-ranging ability to touch upon all subjects whose superstructure should naturally fit this base.[12]

Historically, Christian apologetics display a diverse array of apologetic approaches. Worldview apologetics must selectively utilize this host of tools, expanding and developing them in today's context. The next section explores the current methodological foci of apologetics and how these can be fine-tuned in the Worldview engagement with Advaita Vedanta Hinduism.

Key Methodological Principles

Christian apologetics includes several arguments and principles that fit into diverse methodologies. Some of these key methodologies are now analyzed as broader systems in order to highlight their role in Worldview apologetics. This activity assists in integrating apologetics by utilizing the best tools from each methodology for any given apologetic task. Worldview apologetics will, however, place a singular emphasis upon the contrasting of holistic worldviews in the apologetic engagement. The major methods superbly outlined by Boa and Bowman will be reviewed in light of Worldview apologetics.[13] These approaches include: the deductive Classical, the inductive Evidential, the presuppositional Reformed, and the experiential Fideistic methods. This assessment identifies the role of each approach in Worldview apologetics.[14]

Classical Apologetics

The traditional Classical approach to apologetics begins where people are and it logically reasons out the truth of general revelation. Anselm characterizes the spirit of this method by showing that these proofs are not to cause faith, but come from faith to grow in faith. His ontological argument is still being refined and used today. Thomas Aquinas' five proofs are a fine example of scholastic theology and logical deduction. B. B. Warfield used this effectively in the modern era as does C. S. Lewis' "mere" Christianity. Norman Geisler more precisely refines some of the older arguments today. Peter Kreeft and William Lane Craig have brought this to the forefront today by using it effectively in modern apologetics.

Classical apologetics relies heavily on logic and uses rational tests to determine truth. However, it is markedly different from rationalism which requires everything to be settled on the basis of reason alone. Classical apologetics sees reason at the foundation of theology since faith is eminently reasonable. Thus it uses philosophy constructively in apologetics. Science is seen as primarily compatible with faith and history can confirm

---

[12]Sims, "Evangelical Worldview Analysis," 20: "Fields such as cosmology, archaeology, psychology, sociology, and genetic science support this [CFR] schema, validating its claim as a faithful representation of God's word and creation." No area is beyond the application of the Christian worldview.

[13]Kenneth D. Boa and Robert M. Bowman Jr., *Faith Has Its Reasons: Integrative Approaches to Defending the Christian Faith* (Colorado Springs: Paternoster, 2005). The different views are well summarized in this book. See also Richard Phillips, ed., *Only One Way? Reaffirming the Exclusive Truth Claims of Christianity* (Wheaton, IL: Crossway Books, 2006).

[14]Sims, "Evangelical Worldview Analysis," 22-23. Sims used the CFT matrix after working through Transcendental and Abduction, while the current approach intentionally uses all the methods, which results in a Worldview apologetic that is still not very dissimilar from that of Sims' recommendation.

4

revelation. This approach sees religious experience as reasonable. Worldview apologetics must take advantage of the full scope of logic and reason, especially when it engages with Vedanta which vaunts itself as the supreme philosophy.[15]

Deductive principles used in Classical apologetics progress from broader to narrower claims. The Scriptures then become the basis of authority for apologetics. Apologists often use such a two-step approach: First, using logical arguments they provide the traditional proofs for the existence of God. Second, using this theistic foundation they prove the Christian God of the Bible. They begin with general revelation and end with proving the Scriptures. They can disprove other worldviews and deductively examine the problem of evil. Miracles become the credentials of revelation.

A sample of the Classical arguments for the existence of God is given below. Simply stated, the ontological argument for the existence of God notes that if you can conceive of a perfect being, then such a being must necessarily exist. This takes various forms from contingent to necessary beings. The cosmological argument claims that the beginning of the universe requires some uncaused Cause since we cannot have a past infinite universe with infinite regression. Another version says that anything that exists needs to have an ultimate cause. The teleological argument observes purpose in the universe and identifies that final purpose as God. The moral argument is based on the anthropic principle and notes that the basis of our ethics is God, our ethical Law-Giver.[16]

Worldview apologetics with Vedanta will encounter deductive arguments from Hinduism and must be able to engage these principles with solid reasoning. Some elements of the two-step approach will be more useful than others here. The first step would not be disputed by Hindus and therefore just those distinctive elements of the Christian worldview would need emphasis, such as the moral argument which addresses the character of the Christian God. The second step is vital in any apologetic encounter and particularly to Vedanta, where the historical validity of the Bible and the unique nature of God set up the Christian worldview in contradistinction to the Hindu outlook.

Evidential Apologetics

Evidential approach utilizes facts and evidences, by pointing from these facts to the possibility of God and showing this God to be the Christian God of the Bible. Among its famous proponents, Samuel Butler used the analogous principle from nature to God. William Paley famously used the watchmaker example to show that design in the world points to a designer. The Intelligent Design movement now uses this argument against evolution. William Lane Craig is a classicist who uses data from the Big Bang theory for the origin of the universe. He also uses evidence from historic proofs of the Bible to refute invalid interpretations of this data. Josh McDowell collects and shows a huge volume of data against the non-Christian worldviews. John Warwick Montgomery is the main proponent of the evidential approach today while James Orr, Richard Swinburne, and Clark H. Pinnock also employ this methodology of emphasizing facts.

Evidential apologetics differs hugely from epistemological evidentialism, which demands that all knowledge needs proof. The Evidential method seeks to discover truth from data or evidence that is viewed in a neutral context, in order to show the self-

---

[15]Jonathan Duquette and K. Ramasubramanian, "Is Space Created? Reflections on Sankara's Philosophy and Philosophy of Physics," *Philosophy East & West* 60 (2010): 529.

[16]Boa and Bowman, *Faith Has Its Reasons*, 95-102, 120.

evident truth from these facts. Inductive principles are used in going from narrower to broader claims. The proofs here cannot reach complete certainty, but just a high degree of probability based on cumulative evidence. They begin with scientific data of general revelation and historic data from the Scriptures, to give a high degree of probability to the truths of Scripture. This data is then used to defend theology by critically using philosophy. It shows Christianity vindicated by science and showcases history as the medium of revelation. One's experience of faith is founded on irrefutable evidence.[17]

In presenting the evidence that demands a verdict, Scripture is seen as a source of facts and the uniqueness of Christianity provides an attractive data point. The case for God is cumulative and the problem of evil is handled inductively through specific cases rather than in a general manner. Miracles serve as evidence for God and his work on earth. Some of the scientific proofs include the anthropic principle that shows how the universe is fine-tuned in order to sustain humanity. It is demonstrated through the cosmic constants or through the precise natural laws. Historic evidences validate the data of the Bible and extra-biblical books to exhibit the truth concerning Jesus and his resurrection.

Worldview apologetics should be able to engage the inductive approaches well, with the caveat that each worldview will reinterpret the same data differently without a neutral common ground. Part of Worldview apologetics would be to set the framework to properly interpret the plethora of facts. In relation to Vedanta, this will particularly involve grounding the historic facts in empirically verifiable events. This approach will contrast the mythical and abstract scriptural base of Hinduism which provides its own spectacles to reinterpret reality within its worldview.[18]

Reformed Apologetics

This approach is theologically Reformed in its emphasis on the sovereignty of God and the depravity of man. Its apologetic methodology closely conforms to Reformed theology. John Calvin's theology is the driving force behind this approach, which factors the total depravity of man in its epistemology along with the sovereignty of God in what must define the apologetic content. Herman Dooyeweerd restarted this methodology in the twentieth century and Cornelius Van Til developed it further. Van Til held strongly to what is termed today as presuppositional apologetics. He did not locate logic as self-evident, but rather held that the Scriptures were self-evident, even if logic is rightly used in our understanding of the Scriptures.[19] Gordon H. Clark worked on this in parallel with a higher emphasis on logic, while Alvin Plantinga and Gary North are related to this approach only through their emphasis on special revelation. Plantinga addresses presuppositions defensively as being basic beliefs, but deals mainly with refuting narrow foundationalism by using inductive approaches to logic. While not primarily a Reformed apologist, he is theologically well aligned with this methodology.[20]

---

[17]Ibid., 180-88, 204. Stephen C. Evans, *Philosophy of Religion: Thinking about Faith* (Downers Grove, IL: InterVarsity Press, 1985), 22-23, 27-28. Soft sciences are notoriously reinterpreted. Hard sciences are applied in error, like in relation to the issue of origins in the theory of the multiverse.

[18]Valerie Stoker, "Conceiving the Canon in Dvaita Vedānta: Madhva's Doctrine of 'All Sacred Lore,'" *Numen* 51 (2004): 74.

[19]Cornelius Van Til, *Christianity and Idealism* (Philadelphia: Westminster Theological Seminary, 1955), 13: We "must either presuppose God or presuppose the open universe." See also Tim Grass, "Scripture Alone: 'Is the Bible All We Need?'" *EVANGEL* 25 (2007): 66.

[20]Sudduth, "Reformed Epistemology and Christian Apologetics," 317.

The Reformed arguments presuppose the truth of Scripture and the existence of God. The Transcendental argument presupposes the Scriptures which are used as the standard of truth. This truth is then used to show the impossibility of the contrary, that all other worldviews are inconsistent and lack a rational or evidential basis for their position. The Scriptures stand in judgment of man rather than man judging God and the Scriptures. A neutral ground for evaluating facts and "brute" facts are rejected, as they are always interpreted on the basis of valid or invalid presuppositions.[21]

Sinful man after Adam's fall uses his naturalistic (or more broadly anti-Christian) worldviews through which he sees data. Thus he cannot fairly judge data or reason to determine whether God exists and if the Bible is true. Sinful man is aware of God but suppresses this truth. Thus, epistemology does not just involve processing data, but also includes the ethical response to the truth. The apologist does not just appeal to a neutral court, but rather confronts the rebellious sinner, to return to God whom he knows but refuses to acknowledge. This does not mean that evidences and logic are not used, but they play a subservient role under an intentional foundation of biblical truth.[22]

This method vindicates Reformed theology by moving apologetics closer to Christian philosophy. Christianity stands against false science and revelation is required to interpret history and experience. With Scripture as the foundation, the antithesis between Christianity and non-Christian religions are brought to the forefront. Belief in God is seen as basic. The problem of evil is primarily theological and miracles are revealed by God. The approach is theologically Reformed and bases its actions on the propositions of Scripture.

Worldview apologetics finds a biblical structure in Reformed apologetics for clearly delineating the foundational differences between Christianity and Vedanta Hinduism. While Reformed apologetics can provide a useful framework, it must rely heavily from the other methods to provide specific arguments to false worldviews.

Fideist Apologetics

The Fideistic approach focuses on immediately experiencing truth by minimizing any mediation. Some teachings of Luther initiate this method, but it gains momentum through the works of Blaise Pascal and later Karl Barth who moves the liberal movement back, by looking for experiential faith. Soren Kierkegaard likewise did much to bring back an emphasis on experience which was lacking in spiritually dead churches. Experiential faith is a vital aspect of true religion.[23] Currently, Donald G. Bloesch advocates and uses this method of apologetics.

---

[21]Cornelius Van Til, *A Christian Theory of Knowledge* (Philadelphia: Westminster Theological Seminary, The Presbyterian and Reformed Publishing Company, 1975), 17: "Analogical reasoning sees God as original and man as derivative in knowledge." The Transcendental argument finds its transcendent reference in the transcendent God of Scripture, rather than in reason, in order to critique false worldviews.

[22]Boa and Bowman, *Faith Has Its Reasons*, 290-303, 320. Using science to interpret Scripture fails to understand the shifting sands on which science stands. See also Peter Harrison, "The Bible and the Emergence of Modern Science," *Science & Christian Belief* 18 (2006): 115. Rom 1 provides the broad arraignment of the nature of depravity that colors the unbeliever's vision and allegiance to God. The scriptural references to this are covered in the actual apologetic with Vedanta.

[23]Roe Fremstedal, "Kierkegaard's Double Movement of Faith and Kant's Moral Faith," *Religious Studies* 48 (2012): 211. Mark A. McIntosh, *Mystical Theology* (Malden, MA: Blackwell Publishers, 1998), 96. It is important to distinguish between textual knowledge and experience.

The need for logic, reason, evidence, and even propositional truth of Scripture is rejected as being short of direct, unmediated access to God. This approach can become dangerous when it departs from God's revealed truth. However, it does correct problems in the other approaches when they tend to de-focus from the God of the Bible, evidences, and reason. Thus the divine call alone can initiate a person to obey the truth which makes theology personal. It critiques the god of the philosophers and claims Christianity and reality to be beyond science. Revelation transcends history while faith is experience.

The Scriptures serve as witness to God and Christianity is not just another religion. To know God personally is to know that God exists and the problem of evil is primarily personal. Miracles are seen as God revealing himself. Barth sees the Word of God as distinct from the Bible, to be met personally. Kierkegaard contrasts intellectual faith from genuine experiential faith within the dead Dutch Reformed churches.[24]

Fideism is one approach that does not fit easily with the earlier methods. It tends to minimize objective truth which can be positively dangerous in Christianity. That said it has helpful corrective elements which are extremely useful to augment the other methods. Worldview apologetics must engage finally at the existential level where the individual cannot just acknowledge the right worldview, but also live it. In the contrast between Christianity and Vedanta, the goodness of a life well-lived under God plays a strong role in apologetics. The stubborn will of man is targeted to recognize its state.

Distinctive Apologetic Elements

Before developing an integrated worldview approach from the above methods, the differences between the above views are examined against essential apologetic issues.

The first issue is epistemology of the unregenerate person which seeks to answer what people know apart from regeneration. Apologetics seeks to meet people where they should be met. General revelation from Psalm 19 and Romans 1 show that God has revealed himself through nature. Both Classical and Evidential approaches believe that this must be pressed upon the unbeliever. Suppressed general revelation is the stance of the Reformed approach which agrees that nature does reveal God, but Romans 1 also notes that man suppresses this truth that he already knows. The Fideist says that man can know nothing since he looks for the Holy Spirit to reveal and therefore unregenerate person cannot know anything before regeneration.

The second issue deals with the tools of the evangelist in identifying the best Christian approach which aids a person to be saved. This refers to what things the Christian can do which will aid the unbeliever walk toward God. Classical approaches seek to show that there is a God through reason, which every person can recognize as logical. Evidential approaches seek to show the possibility of God through the evidences given. Reformed approaches note that there is none that seeks after God and therefore the confrontation of the gospel is the only way to assist the unbeliever. They declare, rather than explicate scriptural truth toward unbelieving worldviews, while using logic and data. Fideists believe that the unbeliever must encounter Jesus through the Holy Spirit.

The third issue is closely related, addressing the primary agency or model that the believer can use as the chief means in apologetics. Classical tries to reason logically with man to see God since people are reasonable. Evidential tries to reason with man

---

[24]Boa and Bowman, *Faith Has Its Reasons*, 346-51, 371, 400-02.

scientifically to see God since persons can rightly interpret data or acknowledge its right interpretation, Reformed has a head-on collision with man, confronting falsehood and showing what the unbeliever already knows, but refuses to accept by submitting to the truth. Fideists experience God and hope for the unbeliever to have a similar experience. They demonstrate the truth and state how individuals need to existentially meet God.

The final issue deals with the theology behind each of these apologetic approaches. Classical tends to be predominantly Catholic or Anglican. Evidential is strongly Arminian since it believes man can see and seek God. Reformed is Calvinistic. Lutheran is traditionally fideistic, although Dutch Reformed and modern Charismatics are good candidates. Theological preciseness will play a major role in the extent to which some apologetic formulae tend to be used more than others in Worldview apologetics.[25]

The problems in each of these approaches are mainly tied to any pure implementation of each approach. Their philosophical shortcomings are noted briefly to avoid the dangers of overreaching within these methods. Deductive approaches have premises that are logically argued to lead up to the conclusion. However, no conclusion can rise higher than what the premise affirms. Therefore, no finite premise can lead to infinite conclusions, dealing with the categorical problems of Lessing's Ditch. Inductive approaches use probability which is not the best approach to talk about the authoritative Scriptures and God. Also, man is not neutral in his spiritual state to be merely reasoned with in order to believe in God. The Reformed approach needs flexibility since these truths must be spoken with reason, gentleness, and meekness as required by the biblical mandate. These arguments must be well-thought and the inferences reasonably drawn. Fideists lack a thorough norm and biblical fidelity, despite their corrective emphasis on experience. Fideism cannot stand as a pure apologetic method, when it diminishes the objective verities of Christian faith and reason, but it can supplement other approaches.

Worldview Approach

Integration among these varied approaches tends to take advantage of the strengths of each of the above methods. Among those who developed integrative approaches include Edward John Carnell and Francis A. Schaeffer, who popularized this eclectic method through their active work of evangelism and engaging the world. David K. Clark, C. Stephen Evans, and John M. Frame continue this work by adapting their primary methodologies to accommodate principles from other methods as well, even as Sims developed it. Worldview apologetics will likewise be an integrated methodology.[26]

Worldview integration approaches take one of the above and then develop it using elements from the other approaches. While many in Christendom now attempt it, John Frame is a good example whose approach will be used in the current worldview engagement of Christianity and Vedanta. Frame's perspectivalism uses existential, situational, and propositional corners to address the apologetic problem in the right context. Apologetics can find tighter integration with theology, philosophy, history, experience, and science. By taking advantage of the best possible arguments from all approaches, Scriptures are used as truth when sifting through myth, data, and religious

---

[25]Boa and Bowman, *Faith Has Its Reasons*, 493-95.

[26]David K. Naugle, *Worldview: The History of a Concept* (Grand Rapids: William B. Eerdmans Publishing Company, 2002), 340-41.

claims. The goal is to present the God who makes himself known and showing biblical solutions to the problems of evil. Miracles would act as signs pointing to the truth.

The significant advantage of this approach is that in the church we have one body with many gifts which explains the differences among apologists. Also, in the one world we live in, we have many individuals each differing according to their background and personality. Thus individual apologetic needs differ since we may have one process but will use many stages to reach that desired goal. Likewise, while truth is unique and there is but one faith, the multiplicity of questions requires diverse approaches, tailored to each apologetic problem that one faces, and must be used with great skill and care.

Dangers in Worldview Apologetics

Worldview apologetics can avoid some of the dangers in each method by presenting the Christian worldview as a whole in response to the Vedanta worldview. This can eliminate some of the narrow fissures and rabbit-trails that tend to distract apologetics from its central purpose of honoring Christ while engaging the unbeliever. In addition to the methodology of engaging worldviews as a whole, the spiritual heart commitment of the apologist is addressed using categories of faithfulness. This faithfulness is evaluated both in regards to individuals and to principles that govern Worldview apologetics.

Fidelity in Apologetics

Worldview apologetics could still face similar dangers of the previous methodologies if it is not careful in relation to the key aspect of faithfulness. Three specific areas to watch out include theological, personal, and interpersonal fidelity.

Theological fidelity. Biblical theology must form the foundation upon which a well-reasoned philosophy is built. By reversing this order, theology can be restrained by the strictures of diverse philosophical systems. In seeking to honor Christ in apologetics, one can honor one's tacit understanding of cultural norms while force-fitting eternal truth into these temporal standards. The issue of fidelity here is not primarily to some abstract theology, but rather a fundamental fidelity to God. When God is held in higher regard than all else, valuing God's truth from the Scriptures comes more naturally. This value-pyramid with God on top increases theological fidelity since the fear of others is replaced by a godly fear and faithfulness. Theological fidelity is a vital component of Worldview apologetics and a touchstone on which the apologist constantly measures his defense.

Personal fidelity. Personal fidelity is vital in keeping a good conscience that the biblical mandate requires. From integrity to humility and honesty, one must strive to be faithful in apologetics. Integrity of the apologist is vital in any apologetic encounter. In defending the truth, the apologist must be true to his convictions, even as they get regularly realigned to an increasingly greater biblical awareness. This also keeps the apologist humble. While the apologist does believe that he has a handle on basic truth which the unbeliever lacks, he also knows that he is neither infallible nor omniscient in his representation of God's truth. Thus the apologist can straddle the challenging task of declaring God's truth but doing so with gentleness, aware of one's own finitude. Finally, the apologist must be honest in his speech and actions, which is a logical consequence of personal integrity and humility. Thus the apologist can speak the truth even when it apparently cuts against his own cause, since he knows that God's truth will win irrespective of his own inability to tie all the ends together. These matters of personal fidelity define the standing of the Christian on Worldview apologetics. Without it, the truth may stand strong, but its presentation will be marred by the failure of the Christian apologist to demonstrate what he declares. Christian practice must correspond to Christian preaching.

Interpersonal fidelity. Interpersonal fidelity is the final consequence of theological and personal fidelity. The biblical mandate requires not just gentleness and respect, but also truth-speaking and benevolence toward the unbeliever. When God's love constrains the believer to speak the truth in love, one cannot justify sinful interactions to achieve a godly goal.[27] Thus the Worldview apologist must act with gentleness and respect as befitting an ambassador of Christ to the world. Speaking truth not only conforms the Christian to the image of Christ, but also represents Christ faithfully to the unbeliever, both in word and deed. The Worldview apologist gives to the unbeliever what he himself has freely received – the good gift of God. Thus doing good to the unbeliever in the apologetic encounter and in any other interaction, would put meat to the skeletal claims of the Christian's worldview.

Success in Worldview Apologetics

In closing this introductory chapter on Worldview apologetics, it is helpful to remember what constitutes success and failure in the encounter with Vedanta or any other worldview. As described above, what counts for the Christian Worldview apologist is fidelity to God which translates into a personal and interpersonal fidelity. This fidelity extends to the domains of the intellect, morality, and emotion as briefly noted below.[28]

Intellectual honesty. The Christian is intellectually honest when he is truthful to what he currently knows or believes in. There are some bedrock truths which define a Christian. On these the Worldview apologist corresponds to God's view as presented in the Bible. There are other truths that are either beyond finite sinful man or incorrectly understood by the Christian at a given point in the scale of time and maturity. Christians can be unashamedly honest with what they hold to be true. Yet they can be humble, knowing the possibility of error in their knowledge. Intellectual success is proportional to one's faithfulness to God's revealed truth as understood by the believer and presented without deception to the unbeliever. The apologist fails to the degree that he wanders away from God's revelation in favor of human insight. He also fails to the degree that he suppresses what he believes to be true in order to win an argument with an unbeliever.[29]

---

[27]J. K. S. Reid, *Christian Apologetics* (London: Hodder and Stoughton, 1969), 13-14.
[28]John G. Stackhouse Jr., *Humble Apologetics: Defending the Faith Today* (New York: Oxford University Press, 2002), 146. Norman L. Geisler and Patrick Zukeran, *The Apologetics of Jesus: A Caring Approach to Dealing with Doubters* (Grand Rapids: Baker Books, 2009), 77.
[29]Stackhouse, *Humble Apologetics,* 13. See also George I. Mavrodes, "Jerusalem and Athens Revisited," in *Faith and Rationality: Reason and Belief in God,* ed. Alvin Plantinga and Nicholas Wolterstorff (Notre Dame, IN: University of Notre Dame Press, 1983), 217.

Moral honesty. Moral honesty simply and plainly requires integrity. The Christian apologist succeeds in as far as he imitates God's ethical standards and fails to the degree that he places any other objective other than honoring Christ in his method of apologetics. Genuine humility plays a vital role in the apologetic interaction which can easily become heated when working out the deeply held worldview differences. By remaining humble and honest, the Christian successfully represents the moral component in the clash of worldviews, not just in propositions, but in actual practice.

Emotional honesty. Emotional honesty requires the Christian apologist to persuade the unbeliever to commit to the Christian worldview, without coercing him with purely emotional pleas lacking reasonable content. Emotional humility prevents the superficial transference of one's pathos to the listener without backing it with truth. Attempting to wrongly force the unbeliever's feelings to override what he considers true is an apologetic failure for the Christian. Success here will depend on showcasing the right connection between the content that the Christian upholds and his commitment to the God of that content. The words and actions of the Christian, can then plead for a corresponding commitment from the unbeliever toward Christ.

The success and failure of the Christian Worldview apologetic no longer depends on winning an argument with the unbeliever or even the conversion of the unbeliever. These are matters of skill and God's action respectively. While the Christian desires both, they no longer retain the primacy in the apologetic encounter. Rather, it is Christ's honor and the Christian's fidelity to Christ that take center stage.

This book will apply the principles of Worldview apologetics and engage Vedanta Hinduism with biblical responses of historical Christianity. Vedanta Hinduism is often vaunted as an unassailable mountain by its proponents. Christian apologists have addressed this worldview, typically from the Classical and Evidential frameworks. Christian evangelism in India toward Hindus often uses a Fideistic apologetic. Some of these engagements are reviewed later when identifying helpful and unhelpful approaches from these apologists. The apologetic challenge to Vedanta has not yet been addressed sufficiently by Christian apologists of the Reformed persuasion. A lack in the overall integrated Christian Worldview apologetic to Vedanta will be explored to open up vistas for the evangelization of Hindus.

Advaita Vedanta Hinduism serves as an example to optimally work out the apologetic path in its practical details. The robustness of Christian apologetics is intended to be improved overall through Worldview apologetics, by providing a vigorous and broad apologetic case-study of Vedanta Hinduism. Existential questions facing individuals will be approached in personal apologetics, as an indispensable element of the gospel proclamation. This book will attempt such an evangelistic apologetic response that will strive to be faithful to its biblical mandate while engaging and addressing the Vedanta Hindu with a thorough-going Christian worldview.

With this introduction into the context of Worldview apologetics, the stage is set to review the Vedanta worldview before the task of apologetics can begin contrasting these worldviews.

CHAPTER 2
WORLDVIEW CASE STUDY

Hindu philosophy has had a different trajectory than the western philosophical tradition, but both cherish a rich antiquity of logical and analytical acuity. Vedanta holds a unique position within Hinduism for its complex and sophisticated philosophy. This chapter presents the Vedanta worldview using its main proponents and examines it using its own domestic concepts. After reviewing the major Hindu traditions, the teachings of three individuals will be studied and a progression of the Vedanta worldview observed as a case study of worldview development.

Hindu Philosophic Tradition

The Hindu philosophic tradition relies on various written scriptural sources. The Vedas, the Upanishads, and the Bhagavad-Gita form the common scriptures of all Vedanta philosophy, which is one among six Hindu traditions.[30] Some Vedantins have additional sources of scriptures which will be reviewed later.

The Vedas are ancient scriptures which span a wide range of subjects from religion and rituals, to history and magic. The Upanishads are commentaries on the Vedas, addressing speculative metaphysics. They are called Vedanta or the end of the Vedas. These form the central texts around which the Vedanta philosophy is built upon. The Bhagavad-Gita or simply Gita is set in the epic Mahabharata and commends three paths to liberation – devotion, works, and knowledge, without favoring any one path as better than the others.[31]

Vedantins are the custodians of insights of the Upanishads. Vedanta itself is diverse and includes "Dvaita (dualistic), Advaita (nondualistic), Visistadvaita (qualified

---

[30]The six Hindu philosophic traditions are Samkhya, Yoga, Nyaya, Vaisheshika, Mimamsa, and Vedanta. Some are atheistic and dualistic, others focus on logic or meditation, and still others are empiricist or focus on orthopraxy. Vedanta becomes dominant after the medieval period. For more details see Chandradhar Sharma, *A Critical Survey of Indian Philosophy* (London: Rider & Company, 1960).

[31]P. V. Joshi, *Introduction to Sankara's Advaitism* (Delhi: Motilal Banarsidass Publishers, 2006), 24-26. There is a diversity of opinion here, with some favoring devotion over the other paths.

nondualistic), Suddadvaita (pure nondualistic), and Dvaitadvaita (dualistic-cum-nondualistic)."[32] Three of the more popular Vedantic philosophies will be examined as representative of the Vedanta worldview.

Advaita is the earliest and the most popular of them among the elites.[33] It states that Brahman is the only reality in the cosmos. All else has a degree of unreality. When man breaks the fetters of Maya which gives form to the empirical world, he achieves self-realization. He experiences supreme bliss as all distinction between him and the cosmos disappears. This Brahman is immutable, ineffable, and apart from all human conception.[34]

Visistadvaita also conceives of one ultimate reality, but it has qualities or attributes. Brahman is not undifferentiated, but his qualities find manifestation in humans and the material world, which are his body. Thus humans must love God and realize their relation to God in their liberation.

Dvaita claims that ultimate reality consists of the dualities of Brahman and Atman. This system of teaching sees ontological difference between creature and creator. God's sovereign Will rules the universe and humans must worship their God in devotion. Each of these systems is now studied from the traditions of the principal teacher of the school. Each individual's worldview will be set forth as represented by its adherents.

Sankara

Sankara, Samkara, or Shankara is called the founder of Advaitism. His brief life (A.D. 788-820) was marked by religious passion. His logic is said to be impeccable and his fervor ardent. He won over philosophers by his brilliance, strongly establishing his system across India. He is said to be the first savant to consciously create a sense of unity among the then diverse Hindus, blending sharp logical acumen with deep devotion.

Source

Vedantins' primary source of truth is acknowledged to be the scriptures. Humans have the ability to apprehend truth directly but very few attain it. Ultimately each person attains enlightenment, but that path begins with scriptural revelation. Sankara gives all authority to the Hindu scriptures, but interprets these works using his unifying system of thought by either adding or subtracting words from them. Sankara's writings include metaphysical treatises such as Upadesa Sahasri and the disputed Atma Bodh and Vivekchoodamani.[35] He wrote commentaries on the Gita, Upanishads, and Brahma-Sutras (Sankara Bhashyam). He also composed devotional hymns such as Gita Govinda. Sankara masterfully develops from these scriptures a unified and consistent worldview.[36] Sankara's system of thought is coherent and tight with monism as its supreme truth. He interprets and subsumes all other aspects of the scriptures to fit this solid framework.

---

[32]Karl H. Potter, *Presuppositions of India's Philosophies* (Englewood Cliffs, NJ: Prentice-Hall Inc., 1963), 100.

[33]R. C. Zaehner, *Hinduism* (Oxford: Oxford University Press, 1962), 73.

[34]Joshi, *Introduction to Sankara's Advaitism*, 26-28, 37-38.

[35]Anthony J. Alston, "Samkara in East and West Today," in *New Perspectives on Advaita Vedanta: Essays in Commemoration of Professor Richard De Smet*, ed. Bradley J. Malkovsky (Boston: Brill, 2000), 107-08. Some of these works are attributed to his later followers.

[36]Joshi, *Introduction to Sankara's Advaitism*, 1-5, 17, 24-26.

Epistemology

Knowledge is both sensory and spiritual but each differs in how it is acquired. Most people form their knowledge of the world around them by observation. Very few discern and pursue a deeper reality beyond the sensory world. This lack of spiritual knowledge is seen as the central problem of mankind. Revelation, reason, and intuition form the ultimate criteria of truth for Vedantins. While Brahman is realized by revelation, only a rational person can comprehend the texts of scripture or Shruti. Reason helps to resolve apparent contradictions in scripture. Thus intellectual reason is the critical means of discerning truth from falsehood in the phenomenal world. But pure consciousness or intuition allows the finite self to divest itself of ignorance which sees reality in relation. Sankara values immediate spiritual realization as the supreme criterion of truth.[37]

Living Life

Humanity inherits sorrow by clinging on to the transient forms of life, ignorantly believing them to be stable. Man purifies himself through the hard work of karmic rituals prescribed by the Vedas, in order to cleanse his sins. Devotion to God is also a necessary means to be liberated. But the best means of release is knowledge, which is not just information obtained, but an apprehension of true reality as it consists in the scriptural definition of absolute identity. The individual Self, trapped in the world system, is liberated and it attains pure bliss or liberation by delighting in what is ultimately real, by letting go everything else that is linked to the world.

Enlightenment differentiates the real from the illusory and is an immediate experience, preceded by focused and profound meditation. One can commune with Brahman when one attains the pinnacle of supraconsciousness; progressing in consciousness from reflection, to meditation, to culminate in Nirvikalpaka Samadhi.[38] Thus all of the above means only provide a provisional progress. The only means of final liberation is knowledge, so called, when it realizes oneness of Atman with Brahman:

> [T]here is a moment of transcendent, intuitive realization when even "knowledge" no longer seems the proper descriptive term. It too is transcended as fire burns itself out, not only the fuel that feeds it. The ultimate identity is all that is left.[39]

In more recent times, Ramakrishna spoke of the path to attain enlightenment, relating the absolute end with its relative means, which is vital for liberation:

> A man should reach the Nitya, the Absolute, by following the trail of the Lila, the Relative. It is like reaching the roof by the stairs. After realizing the Absolute, he should climb down to the Relative and live on that plane in the company of devotees, charging his mind with the love of God.[40]

Ramakrishna's disciple Vivekananda developed the path of work on earth, extolling Ramakrishna's life work at the expense of complete unity with Brahman:

---

[37]Sharma, *A Critical Survey of Indian Philosophy*, 287-89.
[38]Joshi, *Introduction to Sankara's Advaitism*, 38-40, 47-50. This is ultimate liberation.
[39]Eric Lott, *Vedantic Approaches to God* (New York: Barnes & Noble Books, 1980), 175.
[40]Mahendranath Gupta, *The Gospel of Sri Ramakrishna*, trans. Swami Nikhilananda (New York: Ramakrishna-Vivekananda Center, 1942), 257. Life in the temporal plane is thus commended.

He would forgo the pleasure of the Nirvikalpa Samadhi even, in order to work for the uplift of the masses. It was the mission and purpose of his life. His was not to be a life of asceticism and retirement but that of intense activity and self-immolation.[41]

World and Maya

Sankara bifurcated reality as practical and transcendent. The practical or lower reality of the world, is not ultimately real, but is real enough for man to work in it. It also reveals God both in and beyond the world. Actions in the world can tend to move one further along the path to liberation, but ultimately one recognizes that it is not truly real. At that stage, no further good works are needed, but only true knowledge, since the world is no longer seen to contain the final destination for the individual.

Sankara formulates a distinct doctrine of Maya, which plays a pivotal role in Hindu philosophy. The Vedas had called Maya the "esoteric power of deities and their magical attributes." Upanishads linked it with "illusoriness." Gita called it "veil of divinity" to create, while Brahma-Sutras used it as a "synonym for dream." Maya causes ignorance, preventing people from comprehending the ultimate reality of Brahman. Maya is infinite divine power, an integral part of Brahman, with divine attributes. Since the immutable Brahman cannot undergo any transformation, it cannot create. The identity of cause and effect requires creation to share in the nature of the creator but the world of change can have nothing in common with an unchanging deity. Maya creates the world, is neither real nor unreal, and it ineffably defies description.[42] Thus,

> The empirical world cannot exist by itself. It is wholly dependent on Brahman, but the changes of the empirical order do not affect the integrity of Brahman. The world depends on Brahman, but Brahman depends on nothing.[43]

For Sankara, the world is a manifestation or projection of Brahman. Thus in the world, karma yoga or works is required for common man to give purpose to his actions and life. However, it is not real in the same sense as Brahman, since true reality is eternal and immutable but the world is temporal and changing. Similes are used to explain this distinction – it is like a rope appearing as a snake, a pot apparently containing or dividing space, or the son of a barren woman. Maya was needed to consistently interpret the scriptures, but some aspects such as its operation or its relation to the Brahman are unknown. In contrast, the Bheda-Abheda philosophy of inconceivable oneness and difference, said that God in his sublime power could create this world without in any way losing his transcendent qualities such as immutability. This led to bhakti yoga which attributed all such power to a personal God.[44]

---

[41] *The Life of Swami Vivekananda by His Eastern and Western Disciples* (Calcutta: Advaita Ashrama, 1955), 185.

[42] Joshi, *Introduction to Sankara's Advaitism*, 2, 4, 41, 55-57, 59-62. Identity of cause and effect is a philosophical rule that will be examined in analyzing the foundations of the Vedanta worldview.

[43] Sarvepalli Radhakrishnan and Charles E. Moore, eds., *A Source Book in Indian Philosophy* (Princeton: Princeton University Press, 1957), 507. See also *Upanisads*, trans. Patrick Olivelle (Oxford: Oxford University Press, 1996), 274: Mundaka Upanisad 2.2.11 states that "It is *brahman* alone that extends over this whole universe, up to its widest extent."

[44] Joshi, *Introduction to Sankara's Advaitism*, 63-68, 94, 100. The simile helps one understand the ontological and epistemological differences between a rope and its appearance as a snake.

16

Sankara's Bhashyam on the Gita explains that the objective of Hinduism was to ensure both material and spiritual prosperity. Sankara divided humanity into the enlightened and the ignorant. Karma yoga is the mandatory means of good works for all except the enlightened, whom gynana yoga or the way of knowledge leads to liberation. Virtue, righteousness, and morality are therefore to be upheld in the world, but by working with detachment from the fruit of one's labor. The enlightened person was able to distinguish the mortal body from his transcendent Self. Advaita claimed that the enlightened sage had transcended the realm of action, but Sankara made karma yoga applicable even to them, thus elevating the role of works. Sankara promoted public welfare by his relentless self-example, but debarred the ordinary person from embracing gynana yoga, despite any such restrictions in the Gita. He required works from ordinary people to purge themselves of their accumulated sins. The ordinary individual must do both mundane and spiritual tasks with the same spirit of dedication to God.[45]

While Sankara never taught that the world was unreal as being illusory, even God or Isvara is a product of Maya. Sankara says that senses and memory can be deceived in their perception of the forms of the world. However the subject or the doubter cannot be doubted.[46] The object and the subject cannot be equated. But superimposition occurs when something observed earlier is remembered and attributed to something else. Malkovsky equates adhyasa or superimposition with modern-day "projection:"

> We project onto the realities of world and self, incorrect notions about their nature, which in turn generates attachment and leads to blind action. This is an innate and universal error, affecting all people.[47]

The world has no existence if viewed apart from Brahman, as most people tend to do. Thus what these people "see" has no existence. However, the world cannot have both existence and non-existence or neither. Sankara invokes Maya, the power of Brahman to explain this mystery. It "belongs to, and is the Brahman, just as the burning power belongs to, and is fire."[48] Individual existence is rooted in this unconscious power of Maya. This existence is lost when one realizes that it is actually part of Brahman. But when viewed separately, Maya neither has existence nor belongs to Brahman. Thus the paradox of the world now transfers to that of Maya. Most Advaitins refer to Maya, avidya, and ajnana interchangeably. Maya can divide itself into opposites of subject and object and has three attributes – sattva (clarity), rajas (activity), and tamas (darkness).[49]

Atman

The Atman or Self is not truly tied to the world, but it needs to transcend the physical and find its true rest in the Absolute Brahman. Sankara does not say that the finite being or ego is identical to Brahman, but rather that the Atman in man is Brahman.

---

[45]Ibid., 103-14. Such works make this world a genuine entity within which to operate.

[46]C. P. Ramaswami Aiyar, *Fundamentals of Hindu Faith and Culture: A Collection of Essays and Addresses* (Madras: Ganesh & Co., 1959), 10-11.

[47]Bradley J. Malkovsky, "Samkara on Divine Grace," in *New Perspectives on Advaita Vedanta: Essays in Commemoration of Professor Richard De Smet*, ed. Bradley J. Malkovsky (Boston: Brill, 2000), 76. Malkovsky seems to relocate grace in Sankara from the theistic to the absolute realm.

[48]P. T. Raju, *The Philosophical Traditions of India* (London: George Allen & Unwin, 1971), 177. A substance and its attribute are variously used in Indian metaphysics and epistemology.

[49]Ibid., 177-80.

The Self controls man's life, despite being beyond the physical world, since it is linked with man and the world through Maya, whose operation is totally beyond comprehension.

Thus Maya is used to defend the nature of the Self just as it was used to defend the creation of the world. In the ultimate sense, there is complete identity between the Self and Brahman.[50] What is perceived is only the Self or the world which are effects and one cannot determine their connection to any cause, be it Brahman or anything else, through the senses. However, Brahman's existence is already known on the basis of it also being the Self. Devout meditation on Brahman effects the Self's release.[51]

Brahman and God

Brahman is the only true absolute reality beyond all predication. With this central worldview, the Advaitin walks through various states interpreting life. Essentially, the attribute-less Brahman is non-different from the world and is identified with Atman. Brahman is the apex of existence, knowledge, and bliss. He is delineated as perfect, without parts, beginning-less, totally beyond the ken of words, cognition, and even conceptualization.[52] Brahman is pure Existence, Consciousness, and Bliss (sat-cit-ananda). Brahman is eternal and beyond all characterizations as Being itself. Brahman is distinguished from God or Isvara as follows:

> The Brahman is the Absolute and is impersonal; but God is not the Absolute, He is personal . . . . He [God] is the Absolute facing the world and knowing it as his object. At the level of the Absolute, there is no distinction between the subject and the object, but at the level of God the distinction obtains. The Brahman creates out of itself the world of souls and matter and faces it . . . He is free and above them [the forces of the world]. Yet an element of finitude enters His being, because He distinguishes Himself from something which He is not. The Brahman as God is called Isvara.[53]

Maya accounts for God emerging in human form in incarnation. Sankara theistically accepted that Krishna, the Supreme Being existed as a man, but his birth is unlike that of the rest of humanity. He accepted God's existence in all manifestations. He even justified idolatry since God permitted being visualized with human attributes. This was allowed to facilitate his worship by man who could focus upon him. God's presence was seen as more pronounced in some places than others. The omniscient, paramount, personal God, as the repository of nobility intervenes to create the world. The personal and impersonal natures of God are contradictory only when thinking within the constraint

---

[50]Joshi, *Introduction to Sankara's Advaitism*, 46-47.

[51]Radhakrishnan and Moore, *A Source Book in Indian Philosophy*, 509-12. See also, Patrick Olivelle, *The Early Upanisads: Annotated Text and Translation* (Oxford: Oxford University Press, 1998), 255: Chandogya Upanisad 6:12 notes how one sees nothing when breaking the tiny seeds of a Banyan tree. The huge tree comes out of what cannot be perceived. Such is the nature of the Self or Atman.

[52]Joshi, *Introduction to Sankara's Advaitism*, 3, 44. Sankara does not equate Brahman and the world in unity. However, in essence, everything finds its base in Brahman when devoid of ignorance. See also R. C. Zaehner, ed., *Hindu Scriptures* (New York: Everyman's Library, 1972), 73: The Brihadaranyaka Upanishad claims that there is "no diversity at all." In its oneness it is immeasurable and firm, "transcending space, immaculate, unborn."

[53]Raju, *The Philosophical Traditions of India*, 178.

of sense and perception, but God transcends our world and has no such limitations at the Absolute level. This paradox is attributed to the operations of the inscrutable Maya.

Since Brahman is the ultimate reality, God is not identical to the Supreme Being for Advaitins. The personal God is a lower-order Being. Man being ultimately no different from the Absolute conflicts deeply with the basic postulate of theism, which regards God as infinitely superior to man. God and Brahman belong to different levels of reality. But the individual self is identified with the supreme Self only for the enlightened and God still exists as an object of devotion for man as long as he considers himself to be a separate individual who is not one with Brahman.[54]

In considering Brahman as both transcendent and anthropomorphic, Sankara again calls it a manifestation of Maya. The division of Brahman into human bodies is similar to the figurative partitioning of space by utensils. The location of water or any other object in a vessel is different from space that exists with or without the vessel.

When considering the creative and destructive roles of Brahman in relation to immutability, Sankara uses the simile of snake and rope. In darkness or Maya the appearance of world is similar to that of a perceived snake. However, the snake disappears and appears as a rope in the light. Likewise the world disappears through enlightenment. When that which lacks reality is gone, the ultimately real is understood.

This explanation does not seem to account for the difference between a mental construct and ontological existence. Equating them degenerates the world into a status of unreality, but Sankara says that the snake is real as an object of one's false imagination. Maya again bears the burden solving the puzzle. It simply restates the issue rather than explain it, since the exact relation between Maya and Brahman remains unexplained.[55] While Maya may seem a convenient placeholder for the mysteries inherent in Brahman, the Vedantins spend considerable effort in explicating its operations.

Liberation

Karma and bhakti are tightly intertwined as two sides of the same coin. Joshi claims that Sankara did not distinguish between bhakti (devotion) and gynana (knowledge), at the final stage of liberation, looking upon bhakti as necessary for gynana. The enlightened one totally surrenders to God, looking upon Him as the sole refuge. Monism merges with theism as karma and bhakti get access to the essential gynana, but bhakti remains necessary along with gynana at the end.[56]

The operation of grace during liberation is under dispute. Malkovsky claims some leap of faith through grace in Sankara's karma, since Sankara speaks of divine grace in numerous random contexts. These cryptic and opaque statements often refer to Brahman as Isvara, and not just to a subordinate Lord as later Advaitins did. Thus the Great Saying, "tat tvam asi" (That thou art) is said to refer to the personal Isvara.

Effort thus becomes indispensable but is insufficient. Both effort and grace are required for liberation. The immutable grace in the creature's depth exists in tension with the personal deity's free response. Sankara seems to interpret predetermination in a manner that favors impartiality and human freedom for purely rational reasons. The devotee has automatic grace in approaching the Lord as when one draws near a fire. But

---

[54]Joshi, *Introduction to Sankara's Advaitism*, 76-84, 138-43.
[55]Ibid., 122-26.
[56]Ibid., 135-37.

from theistic practice, personal Vishnu actively rewards the devotee in grace beyond the demands of karmic justice.[57]

Ramanuja

While Sankara was a bachelor who died a young man, Ramanuja, Ramanujar, or Ramanujam (A.D. 1017–1137) was married, separated, and lived a long life. He fought against the caste system just as vigorously as he opposed the non-qualified monism of Sankara.[58] Julius Lipner commends Ramanuja's profound theology, which is difficult to systematize since it is often condensed and obscure.[59] Ramanuja's theistic Vedanta is defined as the "non-dualism of the qualified Brahman, or simply qualified, non-dualism (visistadvaita)."[60] His determinate Brahman is qualified

> by the atmans and the material world, which together constitute the body (sarira) of the Brahman. The non-duality meant by the Upanisads is that of the one-ness of God, the atmans, and the world, like the one-ness of man who is a unity of body and atman.[61]

Source

Ramanuja's source comes from the Vedantic scriptures, the Upanishads, Brahma-Sutras, and the Gita. He also includes the Tamil scriptures, specifically the Vaisnava puranas, the Pancharatra-Agama and the Prabandham. Ramanuja says "No scriptural texts teach a Brahman devoid of all difference."[62] He clarifies the typical proof-texts of the Advaitins to qualify the monism that they taught:

> What all these texts deny is only plurality in so far as contradicting the unity of the world which depends on its being in its entirety an effect of Brahman, and having Brahman for its inward ruling principle and its true Self. They do not, on the other hand, deny that plurality on Brahman's part which depends on its intention to become manifold – a plurality proved by the text "May I be many, may I grow forth" (Ch. Up. vi.ii.3).[63]

Ramanuja takes "Tat tvam asi," the classic proof text of the Advaitins and says that enlightenment is not knowledge of non-qualified Brahman or absolute identity of a non-differentiated substance. Instead, "Tat" refers to the omniscient Brahman with quality. "Tvam" refers to Brahman having for its body individual selves and matter. This coordination expresses the two-fold form of one substance, while clearly retaining the primary denotation of both words.[64]

---

[57]Malkovsky, "Samkara on Divine Grace," 70-83.

[58]P. T. Raju, *Structural Depths of Indian Thought* (Albany: State University of New York Press, 1985), 438.

[59]Julius Lipner, *The Face of Truth: A Study of Meaning and Metaphysics in the Vedantic Theology of Ramanuja* (Albany: State University of New York Press, 1986), xi.

[60]Raju, *The Philosophical Traditions of India*, 188.

[61]Ibid., 188.

[62]Radhakrishnan and Moore, *A Source Book in Indian Philosophy*, 548.

[63]Ibid., 551.

[64]Ibid., 548-51. The referents in "that art thou" are challenged by different interpreters.

Epistemology

Ramanuja states that perception, inference, and scripture are the three valid means of cognition. He accepted extrasensory perception and that of enlightened persons, but in inference and verbal knowledge he required cognition of an object to have attributes. All cognition is valid in itself; and objects failing to serve their intended purpose represent falsity. P. T. Raju questions the use of the principle of contradiction against other systems which admit false knowledge. But Ramanuja notes that cognition fails its intended purpose. Valid knowledge aids practical interests of life and involves three kinds of consciousness, limited by the inner instrument, its function, and the object. When they coincide, cognition can never be false and is assigned to the Atman. Thus even illusory objects are real and have non-mundane existence. He attempts to reconcile conflicts between perception, inference, and scripture rather than subsuming one under the other. God is known through attributes since knowledge is always "S is P," not just "S." Knowledge involves attribute consciousness, distinguishing subject and object, and nothing indeterminate can be the object of knowledge.[65]

Ramanuja sees language as fact-assertive. It structurally corresponds to reality. The Shruti or divine texts contain veridical information which yields right cognition of their chief object if interpreted literally, despite accommodating figurative interpretation. Also, scriptural correlative predication reveals a differentiated Brahman-reality. The earlier exegesis of "Tat tvam asi" illustrates the relation of identity-in-difference between Brahman and creation.

Liberation of the finite Self is preceded by knowledge of the nature of Brahman and of its own Self. The Atman's consciousness has the Self as knower catching itself at work, being cognitively transitive through introspective self-awareness and self-reflection. The Self acts, enjoys, and suffers in its empirical condition as a personal agent in the samsaric or cyclical state before it attains liberation.[66]

Ramanuja's commentary on the enquiry into Brahman demonstrates the lack of proof for non-differentiated substance. Difference inheres in speech, perception, inference, and in all consciousness. Those claiming substance without difference cannot affirm any "proof of such a substance, for all means of right knowledge have for their object things affected with difference."[67] Sankara's followers tried to prove this, but Sankara refrained from such assertions. Perception cannot reveal mere being, but only one with attributes. Consciousness is an attribute of Being. The agent constantly persists while the attribute of consciousness of sorrow or pleasure, is sublated or negated, persists for a time and ends. The ego or "I" is same as the essential cognizing Self.[68] The Atman's awareness expands rather than contracts in its I-awareness by sharing in the Lord's all-knowingness in moksha. All events are summated and transformed into a fulfilled vision.

---

[65]Raju, *Structural Depths of Indian Thought*, 439-41. Indeterminate knowledge is distinct from determinate knowledge, but it too must have determinations: "in determinate cognition, the determinations are universals or class characteristics, in indeterminate knowledge they are individuals" (ibid., 193-94).

[66]Lipner, *The Face of Truth*, 24-63.

[67]Radhakrishnan and Moore, *A Source Book in Indian Philosophy*, 543.

[68]Ibid., 543-48.

Living Life

Devotion to God is a necessary means for release. For Ramanuja, Vishnu is God and Brahman. Liberation is achieved only by personally understanding Brahman's proper form as having a unique relationship, of identity-in-difference, with creation. The androgynous God has the supernal form as creator and sustainer of finite creatures, being immanent and transcendent, and having a distinctly partitive yet participative relationship. This liberation needs the Lord above to elect and the individual below to respond, as the Katha Upanishad affirms.[69]

World and Maya

The world is real as Brahman's body and Maya is critiqued for its elusiveness in Advaita. Ramanuja refutes traditional Advaidic Maya, saying that the peculiar creative energy of Brahman is not just similar to the fire's power to burn, but that it too must have being. Suffering comes from the Atman forgetting the truth and actively seeking pleasure and knowledge. Thus the problem is ajnana or avidya which is unconsciousness or ignorance, rather than Maya. Avidya is synonymous with karma as both latent and actual action.[70] He questions the appearance of avidya in Brahman to produce the world and jiva, which is the individual self in contrast to the Atman which is the cosmic Self. He says that "ignorance cannot exist by itself, but only as belonging to someone."[71] If belonging to jiva, jiva must exist before avidya to possess it, unlike Maya, but if it belongs to Brahman, then it sullies the perfect Being facing any side. But avidya is just absence of knowledge of the true nature of the jiva and this provides a much better explanation. He thus says that "Maya, as expounded by the Advaitins, is self-contradictory and false."[72] On a positive note, Radhakrishnan and Moore observe that

> Ramanuja fixes his attention on the world, self, and God. For him all these are real, but the world and the selves depend on God. Ramanuja believes in the continued individual existence of the released selves. While Brahman is eternally free from all imperfections, matter is unconscious, and the individual selves are subject to ignorance and suffering prior to release. They (God, selves, and the world) form a unity, as matter and selves have existence only as the body of Brahman. Brahman is the self and the controlling power of the body, which includes the world and the selves. Apart from Brahman they are nothing. The individual self and inanimate natures are essentially different from God, though they have no existence or purpose to serve apart from him or his service. Ramanuja's theory, therefore, is a non-dualism with a difference, namely, that the one Brahman has two forms: selves and matter.[73]

Ramanuja views the world as having its own being as a characteristic apart from Brahman. Prakrti or unconscious matter has the three attributes assigned to Maya – sattva, rajas, and tamas which are akin to substances or even qualities of the mind. In

---

[69]Lipner, *The Face of Truth*, 79-99. Katha Upanishad notes that "Him whom this [Self] chooses, by him it is to be obtained, and to him this Self reveals its form" (ibid., 99).

[70]Karma can be used of individual actions in a positive or negative sense. They can also refer to the samsara or karmic cycle, with the results of action lending to further consequent actions.

[71]Raju, *The Philosophical Traditions of India*, 189.

[72]Ibid., 190.

[73]Radhakrishnan and Moore, *A Source Book in Indian Philosophy*, 508.

creation, the original subtle prakrti in the Atman has its equilibrium destroyed through karma when the "attributes separate, act upon each other and become the world of gross objects."[74] Sattva never exists without the other two attributes. Four levels of being are real: world, dreams, illusions, and hallucinations. For creation, even in their pure state, the Atmans have a body of pure sattva, a very subtle pure transparent substance, different from sattva and unrelated to rajas or tamas. The Atman regains its pure body by seeking to be transparent sattva alone, overcoming rajas' active disturbance and tamas' dark impurity. But ultimately it gives even that up and regains pure sattva. This philosophy is more theological with three kinds of Atmans – in bondage, liberated, or eternally liberated which are the demi-gods and angels of Hindu lore.[75]

Atman

The liberated Atmans enjoy the constant presence of God but enjoyment is possible only if the enjoyer has a body, mind, and senses.[76] The Atman is different from Brahman and is part of its body. It is atomic in size but has an infinite attribute-consciousness. It has two forms of consciousness: an existential-consciousness which is one's own being and an attribute-consciousness which is one's property. The existential-consciousness is the same as the pure I-consciousness or the Atman, but is not the ego, which is the I-consciousness identified with a given form. Thus, the "atman is both the knower and the agent of action, and also the enjoyer of the fruit of those actions."[77] Ramanuja appeals to experience in claiming that I, and not my ego, am the knower of objects. Ramanuja only accepts the "becoming" of the cause into the effect, rather than an identity. Thus, Brahman is seen to transform into the world.

There is no new creation or appearance, but rather a manifestation or becoming of the subtle to gross form. Here only Brahman's body changes while the Atman remains unchanged in both subtle and gross states. Since our own human body changes without our Atman changing, so also one part of Brahman can change without affecting the other. However, Raju takes exception with Ramanuja since the Atman is maintained as the knower, doer, and enjoyer, implying change to the Atman itself and not merely the ego, where he does not follow Sankara's approach. Ramanuja attributes this to the mysterious power of Brahman which remains unaffected and ultimately cannot be understood.[78]

Brahman and God

There is only one true absolute reality and that is Brahman which is non-dual, but qualified or known through attributes. Reality is divided into substance and attribute; into means and objects of cognition; and also into God, spirit and matter. God has five states: Transcendent, Supernal, Incarnation, Immanent, and Idol. God is not just pure Being, but structured and qualified Being, known by every part except prakrti or nature.[79] Ramanuja equates the Absolute Brahman to a personal God who has existence, consciousness, and bliss as his qualities in addition to other great qualities like power and

---

[74]Raju, *The Philosophical Traditions of India*, 191.

[75]Ibid., 191-95.

[76]Ibid., 442-53.

[77]Ibid., 191.

[78]Ibid., 191-93. Ramanuja interestingly identifies the mystery in Brahman rather than Maya.

[79]Ibid., 442-53. Prakrti is divided into sattva, rajas, and tamas.

23

splendor. Brahman is unaffected by the world's evil since the world has an Atman-body relationship to him. The "atmans constitute the body of the Brahman, they are yet different from it."[80] This is not both identity and difference since opposites can never be both true in the same relation. Brahman always existed with the Atmans and the material world. These were subtle before and gross after creation while the gross becomes subtle in dissolution. Ramanuja says, "Chit. That is, the soul. Achit. That is, the body. Both are the attributes of God. Just as a flower possess both fragrance and colour."[81]

Brahman is the one "free from all imperfection and comprising within itself all auspicious qualities,"[82] internally ruling all individual Selves with lordly power. The central formulation is the self-body relationship, described as the Brahman having all intelligent and non-intelligent beings for its body. The individual Self constitutes Brahman's body and has Brahman enter it. Thus the Vedantic phrase "in that all this has its Self" is explained and also the world is consummated in Brahman alone. The Brahman has distinctive qualities and is the only cause of the universe. The individual selves constitute Brahman's body, with unlimited knowledge in their true nature and an essential intuition of the supreme Self. This true nature is hidden by ignorance, which is attributed to a chain of karmic works without beginning; and release is understood as intuition of the highest Self. The infinite regress of karma is problematic. But eliminating ignorance is not just a simple act of cognition, but is done through the grace of the Lord who is pleased with the worshipper's devout meditation. In the Lord's independent act of grace, difference disappears. He grants piety and mercifully provides final release to the selves who apply themselves to the internal aid, thus increasing their happiness to the highest degree.[83]

Liberation

While Sankara esteemed knowledge as highest, Ramanuja gave that place to devotion, although the ethical life of action continues until death. There is no life without action. Thus liberation does not occur in this life and obtains only after death. Ramanuja defines devotion not as feeling, but as continuous knowledge, like being passionately in love. Meditating on verbal conceptual knowledge leads to this devotional knowledge but ethical action keeps the mind pure and above selfishness. Constant knowledge of God is impossible for man. God understands this difficulty and helps anyone sincerely attempting it. The devotee takes refuge in self-surrender to God, as an instrument of God renouncing his actions in the world by active living.[84] Eric Lott defined this thus:

> The devotional relationship, prompted by the supreme Person's perfection, and made possible by his grace, that determines the synthesis of the various means of approach to him.[85]

---

[80]Ibid., 188-89.
[81]Indira Parthasarathy, *Ramanujar: The Life and Ideas of Ramanuja*, trans. T. Sriraman (New Delhi: Oxford University Press, 2008), 56.
[82]Radhakrishnan and Moore, *A Source Book in Indian Philosophy*, 552.
[83]Ibid., 552-55.
[84]Raju, *The Philosophical Traditions of India*, 196.
[85]Eric Lott, *Vedantic Approaches to God* (New York: Barnes & Noble Books, 1980), 184.

Postmortem to liberation in the body, the Self bathes in the refulgence of Brahman, seeing and knowing him as he is, with expanded personal awareness, and fellowship with others likewise liberated. The liberated Self as an accessory of the Lord paradoxically participates in the Lord's sovereignty, bliss, and knowledge. The human form is given a tremendous tribute. This world changes from the source of sorrow under karma before liberation, to a source of unalloyed delight to the cognitively and morally pure Self after. The liberated Self has sensory essential experience of the world in its divine rootedness and the Lord's justice and mercy, but overcomes it beyond karmic sway, the samsara becoming moksha.[86] Ramanuja's soteriology is defined thus:

> Salvation, according to Ramanuja, is not the disappearance of the self, but its release from limiting barriers. The self cannot be dissolved into God. One substance cannot be dissolved into another. However high a man may rise, there will always be God superior to him, whom he should reverence, worship, and adore. The released self has a permanent intuition of God. Its essential nature, which is obscured by ignorance and passion in the state of bondage, is manifested in the state of release.[87]

Lipner sees Ramanuja challenging Advaita in an orthodox and scriptural way, restoring respectability to devotional theism. Ramanuja took the understanding of God further, by providing both content and method, specifically the denotation of naming-words extending to Brahman and the conception of the divine supernal form in the brilliant Self-body model.[88]

Madhva

Madhva or Madhava (A.D. 1197-1276) extends the trajectory that Ramanuja begins on Sankara's doctrines. Philosophically, Madhva's unqualified dualism or Dvaita is furthest from Sankara. Despite his vast differences from Sankara, they still share a few commonalities. Madhva accepted many of Ramanuja's doctrines including rejection of Sankara's doctrine of Maya and acceptance of atomic Atman subservient to Brahman. He accepted the validity of knowledge always and also the difference between Brahman, the Atmans and the world.

Madhva espouses absolute difference (bheda) between Self and God, Self and Self, Self and matter, God and matter, and matter and matter. His dualism is ultimately between Brahman and Atman. Brahman, Atman, and the world are pluralistic. God's controlling power is the unifying principle in his system.[89]

Source

Madhva has similar sources as other Vedantins, with a high view of scriptures as the only source. He sees God as the teacher of the authorless Veda.

---

[86]Lipner, *The Face of Truth*, 24.
[87]Radhakrishnan and Moore, *A Source Book in Indian Philosophy*, 508.
[88]Lipner, *The Face of Truth*, 145.
[89]Raju, *The Philosophical Traditions of India*, 197. The presentation of Dvaita under Madhva is kept minimal since this system serves as a remote foil upon which to contrast the Advaita of Sankara.

Epistemology

Knowledge is intrinsically valid. It reveals the independently real knower and the known. He sees differences in the extent to which even the liberated Selves possess knowledge and enjoy bliss. He accepts perception, inference, and testimony as the three sources of knowledge, like Ramanuja.

Living Life

Enquiry into Brahman shows three classes of action – devotion to God in study, in tranquility, and in realization of the futility of all things apart from Brahman.[90]

World and Maya

The world is eternal and its differences real. Difference is a part of things' essence. Perception requires distinction that makes things unique. Therefore there is no Maya hiding the real as in Sankara's sense. The primal matter, prakrti, transforms from subtle to gross in order to create the body and other material things.[91] Madhva refers to sakti as energy or power. Sakti finds its source in the particular (visesa) in each entity, which distinguishes it from other entities. There are two supreme categories for all entities, the independent and the dependent: "The Brahman alone is independent and has control over everything else, which is subordinate to it. Maya is the Will or desire (iccha) of the Brahman."[92]

Atman

Madhva sees an infinite number of individual, atomic Selfs. Selfs are eternally free, freed, or bound. They act as real agents inwardly controlled by God:

> The self is not an absolute agent, since it is of limited power and is dependent on God. It is by nature blissful, though it is subject to pain and suffering on account of its connection with a material body due to its past karma. So long as it is not freed from impurities it wanders about in changing forms of existence. No two selves are alike.[93]

Brahman and God

The selves and the world are eternal with, but subordinate to and dependent upon God. Brahman is God, the perfect personality primarily called Vishnu, who directs the world. He has a supernatural body, is transcendent as well as immanent, and inwardly rules all selves.[94] God has infinitely good qualities and his essence includes existence, knowledge, and bliss. He creates, preserves, and destroys the universe. He damns some and redeems others as the Lord of karma and is pleased only by bhakti or devotion. He

---

[90]Radhakrishnan and Moore, *A Source Book in Indian Philosophy*, 555-71.
[91]Sharma, *A Critical Survey of Indian Philosophy*, 372-73.
[92]Raju, *The Philosophical Traditions of India*, 197.
[93]Radhakrishnan and Moore, *A Source Book in Indian Philosophy*, 508.
[94]Ibid., 508, 570.

manifests himself to the world and is present in sacred images. Lakshmi is the power of God and his consort.[95]

Liberation

Bhakti is the only means of liberation in love, surrender, and service to Brahman. But God is directly inapproachable and is mediated by Vayu or the Spirit. The divine Will is supreme to set men free or cast them into bondage. Liberation perpetuates the individual Self in release to adore and worship God. The released Self is granted all wishes except the ability to control the world.[96] The goal of liberation that is obtained by both devotion and perception is similar but not identical. Each path reflects the Self's differences – all need hierarchical devotional attachment, but some have specially granted qualities for immediate perceptual vision or knowledge. Devotion still is the means and the end in realizing the essential Being of itself and God. Madhva "insists that devotional dependence is the principal, even the sole, means of 'knowing' Brahman perfectly and attaining liberation fully."[97]

Madhva differs from Ramanuja in not accepting the Atman-body view, as he sees the Brahman completely different from the Atmans forming a complete duality. Madhva is not just a dualist, but is a pluralist with his distinction of the Brahman, an infinite number of Atmans, and material entities.[98]

Madhva's entities have separate existence and are not just qualifications of identity. The attributes are completely real, with Selfs and matter having substantive existence. God is the efficient cause of the world, while prakrti is the material cause.

Selfs are qualitatively and quantitatively plural, differing in degree of knowledge and bliss even in liberation. Liberated Selfs are similar to God and yet vastly inferior. The bliss enjoyed by the redeemed Selfs involves many factors including the nearness and similarity in the location, proximity, external form, and sharing of God's bliss.

What is drastically unique to Madhva and some Jainas is the view that "certain souls like demons, ghosts and some men are eternally doomed and damned. They can never hope to get liberation."[99] Madhva's views are so radical that some see possible Christian influence in his philosophy.[100] This overall progression from Sankara and Ramanuja to Madhva seems to reflect a greater deviation from Advaita's strict monism.

Summary

Eric Lott notes that Vedanta's primary concern is to properly express the perfect being of Brahman as the goal of human existence. Brahman's transcendent perfection circumscribes all existence with immanence. Each interpretation of this immanent transcendence intends to preserve Brahman's perfection. Immanence was scrutinized within causal categories, using mechanisms like Maya for resolving the perfection of Brahman. All Vedantins experientially recognize ignorance or ambiguity in

---

[95]Sharma, *A Critical Survey of Indian Philosophy*, 372-73.
[96]Radhakrishnan and Moore, *A Source Book in Indian Philosophy*, 509, 571.
[97]Lott, *Vedantic Approaches to God*, 189-90.
[98]Raju, *The Philosophical Traditions of India*, 197.
[99]Sharma, *A Critical Survey of Indian Philosophy*, 374-75. They have no escape from samsara.
[100]Zaehner, *Hinduism*, 101.

the finite Self's knowledge of Brahman and use selfhood analogically as the primary model to understand Brahman's being. Each Vedantin had a variant model of selfhood as his determinant analogy.

Vedanta Worldview

Each Vedantin built his worldview tightly and coherently with transcendent consciousness as the lynchpin for Sankara, the Self-body relationship for Ramanuja, and the Self-determining Will for Madhva. All claimed that only scripture reveals the Brahman but used presuppositions in their analogies in order to interpret reality. The monist and the theist differ the most in the categories of ontology, epistemology, and soteriology.

The monist sees absolute oneness of selfhood as ultimately real and the theist establishes Brahman as the supremely glorious, personal Lord. The theist saw Brahman's personal transcendence not as nirguna, but as distinguishing all beings, and this being true of even the liberated Selfs.[101] Equating Brahman with a changing universe or absolute oneness threatened this perfection. Thus ultimately all is real, created by, dependent on, and subservient to Brahman. Devotion and grace are essential in this relationship.

The theism of Ramanuja and Madhva also diverge internally. Madhva rightly agrees with the monist Sankara on a few concepts including the transcendental emphasis around creation. There is a reflective relation of the finite Self to Brahman, where action is different from knowledge and also the avatar is seen as a manifestation rather than a real embodiment. Madhva's emphasis on the Lord's supreme Will controlling all universal entities with innate characteristics is radically different from Sankara and rightly presents divine sovereignty. Although most Vedantins seem to emphasize both works and intuition, Karl Potter sees Vedantins in the categories of progress, leap, and something in-between. Madhva, denying personal effort for moksha requires a leap for liberation; Ramanuja could be progress or undecided; while Sankara has both progress and leap.[102] Alston claims Sankara is closer to experience as he avoids limiting the Absolute with definite conceptions of negative theology as his followers did.[103]

Coherence and Correspondence

Francis Clooney finds realism in Sankara, with three dimensions: The philosophical pinnacle of Brahman, the exegetical study of the Vedas, and the religious faith in the mass of detail on religious realities. The Devatas or angelic beings allegedly provide a mediate understanding of God in the world as declared by the Upanishads.[104]

Ramanuja's system is commendable for its Self-body relational analogy, which brings ontological continuity, through mediated knowledge and experience, to the supremely qualified Brahman. Since creation and its effect-states are real, cause and dependent relationships are also explicable. The assumptions of distinctive Supreme

---

[101]Nirguna refers to the absence of all attributes.

[102]Potter, *Presuppositions of India's Philosophies*, 98,100.

[103]Alston, *Samkara in East and West Today*, 107-08.

[104]Francis X. Clooney, "Samkara's Theological Realism: The Meaning and Usefulness of Gods (Devata) in the Uttara Mimamsa Sutra Bhasya," in *New Perspectives on Advaita Vedanta: Essays in Commemoration of Professor Richard De Smet*, ed. Bradley J. Malkovsky (Boston: Brill, 2000), 30-49.

Being, grace, accessibility, and real devotional agency of the individual have ultimate value in a continuum of being from Brahman, "but only those accepting similar presuppositions are likely to be convinced."[105] Ramanuja has greater inner coherence from a monist view due to the intrinsic inclusiveness of his Self-body model.

In comparing Ramanuja's views with Sankara some take exception to Ramanuja's approach of trying to unify Sankara's Vedantic scriptures and the scriptures of Vaisnava theism. For Sharma these systems can be partially, but not fully reconciled, although Lipner considers the tension rightly preserved.[106] While Ramanuja gives a pregnant immanentism in the best form of monotheism, it retains Sankara's position phenomenally. The highest conception available to finite beings is Isvara alone, despite the highest reality being the determinate Brahman. Thus Ramanuja's Absolute is the concrete personal individual God as identity-in-difference. Ramanuja is said to aspire to but fail in reconciling philosophical thought and religious feeling. This is untrue since a much better realist dimension is now introduced in the nature of God, Self, and the world.

Ramanuja designated matter, Selfs, and God as three interacting realities making the Absolute. However, the Absolute is only identified with God which is one of the three and the substratum of matter and Selfs, which are his attributes. Thus a thing can be both a substance and an attribute, distinguished relatively. Here, Selfs and matter are substances themselves, but also attributes of God. Other Advaitins find this to defy the definition of a substance having independent existence and fault his philosophy as flawed. It is true that the ontological status of God's body is indeed problematic despite his highly specialized classification of sattva.

Ramanuja's Visistadvaita or qualified identity is "identity-in-and-through-and-because-of-difference."[107] This dependent existence is an inner relation, where attributes depend on the substance even as the body depends on the Self. Ramanuja must either give up Advaita or subsume all to be relative to the Absolute. Instead it internally divided as Sharma perceptively diagnoses. This relation is neither pure identity nor pure difference nor both. Prakrti becomes the material cause, but the cause of bondage of Self in karma is inexplicable with the "beginningless" samsara. Reconciling immutability in God and suffering in the body falls short of its objective as Ramanuja is unable to provide a satisfactory answer to these important issues. However, the solution does not seem to rest on absolutism, but rather with that duality in theism that tends closer to Madhva.

Advaita Vedanta

Hinduism as a philosophical worldview has deep roots in the Indian tradition and has been precisely fine-tuned through the logical acumen of brilliant men, relying on their scriptures and their presuppositions. It is awe-inspiring to see the heights that these towering intellectual giants reached.

This chapter broadly outlined the dominant teaching of Vedanta philosophy as seen in Sankara's Advaita, Ramanuja's Visistadvaita, and Madhva's Dvaita. The relative merits and flaws of each system were examined relative to one another. Some of the positive elements of these systems were highlighted along with their problems, demonstrating the keen intellect and passionate devotion of men who lived and developed

---

[105]Lott, *Vedantic Approaches to God*, 192.
[106]Lipner, *The Face of Truth*, 139-42.
[107]Sharma, *A Critical Survey of Indian Philosophy*, 365.

a truly remarkable system. The progression also hints how the journey could further continue toward the ultimately transcendent and yet genuinely immanent God to be envisioned in a consistent, coherent, and correspondent system. Vedanta has at least three strong candidates that contend for the primary position. For the purposes for this book, in light of its popularity among the intellectual elite and its antiquity, Sankara's Advaitism will be retained as the dominant Vedanta worldview, despite its opposition from within Hinduism. Going forward the term Vedanta will refer more specifically to the strands of Advaita which are closer to Sankara.

In the next chapter this worldview will be examined on the basis of key foundational truths from the Christian revelation. Christians have attempted to reach out to the adherents of Vedanta philosophy on various terms and using variegated bases. A historic overview of the rapprochement will be instructive before beginning a robust worldview engagement with Vedanta.

CHAPTER 3
CHRISTIAN APOLOGETICS TO VEDANTA

Christian apologetics with Vedanta Hinduism can take on distinctly diverse patterns. Some tend toward a strong reconciliation, while others disconnect completely from Vedanta. Rapprochement methods showcase the dangers of losing distinctive Christian theology while antithetical methods can argue for reasons other than the Christian gospel. The benefit of learning from contemporary liberal scholarship is explored, while rejecting their overall emphases and defining clear lines that mark the boundaries of Christian Worldview apologetics.

Vedanta and Christianity are arguably polar opposites, when examining their metaphysics, epistemology, and ethics. This is particularly true of Advaita Vedanta which is rather popular and the principal object of our attention.[108] It may be further contended that there exists no fundamental philosophical or theological common ground between the two, making it a contrasting case-study to explore the Reformed Worldview apologetic framework. However, despite *prima facie* differences, there are indeed valid means of communication and points of contact, which make apologetics not only possible, but also necessary.[109]

The challenge for the Christian apologist is to apply the principles of Worldview apologetics by understanding the biblical access points and dividing lines.

At one end, the rapprochement methods aid in determining the points of contact and suggest legitimate means of engagement. At the other end, the methods of antithesis help identify the separating lines between Christianity and Advaita Vedanta. In recommending a faithful approach, the strengths of Worldview apologetics form the base

---

[108]Bradley Malkovsky, "Advaita Vedanta and Christian Faith," *Journal of Ecumenical Studies* 36 (1999): 398-99. Madhva's Dvaita would not be as radically different as Sankara's Advaita.

[109]Sarvepalli Radhakrishnan and Charles E. Moore, eds., *A Source Book in Indian Philosophy* (Princeton: Princeton University Press, 1957), 507: The Christian can agree with the crux of this statement on the relation between God and creation – "The empirical world cannot exist by itself. It is wholly dependent on Brahman, but the changes of the empirical order do not affect the integrity of Brahman. The world depends on Brahman, but Brahman depends on nothing."

within which other apologetic methodologies can be effectively utilized. This chapter will complete the theoretical groundwork from which the actual apologetic shall proceed.

The faithful approach becomes clear once the two sides of rapprochement and antithesis are outlined. Rapprochement is used to signify the advance of any closer connection than biblical Christianity would permit. Antithesis is used of disparities being emphasized stronger than biblical truth constrains the Christian apologist, either propositionally or methodologically.

Any rapprochement involves the danger of compromising Christian truth. However, these bridge-building attempts actually do find key contact points with Hinduism that is often missed by unsympathetic external evaluations of the system. The risks and benefits of rapprochement become apparent by reviewing actual encounters.

The common problem with antithesis is magnifying the differences, by either caricaturing Hinduism or exhibiting mean-spiritedness, without practically reflecting Christian values. Worldview apologetics will seek to avoid these less-than-desirable elements of apologetics, while retaining those genuine and fundamental worldview contrasts that can never be overlooked.

The faithful approach will utilize both contact points and real contrasts without compromising Christian truth or falsifying Hindu beliefs. This Worldview apologetic will focus comprehensively on its intellectual content and also extend to its manner of execution.

Examining Methods of Rapprochement

Unorthodox "Christian" materials are typically unhelpful, since they tend to compromise fundamental tenets of the faith that they purport to defend. However, these unorthodox materials sometimes highlight inherent commonalities between Christianity and Hinduism in the truths of general revelation and *imago dei*. In certain cases, the corrupted instincts may have had an originally positive inclination that could be recovered by closer study. A sharper application of Christian doctrine in the apologetic encounter is invaluable to reevaluate these studies. Additionally, liberal sources often define the opposing Vedanta viewpoint more accurately than conservative material, since they frequently engage sympathetically to fairly depict that worldview. Thus these materials are examined under rapprochement in order to further the Christian understanding of Vedanta Hindus.

It may seem that to represent Vedanta worldview properly, one needs to disengage from core Christian beliefs.[110] This is a valid statistical observation from today's rapprochement. However, biblical Christians can also equitably characterize Vedanta, by examining its beliefs as impartially as any imperfect human can accomplish such a task. This task is best accomplished by viewing it within the Hindu worldview.

There is no neutral point of view except for God alone. The best that finite and fallible Christians can attempt, is to align with God's perspective as best as they can, using scriptural lens. This requires them to view all other worldviews as best as they can from within the perspective of their Christian worldview. In doing so, the slanting of all contrary perspectives appears inevitable. An example may help clarify this conundrum.

---

[110]Karl H. Potter, *Presuppositions of India's Philosophies* (Englewood Cliffs, NJ: Prentice-Hall Inc., 1963), 100. The worldviews are so radically different as to require a complete disconnect.

Imagine this scenario: In country A, the term "short" refers to adults who are less than 4 feet tall. In another country B, "short" now refers to people who are below 6 feet tall. Citizen X of country A is 5 feet tall. Citizen Y of B would call Citizen X short, who would be offended at this insult, assuming that shortness is an undesirable attribute.

This situational conflict is remedied by not restricting one's evaluation purely to the statements made. Any true engagement dives deeper into the definition of "shortness" in each context. It also notes the difference in the underlying presuppositions about the value associated with it. This evaluation more precisely explains how the statement falls short of its intended use either in country A or B.

There are two areas where this illustration falls short. Firstly, philosophical subjects being considered between Hinduism and Christianity are often not as simple as the term "short." Typically they refer to radically different entities that need to be brought on somewhat compatible scales in order to recalibrate the language used. A good example here is God and Brahman. Calibrating these terms can take considerable effort.

Secondly, the issue centers in understanding how any term is used within each worldview. Just as citizen Y must first understand how citizen X understands the term "short," in order to meaningfully communicate, so also the Christian must first properly understand what Vedanta says within its worldview, when speaking about Hinduism. This task is nearly impossible when one constantly views the Hindu worldview through the lens of the Christian worldview.

Using a military analogy, it is insufficient just to look through field-glasses from across the battle-lines. Rather, it requires a covert stepping into enemy territory to survey the land in order to expose the fault-lines. Those who step into enemy territory risk capture, but such engagements are better equipped to attack enemy combatants and spare innocent civilians. The analogy breaks down soon enough. When the underlying presuppositions of the Hindu worldview are exposed and addressed, it will necessarily bring down the entire superstructure, including any truths which are partially aligned with the Christian worldview. Failing to faithfully engage with the Hindu by purely attacking the superstructures in simplicity or falsehood, will unjustifiably alienate the Hindu as their belief is caricatured. Worse, it will also poorly display the Christian worldview with an uncharacteristic callousness, misrepresentation, and lack of charity.

Given this outlook, the engagement of the liberal Christians with Vedanta is explored, rejecting improper concessions but learning from any coincidental connections.

Compromise

Many peaceful engagements with Vedanta trespass along the corridors of Christian truth. The following illustrative examples showcase negatively some ways Worldview apologists must avoid theological compromise in their apologetic encounters.

Paul Tillich's theology seems well-suited as a natural philosophical bridge from Christianity to Vedanta. John Thatamanil connects Tillich and Sankara to foster a conversation between the Christian and Vedanta worldviews. He notes,

> On the Christian side, Paul Tillich serves as a compelling conversation partner for Sankara because the German-American's theological program is deeply informed by precisely those moments within Christian tradition in which God's immanence to the world was most vigorously announced and championed. Tillich's theology

amounts to a twentieth-century distillation of the history of Christian mystical theology.[111]

Those areas where Christendom overemphasized God's immanence become easy access points for contact. This is biblical compromise. Christians must retain the full gamut of scriptural testimony. The underlying failure in Tillich is a rejection of clear Creator-creature distinctions and the resultant, unmistakable dualism of the orthodox Christian worldview. To short-circuit this distinction is to result in a failed enterprise.

Sankara and Tillich share a deep commitment to rejecting theological dualism. Both believe that ultimate reality is not a being among beings. Both believe that human beings find healing when human beings understand their belonging to the divine life. We have also discovered that both traditions are plagued by residual dualisms that are rooted in substantialist ways of imagining divinity. Sankara relapses into dualism by distinguishing sharply between a changeless Brahman and a changing world, and Tillich falls prey to a sharp and tragic dualism when he insists that creatures can only be free if they stand outside the divine life. Adopting a dynamic ontology enables us to overcome these flaws while preserving the deepest intuitions of both traditions.[112]

Thantamanil is discontent with the ontological ground proposed by Tillich and Sankara. He wants to further develop the monism of Vedanta by using dynamic ontology. The danger of lacking deeply anchored roots in biblical theology causes the dialog to fall prey to the seductive underlying monism, which has no place in the Christian worldview. This soldier had no allegiance to begin with and now loses the conflict in being assimilated by the enemy. The metaphysical truth about God and creation is wholly lost.

This danger is more explicitly observed in Anders Jeffner who values a theology resulting from dialog, over and above the prescriptions of scriptural truth:

The Bible gives us help in the search after truth, but nothing is true just because it is found in the Bible . . . a fruitful dialogue leading to theological results must involve an attempt to overcome the idea of a simple scriptural criterion of truth. I think it must go so far that believers clearly disassociate themselves from certain parts of their holy texts.[113]

The irony of this approach is that Sankara would strongly disagree with any scriptural disassociation, as should the Christian. Jeffner finds himself a stranger in a no-man land by attempting to build a bridge of unity without the foundation piles of the

---

[111]John J. Thatamanil, *The Immanent Divine: God, Creation, and the Human Predicament – An East-West Conversation* (Minneapolis: Fortress Press, 2006), 9.

[112]Ibid., 206. For a historic critique, see Robert Watts, *The New Apologetic or, The Downgrade in Criticism, Theology, and Science* (Edinburgh: T. & T. Clark, 1890), vi. Tony Richie, "Hints from Heaven: Can C. S. Lewis Help Evangelicals Hear God in Other Religions?" *Evangelical Review of Theology* 32 (2008): 38-55. It claims that other religions are not totally false, but anything true in all religions is completed in Christ. Lewis' theology of religions seems to bind faithful Christianity and hospitable openness to religious others, opening dialogue with non-Christian traditions to appreciate God's work among everyone, everywhere at all times.

[113]Anders Jeffner, "Truth and Religious Dialogue," in *Truth, Religious Dialogue, and Dynamic Orthodoxy: Reflections on the Works of Brian Hebblethwaite*, ed. Julius J. Lipner (London: SCM Press, 2005), 50.

unshakable Scriptures on either end. He falsely places his confidence in a cooperative theological development at the expense of explicit divine revelation.

Most rapprochements do not boldly give up the Scriptures, but tinker around with scriptural interpretation that manifests itself in ever-changing theology. R. H. Hooker descends to such an effort in attempting to quantify personhood in the nature of God, by recommending a move away from propositions to ecstatic experience.

> Personality in both God and humanity is of eternal significance, but even that final claim must be made in vulnerability and openness. It needs to be purged of anthropomorphism and idolatry, but that is a matter not for more words but for the apophatic way, contemplative prayer, and silence.[114]

Something important must be observed with Hooker. There truly is a tentativeness with which finite man's theology must be held, especially where the *eisegesis* of fallible human thought can corrupt the pristine meaning of the infallible Scriptures. The solution to this problem is getting closer to the text in order to understand it more clearly, if it is indeed God's revelation to man. To resort to experience and negation are not false, but incomplete. They become positively dangerous if done at the cost of exegesis. Hooker's recommended approach is another casualty of war as he ends up naturally favoring Vedanta where experience is often valued as the pinnacle of truth.

Contact Points

There have been strong attempts by Advaita scholars such as Richard De Smet and the tradition of Sara Grant, Francis Clooney, and Bradley Malkovsky who explore the attraction of Advaita from their Catholic backgrounds, conceding to the strength of monistic attraction in varying degrees and from different loci.[115] Neither their scholarship nor sincere experiential commitment to Hinduism is blameworthy. Their failure lies in their weaker commitment to Christian erudition and experience. Some of their writings will be engaged later, but at this point it is sufficient to note how Sara Grant had her Christian theology and experience devolve under Advaita. On the one hand, her bent for non-dualism reclaimed Sankara from the popular monist position of his more radical followers and redefined her own Christian categories in dissolving distinctions by following De Smet's path. On the other hand, her ability to engage and explain the Christian incarnation to the Advaitin is helpful, albeit in a highly qualified sense.[116]

---

[114]R. H. Hooker, *Themes in Hinduism and Christianity: A Comparative Study* (New York: Verlag Peter Lang, 1989), 368. A naturalist example is in Whitney Bauman, "The Problem of a Transcendent God for the Well-Being of Continuous Creation," *A Journal of Theology* 46, no. 2 (2007): 120. Bauman's theology replaces transcendence by secularizing the natural with a "radical materialist" Christianity.

[115]Francis A. Schaeffer, *The Francis A. Schaeffer Trilogy: The Three Essential Books in One Volume* (Westchester, IL: Crossway Books, 1990), 89. Schaeffer critiques the earlier generation of Catholics such as Raymond Pannikar, Dom Bede Griffiths, and others who are influenced by neo-orthodoxy and who proclaimed a synthesis between Roman Catholicism and Hinduism.

[116]Sara Grant, *Towards an Alternative Theology: Confessions of a Non-Dualist Christian* (Bangalore, India: Asian Trading Corporation, 1987), 76-82. She speaks of Jesus reflecting the Father in truth like no other human could, without a false autonomy. However, a methodological problem arises from "mediating theologies" which first mediated Catholic-Protestant disputes. Mediating apologetic methods do not presuppose Christian doctrine as an accepted set of principles, but explain those doctrines using commonly shared principles and values. Christian doctrine now becomes dependent on unbiblical

The annihilation of the phenomenal world is epistemological not metaphysical. It involves not the physical destruction of the world, but the destruction of the *illusion* that the world of *namarupa* is real in the sense of "ultimately real."[117]

Bradley Malkovsky excellently summarizes this range of contact between Vedanta and Christianity. He notes traditional sparks of antagonism before looking at the rapprochements under Richard De Smet and Swami Abhishiktananda.[118] These men exemplify key philosophical and experiential points of contact that will be explored later.

Using Aquinas philosophically, De Smet acknowledges the subordination of reason to Scripture and a high view of God's transcendence. The world is "entirely dependent on its transcendent source,"[119] as Christians readily agree with the Vedantins.

Experientially, Abhishiktananda's elevation of Advaita over Christianity is more dangerous than Sara Grant's Vedantic reinterpretation of her Christian experience. Among others who develop several lines of interaction is Francis Clooney, whose biblical unorthodoxy actually does bring out contacts that can be used in Worldview apologetics.[120]

Examining Methods of Antithesis

The rapprochement reviewed above already showed the need for a strong contrast due the inherent differences between Christianity and Hinduism. However, there are diverse motivations for the antithesis that is developed, not all of which are justified. The goal is to filter out valid means of antithesis for effective Worldview apologetics.

Human nature being what it is with sin, the differences between any two contrasting worldviews are often not handled well, even by using the parameters of goodness within each worldview. A few representative examples below showcase what can be avoided, even when maintaining clear dividing lines in the apologetic engagement.

Confrontation

As one in a vast historical landscape of Hindu-Christian encounters, Sita Ram Goel conveys a visceral response of resentment toward Christian missionaries. Christian mission in India was rightly perceived as antagonistic to Hinduism. Hindu organizations such as the Hindu Tract Society then responded with a spirit of revenge.

They met the (Christian) missionary challenge in their own ways. More and more skeletons were brought out of Christianity's cupboard. The missionaries found it

---

principles. James J. Buckley, "Roger Haight's Mediating Christology," *Modern Theology* 23, no. 1 (2007): 108-11. Haight avoids reductionism, since it cannot explain the doctrines. Since doctrines are not an "accepted" set of principles, what commonly shared principles can be used? Buckley rightly points out that the uniqueness of Jesus "in a different sense than formerly" is no different than Jesus Christ being unique in the same way as any other person. In the case of Vedanta, Jesus just becomes another incarnation.

[117]Sara Grant, *Sankaracarya's Concept of Relation* (Delhi: Motilal Banarsidass, 1999), 77. Namarupa is the world of form and body often used in the Buddhist context.

[118]Malkovsky, "Advaita Vedanta and Christian Faith," 400.

[119]Ibid., 412. The challenge here is the loss of Christian identity and propositions.

[120]Francis Xavier Clooney, *Hindu God, Christian God: How Reason Helps Break Down the Boundaries between Religions* (New York: Oxford University Press, 2001). This handles four themes of God's existence, God's identity, incarnation, and revelation across Christianity and Vedanta.

hard to hide them. They were being given a taste of their own medicine . . . Hinduism was shedding its traditional tolerance and showing hostility towards a sister religion![121]

It is helpful to note that the traditional viewpoint of Hinduism was one of pluralistic tolerance, stemming from its inclusivist worldview. However, in responding to an exclusivistic Christianity, some elements within Hinduism developed a militant evangelism, later manifest in Swami Vivekanada's *tour de force* at the Parliament of World Religions in Chicago in 1893. Tolerance became the necessary truth and Hindu-Christian engagement still reels under that unwarranted burden.

Christian elements of hostility did not aid the engagement either, when lacking a graceful evangelistic mandate or misrepresenting Vedanta. It is instructive to remember the famous encounter of Francis Schaeffer with a young Indian student in Cambridge University, who denied any intrinsic difference between cruelty and non-cruelty. As a Christian student in the group held a kettle of boiling water over the Indian, he promptly walked away. It illustrates the pragmatic problem of Vedanta philosophy, but short-circuits the discussion with deleterious effects.[122] It ignores the mediate concern of the Hindu with karma and asks of a commoner to practice Samadhi. There is a place for the rude awakening to reality, but it cannot dominate the Worldview apologetic to Vedanta.

Contrasts

It is helpful to review the thought of Christian missionaries to Vedantins. They retained a strong biblical view of their identity in stark contrast against paganism.

To be really Christian, to walk daily hand-in-hand with God-in-Christ, is an exacting, searching experience. It is an experience that is soothing but also scorching, quickening but also consuming. 'You only,' said Jehovah, speaking through the prophet Amos to the Chosen People – 'you only have I known of all the families of the earth; therefore I will visit upon you all your iniquities.'[123]

Hogg rightly faults the monist Vedanta as incapable of showcasing the love and holiness of God against the sinfulness of mankind, unlike the later devotional strands of Hinduism. This distinction in the nature of God and man is well worth preserving.

We realize all this far too little; and for that we have no excuse since it is in our Bible. Indian religion also here falls short, but with better excuse since in its sacred heritage there is that which can militate against a full realization. Consider first the more ancient type of reflective religion in India, the more pantheistic or monistic type where meditation concentrates not on a personal Isvara but on the impersonal Brahman, equally present in all things. Is it not obvious that the more vivid the impression which this meditation induces of the incomparable universal Brahman, the more unimportant does man appear in his seeming-separate being, and therefore

---

[121]Sita Ram Goel, *History of Hindu-Christian Encounters* (New Delhi: Voice of India, 1989), 76. The Indian perception of Christian missionaries is ambivalent between religious and social agendas.

[122]Schaeffer, *The Francis A. Schaeffer Trilogy*, 110.

[123]Alfred George Hogg, *The Christian Message to the Hindu: Being the Duff Missionary Lectures For Nineteen Forty Five on the Challenge of the Gospel in India* (London: S.C.M. Press, 1947), 90.

the more unimportant his sins as well as his virtues? There is only one thing that can prevent this result. It will be prevented only if the gravity of the sin is measured not by the stature of the sinner but by the quality of the sinned-against. Of all misdeeds it is sin against confiding love that most inescapably awakens horror and a sense of appalling guilt. And the sins of the finite can be felt as involving an infinite demerit when they are conceived as breach of trust perpetrated against an infinite love . . . . For this reason it is mainly in the Bhakti-literature that we find any uprush of surging penitence and shame for sin.[124]

One must never forget the foundational base of Christianity when attempting to make contact with Hinduism, as the issues of sin and salvation are rightly emphasized.

This contrast need not be limited from the Christian worldview, but can be located directly within the Vedanta worldview. Zaehner has written on the mystical elements of monism and theism, along with overviews of Hinduism. He concludes that monism is not just misguided, but perilous. He contrasts Ramanuja and Sankara to draw out the distinctions of monism. Nicholson finds Zaehner's comparisons tendentious, based on "polemical discourses internal to the compared traditions"[125] where Ramanuja's theism critiques Sankara's monism. This sharp, internal disagreement is further explored by John Sheveland who attempts to find unity between Rahner, Barth, and Vedanta Desika who is a qualified non-dualist follower of Ramanuja.

Qualified non-dualists like Ramanuja and Vedanta Desika charge the Advaita non-dual reading of the Vedas with producing a flawed ontology that, somewhat ironically, is itself a misapprehension with disastrous soteriological consequences. They also hold that Advaita Vedanta tends toward human arrogance and "conceit," thereby compounding its misapprehension of self and God. They suggest instead that the one absolute Brahman is personified as Visnu with his consort Sri; that Narayana has individual souls (cit) and the insentient world (acit) as his dependent but distinct modes; and that Narayana with Sri protect those who surrender the responsibility and burden of their protection to them in a contemplative relationship of love. Pace the Advaitins, the Srivaisnava community holds that release is attained not through contemplation or what is considered Advaitin "esoteric knowledge;" but through entering into a relationship of surrender, love, contemplation of and service to absolute Brahman, personified as Lord Narayana with Sri. Such surrender, moreover, and the love it produces, is itself a form of knowledge, which alone saves.[126]

Francis Clooney summarizes the conflict that Ramanuja finds in Sankara's impersonal monism with regards to liberation from Brahman. As noted in the earlier chapter, these inside debates are helpful tools in identifying error within the worldview.

---

[124]Ibid., 91. This contrast within Hinduism highlights the doxological impact of doctrine.

[125]Hugh Nicholson, *Comparative Theology and the Problem of Religious Rivalry* (New York: Oxford University Press, 2011), 202. The previous chapter developed this idea to a degree.

[126]John N. Sheveland, *Piety and Responsibility: Patterns of Unity in Karl Rahner, Karl Barth, and Vedanta Desika* (Burlington, VT: Ashgate, 2011), 119.

If Brahman is not a person who can respond to devotees, nothing will happen; liberation is not going to occur spontaneously. Recognizing that Brahman is the Lord therefore has both philosophical and religious implications.[127]

Recommending a Faithful Approach

The recommended faithful approach aggregates the points of contact and contrast covered thus far. It additionally provides some new and helpful data points to frame the entire Worldview apologetic.

Contact and Contrast

The contact points begin with varying degrees of similarity in ontological descriptions of reality. The Christian cannot fear to tread upon similarities, as long as they are properly qualified against the deeper underlying differences and within the appropriate framework. It is good to concur on transcendence while disagreeing on how it differs with the radically variant nature of God in each system. As regards contrast, the Christian ought never to try unifying the differences by redefining fundamental truths. His attempts to draw the dividing line must stem from the biblical mandate for the unadulterated truth and also exhibit the right attitudes of gentleness and respect.[128]

Unexpected Faithfulness

The following exchanges maintain the right tension in apologetics between rapprochement and antithesis. The source of these writers could be surprising, given that they are not often associated with maintaining biblical fidelity in cross-religious discussions. Wesley Ariarajah documents the perspective of the ecumenical council in highlighting one element of this tension regarding learning from and difference between Christianity and Vedanta.

The Commission also dealt with the second aspect of Hindu teaching – union with the Supreme Being – in its relation to Christian teaching. Here again it first acknowledged divergence, especially in the Hindu concept of the Supreme Being as that in which the soul loses its identity at the point of self-realization. The Commission, however, went on to say that despite the obvious divergence, the Hindu conception of the Supreme Being and its relationship to the soul challenged some of the inadequacies of the Christian conception, or at least pointed to some of its teaching that had to be expounded and applied in a much deeper fashion. This

---

[127]Clooney, *Hindu God, Christian God*, 71.
[128]Steve Walton, "The Acts – of God? What is the 'Acts of the Apostles' All About?" *Evangelical Quarterly* 80 (2008): 291-306. This article summarizes Acts 17: 22-31, a speech to pagans about God. Paul proclaims Jesus in this narrative framework. The speech expounds a Judaeo-Christian worldview while engaging with Stoics and Epicureans. God is knowable and has revealed himself; He is the creator and sustainer of the world and its inhabitants; He allotted places to every nation; He wants people to seek and find him; idolatry is a false attempt to identify the creator with creation; He calls people to repent as they will be judged by Jesus, whom God resurrected from the dead. Jonathan R. Wilson, "Stanley J. Grenz: Generous Faith and Faithful Engagement," *Modern Theology* 23 (2007):118.

challenge to explore fully the nature of the inner life of the soul in God was seen as the most important impact of the Christian encounter with Hinduism.[129]

It is vital for contemporary evangelicalism to explore more deeply the standing of Christians in Christ. However, this is not something lacking in the Christian conception, but is rather a call to return to the historical and scriptural injunctions of union in Christ, both doctrinally and experientially. The apologetic encounter, however, should place evangelism as a high priority in the dialogue, aside from any self-reflective corrections in its own theology and praxis. Araiarajah further critiques our consideration of finality and uniqueness. Rather than elevating the standards of finality and uniqueness, they recommend that Christ remain ultimate. In order to not dissipate actual practice into vacuous assertions, maintaining that Christ's revelation is as unique and final as Christ, is indispensable in contending for the faith that has been delivered once for all to the saints.

> We advocate neither an easy relativism nor a compromise of the central and challenging elements of the Christian faith. But we do contend that these elements need not necessarily depend on the concepts of finality and uniqueness . . . that it is the uniqueness and finality of Christ which governs, defines, and limits our understanding of and approach to the Hindu.[130]

Peter Feldmeier develops this further from the Catholic perspective of how one learns to ask new questions within one's own worldview. These questions obtain when exploring solutions that the other worldview proposes. They arise from a perceived spiritual richness, such as devotional experience, that may be lacking in contemporary Christianity.

In this book, this subject of further developing one's own theology will not be explored. Nevertheless, reviewing any subject that arises in light of engaging with Vedanta's theory and practice is vital in maintaining an honest communication on those specific areas with those holding the Vedanta worldview.

> Following John Paul's initiative, this text will engage in a kind of comparative theology, examining a number of religious expressions in their own right first and then in comparison with the Christian faith. By crossing over to the religious imagination of other traditions, one can see how they could bring new questions or insights. This kind of engagement is not merely a comparison of religions or doctrines, whereby one recognizes convergences and divergences. It is a juxtaposition to create an ongoing, reflective process of considering religious perspectives anew in the context of encountering other traditions.[131]

On the experiential question, the mysticism of Vedanta is not purely ecstatic, but is also conceptually mediated and therefore can be engaged in discursive apologetics.

---

[129]S. Wesley Ariarajah, *Hindus and Christians: A Century of Protestant Ecumenical Thought* (Grand Rapids: William B. Eerdmans Publishing Company, 1991), 26-27.

[130]Ibid., 211.

[131]Peter Feldmeier, *Encounters in Faith: Christianity in Interreligious Dialogue* (Winona, MN: Anselm Academic, 2011), 18. See also Benjamin Kelly, "Deviant Ancient Histories: Dan Brown, Erich von Daniken and the Sociology of Historical Polemic," *Rethinking History* 12 (2008): 361–82. Hugh Nicholson, "Two Apologetic Moments in Sankara's Concept of Brahman," *The Journal of Religion* 87 (2007): 528. Lluis Oviedo, "Is Christian Theology Well Suited to Enter the Discussion between Science and Humanism?" *Zygon Journal of Religion and Science* 41 (2006): 825. John Polkinghorne, "Where is Natural Theology Today?" *Science & Christian Belief* 18 (2006): 169-79.

Most approaches to mysticism, both historically and in the modern period focus on the kind of contemplation that is ecstatic, that is, it takes someone outside of one's conscious framework. This way of encountering God is said to be apophatic . . . . Knowing God in ways that are conceptually meditated or worked through one's psyche is often referred to as kataphatic.[132]

Feldmeier rightly notes that while the distinctions are fundamental between Christianity and Vedanta, the identifications should not be disregarded, especially in light of the image of God in humans and the dependency of creation upon the Creator.

Christianity retains a clear distinction between God and the soul, Creator and creature. Yet its biblical and theological tradition does point to kinds of identification as well.[133]

Howard Coward brings the exclusivism of the scriptures into sharp focus in both worldviews. Each one makes exclusive truth-claims, but this fact does not necessarily isolate the Christian from engaging truthfully and honestly with the Vedantin.

Both Christian and Hindu scriptures are exclusivistic (that is, only through Veda or Christ is salvation or release possible). Yet in the heart of each scriptural exclusivism there exists a basis for tolerance and dialogue.[134]

Coward brings out the vital differences even in the nature of the scriptures in each worldview. In Christianity, the Scriptures have an origin, being written by human authors under God. In Vedanta, the scriptures are spoken, eternal, and considered authorless. With scriptures as the primary authority in each worldview and them being immensely diverse, one cannot anticipate a facile gloss over their differences. The Christian's task, rather, is to handle the issues rightly by actively leveraging and working through the differences within the context of the Christian worldview.

Worldview

The history of Christian apologetics to Vedanta sampled above showcases the issues of failing to utilize a Worldview apologetic. Piecemeal apologetics lacks a solid biblical framework within which to faithfully address the entirety of the worldview. The Christian cannot examine Vedanta beliefs and experiences without addressing their underlying presuppositions. Furthermore, the radically dissimilar presuppositions of the Christian worldview require a comprehensive presentation of the above arguments and evidences. While this style may not seem to directly engage with individual questions, the overall engagement will actually be more robust since it addresses both the presuppositions and the evidences of Vedanta within its system rather than caricaturing it from the outside or poorly attempting to mediate from a no-man's land. This is precisely the goal of the illustration used of the citizens of countries A and B. The Christian must

---

[132]Feldmeier, *Encounters in Faith*, 25-26. Both forms of mystical experiences are in Vedanta.

[133]Ibid., 127. These identifications need not always be explicitly drawn out, but can be part of the apologetic methodology in engaging the opposite worldview.

[134]Howard Coward, "The Experience of Scripture in Hinduism and Christianity," in *Hindu-Christian Dialogue: Perspectives and Encounters*, ed. Howard Coward (Maryknoll, NY: Orbis Books, 1989), 247.

present his worldview comprehensively to the Vedantin in order to demonstrate the truth of Christianity. Likewise, he must be willing to step into the Vedantin world to provide a compelling argument for the theological and philosophical failure of Vedanta.

Christian arguments will be leveraged from extant apologetic works toward Vedanta Hinduism. The central apologetic thrusts from these materials will form the primary arguments around which any "apologetic sins" will be examined.[135] Most of these works tend to focus on the reasonableness of the Christian faith. They contrast the logical necessity of a real world under a personal God, over against an illusory world functioning under an impersonal reality. These conservative works tend to emphasize Classical and Evidential methodologies, often without comprehensively engaging the worldview. The Reformed or Fideistic apologists lack any substantive engagement with Vedanta.

Reformed works have tended to emphasize the method itself in relation to other apologetic methodologies. These works will provide the framework here to apply Christian apologetics toward the unbelieving Vedanta worldviews since such applications are still few. This book attempts to address these deficiencies by building a broad Worldview apologetic toward Advaita Vedanta Hinduism.

Conclusion

Worldview apologists can learn much from the history of Christian apologetics with Vedanta. This includes avenues that must be actively pursued and excludes those trails which must remain cold. In the next three chapters, the framework used by Reformed apologist John Frame will be utilized to practically demonstrate Worldview apologetics with Vedanta.

Frame's practical framework addresses the entire worldview in three stages. Its sections on proof, offense, and defense will apply the Christian Worldview apologetic to Vedanta Hindus.[136] Thus the Reformed method will outline the apologetic encounter, suitably augmented by all apologetic tools. In order to maintain a higher degree of objectivity, the Vedanta perspective will be presented through the lens of a Hindu, providing their most forceful arguments, even as the Christian worldview is presented through the lens of biblical truth. A final review will evaluate the apologetic encounter.

---

[135]"Apologetic Sins" could be a term used to examine ethical fairness in Worldview apologetics. It would not refer to the practices of one apologetic methodology, say Reformed, in some way or another being superior to another, say Classical or Evidential apologetics. This term is applied instead to Christians sinning while attempting apologetics in general. It can address sinful tendencies inherent within any apologetic method. This is typically noted in regards to attributes such as humility, honesty, and integrity in relation to God and our fellow beings. This book promotes a reflexive study, noting how apologetics in general can avoid the explicit sins of pride and dishonesty, but also the implicit sins which could lack faithfulness and integrity in a comprehensive Worldview apologetic.

[136]John M. Frame, *Apologetics for the Glory of God: An Introduction* (Phillipsburg, NJ: P&R Publishing, 1994), 2, 57. The order of offense and defense are reversed here in light of the dialogical exchange between the Christian and Vedanta worldviews.

CHAPTER 4
PROOF: PRESENTING THE CASE

The actual apologetic engagement commences herein with proof. When two systems of beliefs come into contact, the proponents of each worldview give a fair representation from their worldview to persuade others of the truthfulness of their system. This includes evidences and reasons from within their scriptures and without.[1]

Proof lays out compelling arguments for each worldview.[2] This section provides the unique perspective of the Hindu and the Christian, from inside their own systems. The worldview is laid out in its broadest terms, highlighting key elements of the belief and exposing some of its underlying presuppositions. This representation is central to any Worldview apologetic since the biblical worldview must be presented on its own terms rather than just explained against the context of an unbelieving worldview. The Vedanta Hindu worldview is afforded the same privilege to explain itself.[3]

The encounter represents a Christian with biblical convictions engaging a learned Advaitin convinced of Vedanta's monism. There is mutual respect between the individuals without compromising the convictions of their respective positions. These proofs come primarily from their sources of authority, which are their scriptures. They will use cogent arguments to demonstrate the truth-quotient behind these beliefs using evidence from the scriptures and the world. The Hindu first provides proofs for Vedanta, followed by the Christian. In the Advaitin presentation of the proof for Hinduism, this section actually takes on the position of the advaitin. The arguments are presented from the basic presuppositions of the advaitin, to minimize caricature and misrepresentation. After this presentation, the worldview will be critiqued by the Christian in the offense section and vice-versa.

The proofs are discussed in sufficient detail to provide a consistent, coherent, and corresponding explanation of reality. After the Advaitin presentation, the Christian worldview is convincingly laid out.

---

[1]John M. Frame, *Apologetics for the Glory of God: An Introduction* (Phillipsburg, NJ: P&R Publishing, 1994), 57-60. The Reformed framework can be well augmented with existing Classical and Evidential arguments here.

[2]Ibid., 62-64. Proof is seen as compelling data impressed upon the unbeliever, but not as something that requires the unbeliever to assent based purely on its rational and evidential cogency.

[3]Todd S. Mei, "Heidegger and the Appropriation of Metaphysics," *The Heythrop Journal* 50 (2009): 257-70. The context of propositions is vital in the communication of historical verities.

Vedanta's Basic Beliefs

The Advaitin worldview is monistic. Its central thesis posits that all reality has a unity and manifests the ultimate reality, otherwise known as Brahman. The Hindu scriptures provide this knowledge. The nature of Brahman is gleaned from these past writings and from current experiences. Everything other than Brahman is his expression through the agency of Maya.[4] The atman is the pristine counterpart of Brahman in man. God, as is commonly understood, is located within this framework as a less-than-sovereign deity, necessary for the current state of affairs. The world is in a contingent and transitory state of affairs. It provides the means for man's redemption from the temporary to the eternal state of ultimate reality. Man is confined in this universe, within a physical and spiritual reality, given the tools of works, devotion, and knowledge to work out his release. Reflection leads to meditation which progresses to final realization.[5]

Westerners struggle to grasp Vedanta's intrinsic beauty since their categories of differentiating plurality interfere with the vital task of transcending differences. Some equate Vedanta and pantheism, equating God and the world. A better definition of monism is found in the elimination of differences:

> The term [pantheism] is also used to describe the absolute monism of Advaita Vedanta Hinduism, which holds that the whole of reality is identical with the one Absolute that is God, and that the distinctions we draw between objects are just part of appearances.[6]

This definition is closer to the mark of monism which is the "metaphysical view that reality is fundamentally one."[7] Monistic Advaita Vedanta is nondualistic.

Scriptures

The Vedantic worldview is built on the foundation of the Vedas, Upanishads, and the Baghavad Gita. All Advaitins affirm that the Veda is eternal and of divine source.[8] Vedanta doctrines are developed on the sure footing of divine revelation. When one's destiny is on the line, that lifeline ought to be the best one available. No better standard can be commended for the scriptures than one which directly shares the divine attribute of being eternal. The eternality of the Vedas may seem difficult to comprehend.

---

[4]C. P. Ramaswami Aiyar, *Fundamentals of Hindu Faith and Culture: A Collection of Essays and Addresses* (Madras: Ganesh & Co. Private Ltd., 1959), 10-11. See also Bradley J. Malkovsky, "Samkara on Divine Grace," in *New Perspectives on Advaita Vedanta: Essays in Commemoration of Professor Richard De Smet*, ed. Bradley J. Malkovsky (Boston: Brill, 2000), 76. See also P. T. Raju, *The Philosophical Traditions of India* (London: George Allen & Unwin, 1971), 177-80.

[5]P. V. Joshi, *Introduction to Sankara's Advaitism* (Delhi: Motilal Banarsidass Publishers, 2006), 38-40, 47-50. The temporal state governed by karma involves reincarnation in samsara.

[6]Stephen C. Evans, *Pocket Dictionary of Apologetics & Philosophy of Religion* (Downers Grove, IL: IVP, 2002), 88. Despite being an outside source, this definition is helpful.

[7]Ibid., 8. Evans further notes: "According to Advaita Vedanta, ultimate reality is one – the absolute divine unity of Brahman that is beyond description in language. The human soul, or Atman, is identical with this absolute reality, and enlightenment or deliverance involves a realization of this oneness. At the level of appearance, objects in the world seem to be distinct from such things as the self and a personal deity" (ibid., 77).

[8]K. Satchidananda Murty, *Revelation and Reason in Advaita Vedānta* (Grand Rapids: Eerdmans Publishing Company, 1959), 33: "Veda is eternal, but renewed at the beginning of each world-cycle."

Its source is Brahman but it is without any temporal beginning. The Vedantin scriptures stand on a platform of true infallibility that no other religious book can claim, since there is no instrumental error in its creation by humans. Francis Clooney summarizes this well:

> A Veda composed by human authors would depend on them and be fallible as they are, and even divine authors may have intentions not perfectly expressed in their words, or may even intentionally obscure what they mean . . . . The Veda in effect uses the instrumentality of an "author" to express itself.[9]

Hinduism is among the oldest of living religions. The written scriptures deliver an ancient oral tradition of the eternal words.[10] Among the various extant religious works, none compare to the Hindu texts for their ideal communication of the infallible and eternal truth from before human history.

Brahman

Brahman is the apex of existence, knowledge, and bliss; delineated as perfect, without parts, beginning-less, totally beyond the ken of words, cognition, and even conceptualization.[11] Although incomparable, taking Anselm's line, Brahman is "that than which" nothing greater can be conceived. While Anselm sought to show that existence is an attribute of perfection that surpasses the mere conception of God, Brahman exceeds all attributes, by being *that* which truly exists. A few relevant attributes help exemplify Brahman as the source of all reality – these are eternality, the basis of all being, and immutability.

The ultimate being does not share its existence with any other entity. This ultimate being is necessarily eternal because anyone who begins to exist is contingent and dependent on someone else to cause their existence. Since Brahman is ultimate and eternal, Brahman is also self-existent. If Brahman is the only ultimate reality, Brahman must be the source of all being and the ultimate cause for everything. Brahman's eternality and source of being are thus linked in being the solitary ultimate reality.

The sticking point is immutability. The changes regularly observed in the world seem necessary in Brahman for any causal creation. One option is to deny any causality which results in skepticism. Another is to identify causality in Brahman. Causation implies participation and change. Change is undesirable in Brahman for it involves moving up or down in perfection. The identity of cause and effect requires creation to share in the nature of its creator, but the world of change can have no essential

---

[9]Francis X. Clooney, "Why the Veda has no Author: Language as Ritual in Early Mimamsa and Post-Modern Theology," *Journal of the American Academy of Religion* 55 (1987): 660. Clooney also notes, "Authorlessness allows one to concede these points without the risk of damage to the Veda; it does not really matter what an apparent author may have intended, since what actually is constructed in language according to the rules of language and gleaned from it by the rules of interpretation transcends the author's intentions and only by chance coincides with what this author may have meant" (ibid., 664). Sankara merely insists from the Brahma Sutras of Badarayana that Brahman is the Veda's source and cause. Later Vedantins called Brahman the material cause of the Vedas but not its author, just as the potter forms the clay into an object but does not create it. There is "no meaning beyond the words and the sacrificial actions themselves; one cannot appeal to a pre-verbal intention to get beyond the words" (ibid., 680).

[10]M. Hiriyanna, *Outlines of Indian Philosophy* (Delhi: Motilal Banarsidass Publishers, 2009), 14. Hinduism is among the oldest living organized religions, with its Vedas being written around 1500-800 B.C. Even skeptical authors like Danielou accept that its oral tradition significantly predates the written texts, for its roots. Alain Danielou, *A Brief History of India* (Rochester, VT: Inner Traditions, 2003), 24, 46.

[11]Joshi, *Introduction to Sankara's Advaitism*, 3, 44.

commonality with an unchanging deity.[12] Vedanta resolves causation with Maya, the power of Brahman, creating the world.[13]

Samkara puts the objector's argument in the form of a dilemma: either Brahman had a purpose in creating the world or he didn't. If Brahman created the world for a purpose, then there must have been some goal; Brahman must be lacking something. But if that were the case, then Brahman would not be perfect.[14]

Brahman's nature solves this dilemma. Brahman is immutable. Brahman is eternal. Brahman is the ultimate source of all Being. As immutable, Brahman is not just the source of all being, but being itself. Since Brahman is existence itself, it is improper to designate any attributes to Brahman. Personality with its intentionality and restrictive attributes are subsumed in a greater existence, which is impenetrable to humans who necessarily think and live under the personal and transmuting conditions of life.

For example, today's scientific community seeks to answer the underlying reason for evolution. They cannot successfully locate it in mindless matter. They no longer trust the personal Christian God as a god-of-the-gaps or a dualistic ghost-in-the-machine for the nature of mankind. Untraceable and invisible, Brahman is Being itself, the unifying truth behind all reality. Brahman has compelling explanatory power for all reality, not just in the specific empirical proofs which are sought for in other worldviews.

Atman

The identity of the self is enigmatic. Humans are not merely static matter since the body changes dramatically from conception and birth to death and disintegration. They cannot be just mind, since the changes of the mind are even more radical than those in the body. Neither body nor mind affords any common kernel of identity to hold it together. The identity of man rests in something else within which remains constant. That identity is recognized by Vedanta as atman.

With Brahman as the ground of all reality, mankind naturally identifies with Brahman. Sankara does not say that the finite being or ego is identical to Brahman, but rather that the atman in man is Brahman. Atman is the counterpart of Brahman in man, as the pristine being mysteriously connected with the individual ego. Christians recognize the spark of the divine in humanity as *imago dei*. Vedanta identifies that capacity for the divine firmly in the atman. The atman in each person needs to find release in Brahman.

Naturalistic scientists tend to center the immaterial being of man in physical matter. The connections of the will and intellect point to something beyond what physical senses themselves can identify. Proofs for the atman are necessarily negative proofs as

---

[12]Chandradhar Sharma, *A Critical Survey of Indian Philosophy* (London: Rider & Company, 1960), 261. God, matter, and souls are examined for being infinite and for causal relation to one another in using the identity of cause and effect.

[13]Joshi, *Introduction to Sankara's Advaitism*, 2, 4, 41, 55-57, 59-62. Identity of cause and effect is one philosophical rule that will be examined in analyzing the foundations of the Vedanta worldview. Maya is seen as neither real nor unreal, a mysterious work of Brahman.

[14]Frederick F. Fost, "Playful Illusions: The Making of Worlds in Advaita Vedanta," *Philosophy East and West* 48 (1998): 393. Sankara addresses the objector in the Brahma Sutras of Badarayana in 11.1.32 where "an objector presents the following argument: Brahman cannot be the cause of the world because to cause or create involves motives or purposes (and if Brahman has either, He is imperfect)" (ibid., 393).

there is no other valid explanation. Like Brahman, there is something that exists in humans, which cannot be identified with matter. The scriptures call it the atman.

Brahman is the truth of the universe; the atman is the truth within. "*Atman* as the soul or self is the inmost truth of man."[15] Vedanta explains the mystery of the atman as centered in the conscious self which transcends the function of the mind.

> *Atman* (the self) is the innermost individual being characterized by individual consciousness (*Chitta*). The essence of personality is something beyond body, life, mind and intellect. It is *Atman*, the self. Its chief attribute is consciousness.[16]

The familiar self of the empirical senses is distinguished from the atman, the immaterial and metaphysical self, which is ontologically identical to Brahman.

> The concept of "real self" in Hindu thought is the Atman, a nonmaterial or metaphysical self, as opposed to the material, experiential forms of the empirical self, involving sensations, desires, and thoughts. The empirical self is viewed as hierarchically lower than the metaphysical self.[17]

The atman provides the ideal conception of human identity even as Brahman provides the ideal concept of God. The value ascribed to people finds its supreme basis in its grounding in Brahman and the atman. This identity unifies all reality under one supreme rubric. In a naturalistic universe, humans annihilate after physical death, being sustained only by material entities. Christians cannot clearly delineate mankind's final estate since they shy away from identifying the image of God in humans as God. Jesus knew that identity in himself, making him truly God.[18]

God

With an immutable Brahman not readily accessible, humanity's need for communication with the divine is fulfilled in Isvara or God. God is the aspect of Brahman facing the world, not that different from the god of most theistic religions including Christianity. There is passionate beauty in the personal God, *Isvara*. He is incarnate in various forms, places, and times. However, the emphasis is on the binding principle of this world instead of the many gods of polytheism.[19] Mankind's need of God's grace is well understood in Vedanta. Man bound in ignorance cannot rise beyond his folly without help from God. God's operations are visualized using the metaphor of a stage actor:

---

[15]Kalpana Srivastava, "Human Nature: Indian Perspective Revisited," *Industrial Psychiatry* 19 (2010): 78. Also, "unveiling the truth was subjective and often it was based on introspection" (ibid., 80).

[16]Ibid., 80. Srivastava further notes: "The self exists before, in and after the various states of consciousness: wakeful, dream and sleep. Denial of consciousness means denial of everything else. Hence, mind and self are not identical" (ibid., 80). Also: "Mind in the Advaita is described as the internal organ . . . . The five [external] sense organs [of action and perception] have as their objects, sight, hearing, touch, taste and smell. Mind is capable of establishing contact with all the external organs" (ibid., 81).

[17]T. S. Saraswathi, "Hindu Worldview in the Development of Selfways: The 'Atman' as the Real Self," *New Directions for Child & Adolescent Development* 109 (2005): 44.

[18]Sara Grant, *Towards an Alternative Theology: Confessions of a Non-Dualist Christian* (Bangalore, India: Asian Trading Corporation, 1987), 76-82.

[19]Sharma, *A Critical Survey of Indian Philosophy*, 16, 280.

Isvara conjures a world very much like an actor creates a scene on the stage, but finally the play shows itself as not being fully real, or perhaps better, as pointing to something beyond itself, namely, to Brahman as nirguna.[20]

This grace is given through a subordinate deity who appeals to humanity with perfect personality to lift it up. Isvara is transcendent and immanent. Most religions fail to recognize the limitations of a less-than-perfect personal God to exemplify the absolute Brahman. Vedanta scriptures recognize the identity and role of God as Lord of Maya, while preserving his subordinate function with regards to the impersonal Brahman.

Westerners with a Christian heritage seem to be losing their preference for a personal God in deference to an impersonal intelligence.

Over 90 percent of Americans check "yes" when asked if they believe in God. But increasingly they see God as an abstract, non-personal force or intelligence, as opposed to an anthropomorphic deity.[21]

They are exchanging their worship of Isvara, for a nascent awareness of Brahman. Instead of losing Christian doctrinal purity, this trend vindicates mankind's intuition that transcends the personal God, to seek the ultimate truth in Brahman. To achieve this, the relationship between the world and Brahman must be understood.

World

The world is dependent on Brahman for its existence. It has no reality outside of Brahman. This world of change relies on the ontology of the unchanging Brahman. At one end is the full differentiation and variation inherent in the world. At the other end is the undifferentiated and changeless Brahman. These seemingly antithetical properties are tied together by Maya. The invariant Brahman as the ground explains the deep-seated unity apparent in the world. Science identifies these laws binding diverse phenomena.

It may seem counter-intuitive that the force bringing the apple down from the tree is the same one that sustains the moon's orbit around the earth. Yet those very diverse phenomena have one underlying law at work. While physical phenomena are open to discovery by empirical experimentation, the operation of Maya is understood by revelation and experience. Maya is understood both positively and negatively.

According to Sankara then, the doctrine of Maya implies positively that there is but one undifferentiated pure Being which is identical with the real world of men. In the ultimate sense, the absolute is the same as this phenomenal world of Becoming. Negatively, Maya refers to the world as it is. It would then imply that the world is

---

[20]Gerald James Larson, "Indian Conceptions of Reality and Divinity," in *A Companion to World Philosophies*, ed. Eliot Deutsch and Ron Bontekoe (Malden, MA: Blackwell Publishers, 1997), 257. Nirguna is the lack of any form in Brahman while Sarguna is the perfection of attributes in Isvara: "Isvara is 'qualified' Brahman who is the creative manifestation of maya, the mighty force that creates all of the determinate forms which represent the 'play' of Brahman."

[21]Philip Goldberg, *American Veda: From Emerson and the Beatles to Yoga and Meditation – How Indian Spirituality Changed the West* (New York: Harmony Books, 2010), 22. Goldberg also notes: "In the 2001 Beliefnet survey cited above, 84 percent saw God as "everywhere and in everything" as opposed to 'someone somewhere.'"

an appearance mysteriously caused and sustained by the inexplicable energy of Brahman, the Absolute, which, however, is not in the least affected by it.[22]

There are various ways of explaining this world as it is. F. H. Bradley develops Sankara's analogical explanations for our understanding in the modern physical realm.

For Sankara, as for [F.H.] Bradley, Reality is the cause of the world in the sense in which for modern physicists the bunch of corpuscles or waves in front of me are the cause of what appears to me as a table, a notebook, a pen, a heap of papers, etc. The emergence of these articles is true to my perception; however, they do not have any reality per se, that is, they are only the manifest forms of something discrete and vacuous.[23]

Science struggles to explain the nature of light as waves and particles. Solid matter is made of atoms with the sub-atomic particles in constant flux. There is a distinct difference between the metaphysical realities of objects in relation to their appearance, as their observation is often tinged with ignorance, which is a limitation in the observer. Spiritual bondage inheres in separation from Brahman, being constrained by the world.

Sankara could not possibly be unaware of the logical implication that if Brahman is not subject to causal determination, then the world, for whose being Brahman forms the ground (adhistana), also ought to remain free from causality. Yet, it cannot be denied that we perceive the world as universally governed by the sequence of causes and effects. To show, therefore, that the causal order of the universe is quite compatible with the non-causal Supreme Being is the principal endeavor of Sankara's system. And fundamentally, he like Bradley, succeeds in this endeavor inasmuch as he regards our world-experience as having no status beyond the confines of our ignorant or naive selves. Being inseparable from our bondage-oriented life, the world responds to our natural dispositions, and makes us incur punishment on ourselves according to the deeds done by us. For Sankara, the appearance of the world has a moral significance. It is as if the result of our being alienated from the Absolute.[24]

This ignorance of Brahman impacts our ethics since we live unaware of the broader purpose of existence. The consequences of our actions on earth are self-inflicted when living without realizing the true nature of Brahman, atman, and the world itself.

Man and Liberation

Both the Christian and the Hindu see humanity stuck in the morass of pain and suffering in the world, along with its joys and pleasures, living in anything but an ideal situation. Ignorance causes this lamentable state of mankind. Knowledge which is understood and then lived out dispels ignorance, liberating the atman.

---

[22]Paul David Devanandan, *The Concept of Māyā: An Essay in Historical Survey of the Hindu Theory of the World, with Special Reference to the Vedanta* (London: Lutterworth Press, 1950), 113. Sharma, *A Critical Survey of Indian Philosophy*, 274, notes further characteristics of Maya.

[23]Ramakant A. Sinari, *The Structure of Indian Thought* (Springfield, IL: C. Thomas, 1970), 110. Bradley deals with issues of appearance, causality and illusion in relation to the world and Brahman.

[24]Ibid., 110. The laws of cause and effect seem to punish our alienation from Brahman's true bliss. The attributeless Brahman does have supreme bliss, knowledge, and existence (Sat-cit-ananda).

Just as dreams appear to be true as long as one does not wake up, so, the identification of oneself with the body etc. and the authenticity of sense-perception and the like in the waking state continue as long as there is no Self-knowledge.[25]

The "waking up" from this world into true reality affords release. Vedanta identifies the cognitive components in man more precisely than Western philosophy or psychology. The self is knower (kshetrajna), the seer (drasta), the witness (sakshi), and the immutable (kutastha).[26]

Man is liberated from the karmic cycle of reincarnation through realization of the truth. In this goal his efforts are aided by grace from God. He is freed from the thrall of karma and realizes the truth which sets him free. This process is through negation until the truth alone remains, rather than any positive affirmation of aspects of divinity.

The Self is left over by negating the body etc. by the *Sruti*, "Not this, not this," so that one may have the Knowledge of the Self which is devoid of all attributes. Ignorance is brought to an end by this Knowledge.[27]

This knowledge is not obtained instantaneously for liberation. It is not to affirm intellectually, but to grasp true knowledge with all of one's being, to experience and live it as Sankara says: "That means to liberation, viz. Knowledge, should be explained again and again until it is firmly grasped . . . indifferent to everything that is transitory."[28]

Liberation is effected by Bhakti, Gynana, and Karma; these correspond to devotion, knowledge, and action. The path of devotion to God consumes the devotee until he attains union with the divine. The path of knowledge merges the knower with the known. The path of works disciplines and prepares the doer to live life such that union with Brahman becomes possible. This liberation is not purely works-based so as to follow a mechanical path. Rather, divine grace finally liberates the seeker after truth.

Samkara does not teach that liberating knowledge dawns automatically given the proper mental and moral dispositions and a proper grasp of the mahavakyas. It is rather the case that the fully pure and quiescent sadhaka can only await the breakthrough into the higher consciousness in passive and trusting expectation, continuously inspired by the desire to know Brahman, fully aware of its inability to reach the goal through unaided effort.[29]

This liberation is not to be simplified into some objectified divine transaction. Grace is no longer grace if mandated upon the giver, as Malkovsky rightly notes.

---

[25]Sankaracharya, *A Thousand Teachings: In Two Parts: Prose and Poetry of Sri Sankaracharya*, ed. and trans. Swami Jagadananda (Madras: Sri Ramakrishna Math, 1949), 117.

[26]Srivastava, "Human Nature," 80. Srivastava further notes: "The composite whole of *chit* and *achit* (consciousness and matter), *kshetrajna* and *kshetra* (knower and known), *karta* and *karana* (doer and its instrument) is the total personality called *Jiva* and *Jivatman* - the embodied self. *Jiva* (the individual), *Purusha* (the person), *Samsari* (the worldly person), *Vijnanaghana/Vijnanatma, Prajna, Atma/Pratyagatma, Sariri, Karta, Bhokta*, and *Kshetrajna* are synonymous" (ibid., 80).

[27]Sankaracharya, *A Thousand Teachings*, 84.

[28]Ibid., 2.

[29]Bradley J. Malkovsky, *The Role of Divine Grace in the Soteriology of Śankarācārya* (Boston: Brill, 2001), 382. Grace in Advaita Vedanta has been emphasized much more recently.

May it be that, on the one hand, Samkara is compelled by his personal experience to witness to the reality of grace, but, on the other hand, he recognizes the impossibility of objectifying what is properly the mystery of liberation?[30]

Humans recognize an underlying reality and worth that ought not merely be reduced to the physical. They yearn for something more fundamentally valuable. Vedanta explains what this unifying truth is. Mankind is in different stages of his progress – some appreciate it sooner than others, but all can recognize the attraction for this unity in all aspects of life. As the world struggles to understand the unity transcending the races, languages, cultures, and yes, even ethics and religions, they will one day attain to a perfect knowledge of that unity when that which divides loses its existence to perfection.

Christianity's Basic Beliefs

The Christian thesis rests on the absolute, personal, and Triune God. This worldview is founded on the inerrant and infallible Scriptures.[31] God is an autonomous person separate from all his creation. Humans are created by God in his image, but despite their original purity, after Adam's fall they are in a state of sin, separated from God and requiring redemption. This salvation of humanity is accomplished through a historic act of Jesus Christ who paid the penalty for sin, restores individuals who are remade and ultimately restores all creation to an eternal state of purity to enjoy God forever.[32] These truths are consistent, coherent, and correspond to reality.[33]

Scriptures

The Scripture is self-evident truth.[34] Everyone's authority rests upon some external basis and the Christian's certain knowledge comes from the Bible. This verity is foundational for each individual's spiritual state and life before God.

From childhood you have been acquainted with the sacred writings, which are able to make you wise for salvation through faith in Christ Jesus. All Scripture is

---

[30]Ibid., 402.

[31]See Norman Geisler and William C. Roach, *Defending Inerrancy: Affirming the Accuracy of Scripture for a New Generation* (Grand Rapids: Baker Books, 2011). See also, *The Proceedings of the Conference on Biblical Inerrancy 1987* (Nashville: Broadman Press, 1987). The apologetic is presented to an Advaitin from a specific Christian tradition, in this case, Reformed Christianity.

[32]G. C. Berkouwer, *Man: The Image of God* (Grand Rapids: Wm. B. Eerdmans Publishing Company, 1962), 349.

[33]Ronald H. Nash, *Life's Ultimate Questions: An Introduction to Philosophy* (Grand Rapids: Zondervan, 1999), 228-30. The nature of truth is defined in terms of correspondence to reality. However, the tests or justification for truth include both coherence and correspondence, since each theory has its own limitations and advantages. True statements must correspond to metaphysical reality. The statements of truth in any worldview must cohere rather than disagree with one another. Thus each belief is also tested in light of other beliefs, especially when it is difficult to examine one's beliefs outside one's system of belief. See also Simon Blackburn, *Oxford Dictionary of Philosophy* (Oxford: Oxford University Press, 2005), 65. For another definition, see Louis Arnaud Reid, "Correspondence and Coherence," *The Philosophical Review* 31(1922): 39-40: "Coherence might be described as an intellectual and mental, correspondence as a practical, test of truth." Reid requires both coherence and correspondence as fundamental tests of true propositions. See also J. P. Moreland and William Lane Craig, *Philosophical Foundations of a Christian Worldview* (Downers Grove: IL, Intervarsity, 2003), 121-22, 142.

[34]Self-evident implies that when activated by the Holy Spirit, the words of Scripture convey their meaning to the believer in a basic or direct manner.

breathed out by God and profitable for teaching, for reproof, for correction, and for training in righteousness, that the man of God may be competent, equipped for every good work.[35]

This written revelation from God transcends experience today, even that which is unmediated between an individual and God. It illumines ignorance and dispels evil.

And we have something more sure, the prophetic word, to which you will do well to pay attention as to a lamp shining in a dark place, until the day dawns and the morning star rises in your hearts, knowing this first of all, that no prophecy of Scripture comes from someone's own interpretation. For no prophecy was ever produced by the will of man, but men spoke from God as they were carried along by the Holy Spirit.[36]

The central attraction of God's Word is its truth. This truth is eternal. "The sum of your word is truth, and every one of your righteous rules endures forever."[37]

Not only does the Scripture make such large claims, but it also corresponds to reality. Unlike the mythical nature of Vedantic scriptures, which place little value on historic facts, the Bible is a historic document which makes true biographical and geographical claims that are authentic and corroborated.[38] Its chief characters are situated in time and space. God's truth is vindicated through the lived actions of these individuals, rather than in picturesque but untethered parables. Unbelieving Bible critics have yet to discredit the historicity of the Bible after centuries of attack.[39] The frank evaluation of biblical characters presents the nature of the God of the Bible as impartial in applying his eternal truth. The Bible represents a verifiable case-study of eternal truth in human lives.

Most other ancient books are not nearly so well authenticated [as the Bible]. New Testament scholar Bruce Metzger estimated that the *Mahabharata* of Hinduism is copied with only about 90 percent accuracy and Homer's *Iliad* with about 95 percent. By comparison, he estimated the New Testament is about 99.5 percent accurate.[40]

---

[35]2 Tim 3:15-17. Paul traces Timothy's salvation through the God-given Scriptures.

[36]2 Pet 1:19-21. Peter here commends the Scriptures over his mountain-top experience.

[37]Ps 119:160. Ps 119 works out the importance of scriptural revelation.

[38]This statement does not mean that every statement in the Bible is corroborated by archeology or other methods. Rather, it means that several of its claims have withstood the test of time and have been affirmed outside of the Scriptures. For more details, see N. T. Wright, *The Resurrection of the Son of God* (Minneapolis: Fortress Press, 2003). For a recent update of a classic work see Cyrus H. Gordon and Gary A. Rendsburg, *The Bible and the Ancient Near East* (New York: W. W. Norton & Company, 1997). For additional details see Jack Finegan, *Light from the Ancient Past: The Archeological Background of the Hebrew-Christian Religion* (Princeton: Princeton University Press, 1951) and W. F. Albright, *From the Stone Age to Christianity* (Baltimore: John Hopkins Press, 1940).

[39]See David R. Hall, *The Seven Pillories of Wisdom* (Macon, GA: Mercer University Press, 1990). See also K. A. Kitchen, *On the Reliability of the Old Testament* (Grand Rapids: Wm. B. Eerdmans Publishing Company, 2006) and W. F. Albright, "Archeology Confronts Biblical Criticism," *American Scholar* 7 (1938): 176-88. See also Merrill R. Unger, *Archaeology and the Old Testament* (Grand Rapids: Zondervan Publishing, 1954), along with G. E. Wright, *Biblical Archeology* (Philadelphia: Westminster Press, 1957).

[40]Norman L. Geisler, *Baker Encyclopedia of Christian Apologetics* (Grand Rapids: Baker Books, 1999), 532-33. See also Bruce M. Metzger, "Trends in the Textual Criticism of the Illiad, the Mahabharata, and the New Testament," *Journal of Biblical Literature* 65 (1946). The percentage is

While more evidences can be provided, this section concludes with prophetic fulfillment. What was foretold in the earlier portions of Scripture can often be historically verifiable in the latter portions of Scripture and in secular history.[41] These include the rise and fall of nations and the predictions concerning Jesus Christ.[42] Thus the fundamental claim made for the Christian Scriptures is one of truth. The Bible represents metaphysical verities which correspond to reality. This claim is made not just because of cohering evidences, but as God's Word, it is expected to be true in all its parts. One can accept the greater claim and then examine how all the lesser details correspond well with actuality. One begins by trusting God's Word which is confirmed in greater measure as each of its individual statements is validated in its correspondence to reality.

Common reason tells us that we must first have a general proof that Scripture is God's Word, and argue thence to the verity of the parts, and not begin with a particular proof of each part. It seems that you would argue thus: This and that text of Scripture are true, therefore they are God's Word. But reason telleth you that you should argue thus: This is God's Word, therefore it is true.[43]

God

God is the central theme of the Bible. God is not hidden away, but plainly known to all who inhabit our world. Vedantins can acknowledge some of these claims:

The heavens declare the glory of God, and the sky above proclaims his handiwork. Day to day pours out speech, and night to night reveals knowledge. There is no speech, nor are there words, whose voice is not heard. Their voice goes out through all the earth, and their words to the end of the world.[44]

No person can escape all of nature pointing to God as its creator. There is no one who is outside of this communication of creation about its creator. However, this general knowledge of God as creator is insufficient to understand God's being, character, and actions as revealed in the Bible. God reveals himself in the Scriptures with positive and absolute truths, rather than in a qualified or negative sense alone. Yet there also remains mystery in God, in those areas where God has chosen not to reveal of himself,

---

calculated using the ratio of the number of variant Greek words against all the Greek words used. Using variants C and D arrives at 99.5% while using all variants A-D brings the accuracy down to 97%.

[41] The note on secular history refers to events such as Daniel's prophesy about the four kingdoms from the Babylonians to the Romans which have since come to pass. See, for example, Daniel-Rops, *Israel and the Ancient World: A History of the Israelites from the Time of Abraham to the Birth of Christ* (London: Eyre & Spottiswoode, 1949). See also W. F. Albright, *Archeology, Historical Analogy, and Early Biblical Tradition* (Baton Rouge: Louisiana State University Press: 1966); G. E. Wright, "Archeology and Old Testament Studies," *Journal of Biblical Literature* 77 (1958): 39-51; K. A. Kitchen, *The Bible in Its World: The Bible and Archaeology Today* (Eugene, OR: Wipf & Stock Publishers, 2004).

[42] The prophesies in the books of Isaiah, Jeremiah, and Daniel document some international rulers under God's prediction and sovereignty. The prophesies concerning Jesus Christ in the Psalms and Isaiah are impossible to deny in light of their fulfillment in the New Testament.

[43] I. D. E. Thomas, *The Golden Treasury of Puritan Quotations* (Simpsonville, SC: Christian Classics Foundation, 1999), 37-38. Thomas quotes from Richard Baxter, *The Practical Works of Richard Baxter* (London: James Duncan, 1830).

[44] Ps 19:1-4. This passage and Rom 1 explain the general revelation of God.

for his own good purposes or where humanity lacks the capacity to grasp God's nature and action. The Trinitarian nature of God is known only by revelation.[45]

God is absolute. There is no entity above or behind God. This God is one. He exists eternally as the Father, Son, and Holy Spirit who are three persons in the Trinity. Far from being a metaphysical conundrum of equating one and three, they are one in divinity and three in personhood. This unity and plurality in the Godhead avoids the difficulty of relationships in the monistic absolute. There is no essential change in God by relating to creation for there is an eternal communication of love within the Trinity. This relation extends uniquely to the world. The world is currently in a state of condemnation, but finds hope through Jesus Christ, the Son of God who is both God and man. Jesus is also the savior of the world and will judge it ultimately.

> For God so loved the world, that he gave his only Son, that whoever believes in him should not perish but have eternal life. For God did not send his Son into the world to condemn the world, but in order that the world might be saved through him. Whoever believes in him is not condemned, but whoever does not believe is condemned already, because he has not believed in the name of the only Son of God.[46]

Creation communicates the Creator to all humans intrinsically, rather than inferentially.[47] This awareness of God bears upon all humans who conceive various objects of worship, based on what they imagine and adore in their hearts.

A few well-known lines of reasoning help flesh out the nature of God. The teleological argument infers from design to an intelligent designer, rather than Vedanta's abstract being behind creation. Teleology points to a goal or object that requires a goal-giver and final cause. It elaborates the implicit reasoning from Psalm 19 and Romans 1.

1. All designs imply a designer.
2. There is great design in the universe.
3. Therefore, there must be a Great Designer of the universe.

Any designed object points to the intelligence of its designer. The complexity of design is proportional to the intelligence producing it. Simple one-cell animals, for instance, contain more complex information than Webster's Unabridged Dictionary.[48]

While teleology begs intelligence, the moral argument requires a moral God rather than an amoral being. Living with good categories demands an ethical law-giver.

1. Everyone assumes a universal moral law. Without this, life becomes unlivable: Moral disagreements cannot exist. Moral criticisms lose meaning. Promises and

---

[45]Matt 28:19 commands, "Go therefore and make disciples of all nations, baptizing them in the name of the Father and of the Son and of the Holy Spirit."

[46]John 3:16-18.

[47]Alvin Plantinga, *Warranted Christian Belief* (New York: Oxford University Press, 2000), 170-75. The typical proofs for God's existence are not required with the Vedantin who acknowledges the existence of God, but denies the specific nature of this God. The teleological and moral arguments will be employed to press the difference in understanding on the nature of God. These inferential rather than intrinsic arguments should resonate with those already predisposed, as will be drawn out later.

[48]Geisler, *Baker Encyclopedia of Christian Apologetics*, 277–78. If intelligent humans produced the dictionary, it certainly requires a much more intelligent being to create the entire universe, far more complex and diverse than any single-celled animal.

treaties can no longer to be upheld. We would justify rather than excuse our violation of the moral law.

2. A universal moral law presupposes a universal Moral Law Giver. This Law Giver gives moral commands and is interested in our behavior.
3. This universal Moral Law Giver must be absolutely good in order to have lasting meaning. Otherwise we could sacrifice our lives for what is ultimately less than right. The source of all good must be absolutely good, since the standard of all good must be completely good.
4. This implies an absolutely good Moral Law Giver.[49]

Like Scripture, the existence of God explains observed life, from creation to ethical standards. A moral, intelligent God does not exist because one observes morality and design in life. On the contrary, by believing in a moral and intelligent God, all that is observed, including morality and creation make complete sense.

Creation

Creation may be a complex mystery in Brahman, but the God of the Bible creates simply and unequivocally, by divine fiat. God speaks the universe into existence. Existence comes from non-existence. From nothing comes everything. It is not a divine fashioning of eternally co-existent substance, but the brand new creation of visible and invisible entities from absolute nothingness. This demonstrates the immense power of God. Creation differs from Vedanta in rejecting the identity of cause and effect. While God acts in creating time, space, and matter, his essential nature is unchanged by this creation. Creation also does not add to God's being, purpose, or his self-existent goal.

> In the beginning was the Word, and the Word was with God, and the Word was God. He was in the beginning with God. All things were made through him, and without him was not anything made that was made. In him was life, and the life was the light of men. The light shines in the darkness, and the darkness has not overcome it.[50]

Creation serves God, but God does not need this creation to add to his essential nature. Jesus Christ is the creator of both the visible and invisible, of persons and matter. Creation finds order from the nature of God and is sustained by God.

---

[49]Ibid., 500. Everyone presupposes morality: This presupposition of morality and a good moral law-giver makes intrinsic sense, as was developed by C. S. Lewis. Inferentially, alternate solutions to the problem are unsatisfying in every non-Christian worldview, especially Advaita Vedanta. See especially C. S. Lewis, *The Abolition of Man* (New York: HarperCollins, 2001), 83-99. See also William A. Dembski and Michael R. Licona, eds., *Evidence for God: 50 Arguments for Faith from the Bible, History, Philosophy, and Science* (Grand Rapids: Baker Books, 2010), 20-21. For an atheistic view on morality see: Richard Dawkins, *The God Delusion* (Boston: Houghton Mifflin Company, 2006), 211-14. A Christian response is presented in Ian S. Markham, *Against Atheism: Why Dawkins, Hitchens, and Harris are Fundamentally Wrong* (Malden, MA: Wiley-Blackwell, 2010), 59.
[50]John 1:1-5. Perfection is not a mechanical equation tied to immutability in all spheres. Thomas V. Morris, *Our Idea of God: An Introduction to Philosophical Theology* (Downers Grove, IL: InterVarsity Press, 1991), 141, 154. God is free to create while creation is dependent upon God.

He is the image of the invisible God, the firstborn of all creation. For by him all things were created, in heaven and on earth, visible and invisible, whether thrones or dominions or rulers or authorities – all things were created through him and for him. And he is before all things, and in him all things hold together.[51]

The world therefore is neither eternal nor self-existent. However, it is real in all senses of the term in its existence. It comes into existence by the creative power of God and reflects the wisdom of God in all its beauty and order. Its continued existence is not intrinsic to itself, as it depends wholly upon God.

For Vedantins, this dependency should be self-evident. However, the nature of the creator God is better exemplified in Christianity. The order and design of the universe reflect a purposeful creation with a reflection of God's attributes in contrast to a random, chaotic, and disordered universe that can be expected without the biblical God.

Humanity

Reflecting on creation, the undesirable elements of the world are not hard to miss. Tsunamis and earthquakes seem like anomalies at one end, while the wickedness of humans can reflect greater evil than good. Justifying goodness and order in this context can challenge the commendation of the biblical God, since disorder and evil can defy it in apparent chaos. The Bible explains the origin of the universe to be good and ordered, in keeping with the nature of God. The disorder observed today is explained in the historic "fall" of mankind and the universe from its original state. Humans deliberately turned away from God and brought a curse upon the earth and upon themselves.[52] It is true that one observes both order and disorder in the world. They are both best accounted for in the Christian worldview.

Human sin is said to be the most empirically verifiable truth. No person can claim to be without the taint of sin for its effects are visible on every street.[53] Given the holy nature of God revealed in the Scriptures, the sinfulness of mankind becomes the chief obstacle for humanity's restoration with God.[54]

---

[51]Col 1:15-17. God's creation of time and his action in time and space follow his eternal decree. God's nature and sovereign purposes are eternally immutable, but his actions are not artificially limited by a human need to restrict all action and all intent in order to conform to some static unchanging being. The personal nature of God reflects this common sense view of the perfect state of God in action.

[52]John S. Feinberg, *No One Like Him: The Doctrine of God* (Wheaton, IL: Crossway Books, 2001), 640. Gen 1:31a notes the original state of the created universe: "And God saw everything that he had made, and behold, it was very good." After the disobedience of Adam and Eve which is recorded in Gen 3, Paul summarizes the current state of sin and death in humanity in Rom 5:12 – "Therefore, just as sin came into the world through one man, and death through sin, and so death spread to all men because all sinned." Paul then observes in Rom 8:20-22 the far from ideal state of all creation: "For the creation was subjected to futility, not willingly, but because of him who subjected it, in hope that the creation itself will be set free from its bondage to corruption and obtain the freedom of the glory of the children of God. For we know that the whole creation has been groaning together in the pains of childbirth until now."

[53]Gilbert Keith Chesterton, *Orthodoxy* (London: John Lane Company, 1909), 22. Sin is "the only part of Christian theology which can really be proved" (ibid., 24). Modernist theologians "essentially deny human sin, which they can see in the street" (ibid., 14). Sin is offense against God which moderns reject to translate sin into the human plane. Vedantins accept God but sin's reality is masked without an absolute, holy God.

[54]Lev 11:44 states, "For I am the LORD your God. Consecrate yourselves therefore, and be holy, for I am holy." Lev 20:26 notes, "You shall be holy to me, for I the LORD am holy and have

Humanity is not in a copacetic state before God. It is under God's judgment for its false worship. It receives God's wrath today, evident in mankind's loss of restraint to impurity, spanning from homosexuality to every other observed form of evil.

They are filled with all manner of unrighteousness, evil, covetousness, malice. They are full of envy, murder, strife, deceit, maliciousness. They are gossips, slanderers, haters of God, insolent, haughty, boastful, inventors of evil, disobedient to parents, foolish, faithless, heartless, ruthless.[55]

This charge is not only against those who exhibit these specific forms of evil. Sin is endemic, beginning with the rejection of God. Sin finds diverse expression in each individual, "for all have sinned and fall short of the glory of God."[56]

Theologians such as Calvin clarify God's view of humanity's professed quest for truth. Man's epistemic system is flawed and incapable of rightly ascertaining truth.

Yet this disfiguring [of understanding, judgment, and will] does not go so far that we may judge man's understanding to be continually and completely blinded, for this contradicts common experience. Calvin cites man's desire to investigate truth, though this very search shows how unfit fallen man is to search for truth and to find it.[57]

The will and mind of man are impacted by the fall. Man reasons fallaciously to reach wrong conclusions, often based on improper assumptions. Contrary to Vedanta, this mental deficiency is not ignorance, but sin. Yet, the image of God in persons was not annihilated. Otherwise "man could not be a sinner at all . . . if he were not still God's image. Sinning presupposes rationality and voluntary decision. Animals cannot sin."[58]

This situation is tragic since man is incapable of addressing his deep-seated sin by himself. His sin-tainted will is incapable of rejecting future evil, just as he lacks the resources to pay for all his past misdeeds. Each offense against his infinitely holy creator God requires an infinitely mortal penalty to satisfy justice, if such recompense were even

---

separated you from the peoples, that you should be mine." Isa 6:3 declares God's holiness: "And one called to another and said: 'Holy, holy, holy is the LORD of hosts; the whole earth is full of his glory!'"

[55]Rom 1:29-31. Rom 1:18-32 contains the entire indictment of God against humanity.

[56]Rom 3:23. Both the universal condemnation of mankind and its redemptive hope are noted in verses 23-25. See also Wayne H. House and Joseph M. Holden, *Charts of Apologetics and Christian Evidences* (Grand Rapids: Zondervan, 2006), Chart 9: "Depravity is total, it is extensive (to every part), and it is intensive (rendering every human faculty unresponsive to God)."

[57]Berkouwer, *Man*, 151. Berkouwer notes: "It is not a simple matter to obtain a clear insight into Calvin's precise meaning when he speaks about divine grace and divine gifts to man. He distinguishes between natural and supernatural gifts (II, II, 12); man lost the latter (faith, love, righteousness) but kept the former (understanding, judgment, will), though these were disfigured and darkened" (ibid., 151).

[58]Gordon Haddon Clark, *The Biblical Doctrine of Man* (Jefferson, MD: The Trinity Foundation, 1992), 72. Clark also notes: "The effect on the mind is not ignorance as such, for Adam was extensively ignorant before the fall. Before the fall Adam may have reasoned relatively little, but his syllogisms were all valid. Afterward he fell into fallacies . . . . Sin had no effect on logic. Logic is the form of God's thought . . . . It is the sinner, not the logic that is mistaken. He often chooses false premises. Yet even moral judgments are a species of judgment and are thus subsumed under general intellectual activity. One result of the fall, then, is the occurrence of incorrect evaluations by means of erroneous thinking" (ibid., 77). See also Bernard Ramm, *Varieties of Christian Apologetics* (Grand Rapids: Baker Book House, 1982), 184: "The most drastic effect of sin upon us is with reference to the darkening of our natures in their understanding."

possible. No person is able to remedy the past or address the future. Even as humanity's need is desperate, mankind's hope is strong in the person of the God-man Jesus Christ.[59]

> For in him [Jesus Christ] all the fullness of God was pleased to dwell, and through him to reconcile to himself all things, whether on earth or in heaven, making peace by the blood of his cross . . . . And you, who once were alienated and hostile in mind, doing evil deeds, he has now reconciled in his body of flesh by his death, in order to present you holy and blameless and above reproach before him.[60]

Redemption

Jesus Christ is the one hope for all humanity. What cannot be accomplished by sinful man, God accomplishes through the sinless Jesus. As man, he identifies with humanity. As God, he is able to pay for the sins of many. As man, he lives a perfectly righteous life. As God, he provides his righteousness for many. For those who trust in him, his death is their vicarious punishment. His resurrection grants them his life for eternity. Humanity in deepest darkness finds its bright and only true light in Jesus Christ.

> Now the law came in to increase the trespass, but where sin increased, grace abounded all the more, so that, as sin reigned in death, grace also might reign through righteousness leading to eternal life through Jesus Christ our Lord. [61]

The medieval notions of hell may seem unpersuasive and the Christian claims may sound cliché today. However distorted by its historical messengers, the central message remains unchanged. Jesus still saves people today through the gospel, the Good News. This biblical message of forgiveness is given to unbelievers, in order that God may grant them newly regenerated hearts. With new ears to understand it, they repent from their sin and believe in God's provision of redemption in Jesus Christ. This redemption is categorical as the unbeliever is brought into God's kingdom once and forever.[62]

The central problem of apologetics is that no one is able to listen to God today. God is not obscure or hidden in an illusory world, but the recipients of God's grace need God's work done in them, when they will rightly respond to God's call of salvation. "My sheep hear my voice, and I know them, and they follow me."[63]

The Christian confidently hopes for eternity in heaven with God. He is granted a new existence in this world, to enjoy new life right here on earth. The Christian is

---

[59]Rom 5:15-19 notes how God's redemption is a "free gift" obtained only in Jesus Christ. See F. F. Bruce, *Jesus and Christian Origins Outside the New Testament* (Grand Rapids: Eerdmans, 1974).

[60]Col 1:19-22. In Col 1:15-29 man's chief sin is rejecting God; his only hope is forgiveness in Christ. See also Donald E. Hartley, "Essential Doctrines: The Implications of the Fall: Romans 5:12," *Areopagus Journal* (2009): 16.

[61]Rom 5:20-21. Verses 12-21 highlight the unique way of salvation through the unmerited grace of God.

[62]John 5:24 notes: "Truly, truly, I say to you, whoever hears my word and believes him who sent me has eternal life. He does not come into judgment, but has passed from death to life." Every individual either belongs to God's kingdom or is aligned against God.

[63]John 10:27. Verse 29 notes the calling of and security in God: "My Father, who has given them to me, is greater than all, and no one is able to snatch them out of the Father's hand." James W. Sire, *A Little Primer on Humble Apologetics* (Downers Grove, IL: IVP Books, 2006), 42-43. See belief causation in William Alston, "Psychoanalytic Theory and Theistic Belief," in *Philosophy of Religion: An Anthology*, ed. Charles Taliaferro and Paul J. Griffiths (Malden, MA: Blackwell Publishing, 2003), 123-40.

forgiven of all his sins. Yet on earth he is not sinless. He sins less as his transformed heart makes God and God's pleasure the center of his affection, rather than his self or his sin.

Serving Christ instead of sin, the Christian is sensitive to sin and progressively reflects Jesus Christ in increasing measure on earth. Tensions still remain between desire for the things of God and struggle with temptations. There is an eager anticipation of the culmination of history in a new heaven and a new earth, while enjoying life in this world under God today. The Spirit of God directs the life of the Christian, granting communication with God that imperfect humanity struggles with.[64]

In closing the Christian worldview, it must be reiterated that redemption on earth is not its pinnacle. All creation longs for the final redemption. This is accomplished not through the salvation of all, but of some individuals in the return of Jesus Christ.

The ultimate Christian apologetic rests in the person and life of Jesus Christ. A historical man, he lived an extraordinary life, making enormous claims. His death, burial, resurrection, and return are the central themes of all Christianity. They remain historic yet supernatural events that demand all humanity to submit to God.[65]

Apologetic Review

Having presented the proof from each worldview, the first stage of the apologetic encounter is reviewed. Before looking at the content in the discussion of the belief systems, the degree to which the application matches the theory of Worldview apologetics is first reviewed. Examining the proof section from the theory of Worldview apologetics, some salient points are highlighted.

Firstly, each worldview was presented from within the context of its own belief system. This is true for Vedanta and Christianity, but the Christian presentation is examined here. The Christian worldview was primarily presented from the viewpoint of the scriptural presuppositions. The Scriptures formed a major portion of the data.

Secondly, the worldview presentation was tailored to make it persuasive to the Vedanta worldview. The Christian worldview proof was presented differently than would be presented to a modernist or postmodernist skeptic, agnostic, or atheist.

The traditional proofs for existence of God are unnecessary since the Hindu already believes in the existence of a supreme being. Establishing the need for the Scriptures is also superfluous since the Hindu sees the need for revelation. Typical Christian apologetic arguments were either eliminated or modified for those which directly appealed to or conflicted with the Vedanta worldview.

Thirdly, the typical classical or evidential arguments were given a presuppositional base. By presupposing the truth of the Christian worldview, the

---

[64]Rom 8:18-30. The Spirit intercedes for the believer in his weakness in the will of God. Christians find today's suffering incomparable to the glory of eternity when corruption turns to freedom. This hope is not just a wish, but confident trust in God. It remains a hope since we do not see it yet.

[65]Col 1:15-29. The Bible calls Jesus the head of the church, the preeminent one in whom the fullness of God dwells, who brings peace by his death on the cross on behalf of sinners. God is pleased with the substitutionary death that places their sin upon Christ who pays its penalty and rises from the dead. These alienated, evil doers are made blameless and holy by Christ, granted Christ's righteousness. This is the Gospel or Good News. This is not purely a metaphysical theory, but a verifiable event in time and space. Jesus Christ and his resurrection are central without which there is no Christianity. With the reality of Jesus Christ, there is no hope for any other religion or means to peace with God, since one cannot reject God's provision for one's own and hope to outsmart God or ask for special pleading.

presentation was neither purely rational nor academic. It was given a distinctly evangelical thrust, even if it seemed less persuasive in relation to traditional apologetics.

Finally, the proof section minored on providing arguments within the opposing worldview. However, the presentation was tailored to make the Vedantin consider the simple Christian worldview in its entirety, contrasting key presuppositions in order to provoke questions on the validity and cogency of each worldview. The personal God and the historic events of redemption in Jesus Christ were emphasized for a convincing explanation.

Commonalities

Apologetic honesty would require the observation that even the most deviant systems have to take God's truth to pervert it. This "taking of God's truth" is necessary because even unbelievers live in God's world. Their metaphysical views must relate to the existing ontology created by God. Their epistemology depends on the way that their minds have been created, however distorted by the fall. However, any commonality does not provide a basis for building a neutral worldview from any presumed common ground. Rather, these points of contact are recognized within the larger framework of Worldview apologetics. This framework includes the transitory state of the current world, the need for redemption, and the existence of God. However, each of these needs to be severely qualified from within each worldview.[66]

The reliance of the Vedantin on the scriptures makes a powerful case for authoritative revelation from God. There is agreement that mankind is incapable of finding truth apart from God's revelation. The communication of God is vital in both worldviews. The desire for the Vedantin to preserve the perfection of Brahman is similar to the Christian's desire to preserve the divine attributes of God, in accordance with the Scriptures. The reality of humans that extends beyond the physical existence is crucial to both Christianity and Vedanta. The contingency of the world upon God and the grace of God for liberation form common themes in both worldviews.

The Christian worldview will attribute these commonalities to the epistemological base that Christianity identifies in the fallen world. All people have the image of God in them. The world they observe around them is created by God. Their fallen nature will not accurately acknowledge God, but it can recognize some aspects of God and of reality that concur with the Christian worldview. The Vedanta scriptures showcase some of these truths along with falsehood, reflecting the human wisdom that correctly identifies certain verities. The absence and corruption of key truths make Vedanta not a sister faith of Christianity, but a radically opposite worldview.

Difficulties

The above common points do not permit any rapprochement since the conflicts between the two worldviews far exceed any lasting contact. First and foremost in the conflict, is the nature of the Supreme Being called Brahman and God in the two systems: Brahman includes all reality, bliss, is ultimately attributeless, and impersonal, while the Christian God is distinct from creation, holy, Triune, and eminently personal. Among

---

[66]John G. Stackhouse Jr., *Humble Apologetics: Defending the Faith Today* (New York: Oxford University Press, 2002), 13.

other differences are the nature of man in God's image, but not divine; the nature of the problem in the universe, the means of redemption, and the final end of all creation.[67]

Specific arguments will be made against each contention in the offense section. Among these is the nature of true scriptures. The inviolate presuppositions will be exposed and the unsupportable superstructures checked. In the Vedanta worldview the nature of Brahman as the Supreme Being conflicts severely with the Christian God. It is impossible to reconcile the two views of the ultimate being in any measure. Failing to understand the true nature of God, the alternate Vedanta presentation is an idol, created in accordance with the will and desire of humans, rather than the true revelation of God. On this foundational falsehood the Vedanta worldview will be charged in the offense section.

Conclusion

This chapter presented one way in which Worldview apologists can present the Christian arguments to a Vedantin. At this stage, the engagement is far from over. The data of each worldview is presented simply and comprehensively in order to connect best with the opposing worldview.

While making minor connections, the presentation has remained mainly within the mainstream of each worldview. The next two stages however, will involve an active interaction with the opposing worldview since offense involves showcasing the failure of that worldview in its own terms and defense responds to any similar charges within one's own worldview.

---

[67]Alfred George Hogg, *The Christian Message to the Hindu: Being the Duff Missionary Lectures For Nineteen Forty Five on the Challenge of the Gospel in India* (London: S.C.M. Press, 1947), 34.

CHAPTER 5
OFFENSE: HIGHLIGHTING THE STRENGTHS

Establishing the bases of each worldview does not complete the apologetic encounter. Since the adherents of each worldview believe in the ultimacy of their view, they contrast their viewpoints against those of the other system.[1] The Hindu system will first make its strongest case why it is better than the Christian worldview, by pointing out its deficiencies. This is then followed by the Christian making his case. The offense section of apologetics utilizes the methods such as *reductio ad absurdum*, "impossibility of the contrary," logical fallacies, inconsistencies, incoherence, and failure to correspond. It will engage the opposing worldview within itself and attempt to show where its foundations are weak and the superstructure unsupportable in its worldview. It will also contrast why its own worldview is satisfactory.

Vedanta's Challenge

Vedanta has established its value as a unifying monistic system grounded in an impersonal, all-inclusive, and supra-rational reality. The Christian worldview suffers significantly by failing to present a fulfilling view of an absolute personal God.

Monism

Christianity claims that God alone necessarily exists and that everything else is created by God *ex-nihilo*. Everything is claimed to be sustained by God, but is not God. What is this world fundamentally? If it is made in time and will be lost in eternity; then matter, plants, and animals are less than substantively real. They are not very different from the world developed by Maya. They need to be an extension of the divine or divine itself if real in any significant sense. Vedanta recognizes that from the perspective of ultimate reality, the current world of Brahman appears ephemeral; while Christianity claims a lesser essence but a greater reality for the world's substance without proper justification.

The image of God in humans partially straddles this problem but fails to grant reality to all non-human entities. Christianity still fails to clearly identify the actual worth of man. If constructed from clay and breathed in by God, then his dual nature seems

---

[1]John M. Frame, *Apologetics for the Glory of God: An Introduction* (Phillipsburg, NJ: P&R Publishing, 1994), 57, 82, 191-93. This showcases the errors within the false worldview.

schizophrenic. His body must perish and his spirit identified with the unspoiled Atman, if indeed he has the breath of God in him. The lack of a monistic principle requires a complex theory to re-create man's body for eternity.

Vedanta's monism has a strong attraction to those who want to unravel mysteries. Science looks for unified approaches to resolve diverse phenomena. Unlike various systems that posit multiple independent realities, monism is simple and clear. There is one reality that is eternal. This reality is instantiated in various observed forms. Humans and the world have Brahman as the substratum from whom they gain existence and in whom they will ultimately dissolve. The resolution of differences involves understanding how these entities relate to one another and how one may transcend the differences to return to a complete unity. Monism posits an intuitive beauty in the presentation and resolution of problems. However, non-monistic Christianity provides a complex system of details to explain how independent realities came to be and where they are headed.[2] The more complex the system, the greater suspicion it garners.

Personality

Reality is ultimately impersonal. Personality as we understand it is far from perfect. Personality involves change. Change introduces deviation from one state to another, either gaining or losing perfection in the process. Personality thus becomes one of the manifest forms of reality that is contingent, lacking perfection. Whether in man or in God, this transitory handling of relationships will no longer be necessary when the consciousness of the individual is absorbed in the ultimate consciousness. Like all underlying laws governing the universe, the essence of being must be impersonal. One can trust in the forces of gravity to endure, even when today's advanced technologies created by persons fail and are replaced by incremental improvements. The failure is ascribed to the source of these systems, which is fallible personality. Christianity projects a super-person who lacks any human flaw or limitation. However, this projection fails to metaphysically reconcile the concept of a person with the concept of perfection.

Personality is inherently limited by its choices and its changes. The Christian Scriptures include paradoxes of the covenant love of God for Israel contrasted with his rejection of the rest of humanity. They also speak of God changing his mind, introducing the very limitation which they claim that God is without.[3] They speak of God responding to human action, especially prayer, while positing that God sovereignly executes what he ordains from all eternity. By positing a person, Christianity fails to rest in an ultimate source of perfection that Advaita Vedanta has in the impersonal Brahman.

Any personal system like Christianity is explained as a subset of the overall impersonal scheme of Advaita Vedanta Hinduism.[4] Vedanta has Isvara or God as

---

[2] Bradley J. Malkovsky, "Samkara on Divine Grace," in *New Perspectives on Advaita Vedanta*, ed. Bradley J. Malkovsky (Boston: Brill, 2000), 76. Brady further notes: "We project onto the realities of world and self, incorrect notions about their nature, which in turn generates attachment and leads to blind action. This is an innate and universal error, affecting all people" (ibid., 76). The Christian theology of creation, fall, and redemption involves much complexity from the Advaitin perspective. These critiques are customized from diverse Advaitin arguments.

[3] Gen 6:6 says, "And the LORD was sorry that he had made man on the earth, and it grieved him to his heart."

[4] P. T. Raju, *The Philosophical Traditions of India* (London: George Allen & Unwin, 1971), 178.

Christianity does. However, this God is Brahman facing the world, while the absolute Brahman is impersonal and beyond the limiting attributes of the Christian God.

Inclusivity

With Christianity subsumed under it, Hinduism becomes inclusive of all religions and even irreligion. Hindus do not seek to actively convert Christians. Just as all rivers end in the ocean, so also any attempt to worship God is a gift of God's grace which draws man closer to Brahman.[5] Every human estate finds its place in the continuum of Vedanta Hinduism. This comprehensive feature of Hinduism is attractive to many who intuitively long for the beauty of inclusivity. Many religions may claim to include the reality of other faiths, but only do so in an exclusive or partially inclusive manner.

Christianity provides no hope for the larger mass of humanity which is ignorant of the Christian gospel. Many pass on to an eternity of suffering, for their crime of being created by the Christian God. Even the Christian Scriptures seem to equivocate on this, finding some whose righteous acts were seen by God as acceptable before they believed in Jesus Christ or used the means ordained in the Old Testament.[6] If salvation is only through faith in Jesus Christ and all are de-merited sinners before God, then God's response to the actions of men like Cornelius, Noah, and Naaman are symptomatic of inconsistencies. Either the threat of hell for all outside of Christ is just an empty threat or the redemption of those in the Scriptures before Christ acts point to error in the Christian Scriptures or theology or both. At face value, the eternal suffering of the ignorant tribes makes the exclusive claims of Christianity not just unpalatable, but also irreconcilable with its claims of a God of love, mercy, and grace.

Only Hinduism has a way of acknowledging positively the situation with a thoroughgoing inclusiveness.[7] Without the limitation of just a single lifetime to attain perfection, humanity can progress through reincarnation until what Brahman begins culminates in Brahman. None are lost, but all of creation ultimately returns to Brahman.

Rationality

Despite its seemingly irrational approach to life, especially in the apparent illusory nature of the external world, Vedanta Hinduism is eminently rational. Among the philosophers of Hinduism, many categories exist in the ancient languages for concepts

---

[5]R. C. Zaehner, *Hinduism* (Oxford: Oxford University Press, 1962), 101.

[6]Acts 10:1-4 says, "At Caesarea there was a man named Cornelius, a centurion of what was known as the Italian Cohort, a devout man who feared God with all his household, gave alms generously to the people, and prayed continually to God. About the ninth hour of the day he saw clearly in a vision an angel of God come in and say to him, 'Cornelius.' And he stared at him in terror and said, 'What is it, Lord?' And he said to him, 'Your prayers and your alms have ascended as a memorial before God'"; 2 Kgs 5:17-9 notes, "Then Naaman said, 'If not, please let there be given to your servant two mules' load of earth, for from now on your servant will not offer burnt offering or sacrifice to any god but the LORD. In this matter may the LORD pardon your servant: when my master goes into the house of Rimmon to worship there, leaning on my arm, and I bow myself in the house of Rimmon, when I bow myself in the house of Rimmon, the LORD pardon your servant in this matter.' He said to him, 'Go in peace.'" Gen 6:9b says that "Noah was a righteous man, blameless in his generation. Noah walked with God."

[7]Sara Grant, "Contemporary Relevance of Advaita," in *New Perspectives on Advaita Vedanta: Essays in Commemoration of Professor Richard De Smet*, ed. Bradley J. Malkovsky (Boston: Brill, 2000), 160-63.

that lack equivalence in other systems.[8] It is often this lack of ability in other systems to handle the supra-rational nature of Hinduism that is caricatured as irrational. It just means that the expansive Vedanta categories do not fit within the narrow Christian taxonomies. When the system as a whole is viewed from any point within it, there is an intricate web of reason that finely holds the entire worldview together.[9]

It is the Christian worldview that seems to fail a simple test of rationality. The Christian gospel appears very direct. It appears consistent and coherent and even to correspond with observed reality. However, its claims are not simple but simplistic. It dismisses a vast majority of people to heartless suffering today and to an eternally inferno, when the universe is apparently governed by a loving, and all-powerful God.

The problem of evil has been the historical Achilles heel of Christianity despite the best attempts to redeem this conundrum; Christians divide over their stated reasons, even as the Scriptures seem to contradict themselves over this fundamental problem. Is God sovereign? If so, how does he avoid being the ultimate cause of all evil? Yet this God does not sin. Vedanta by-passes this entire problem by having two spheres of activity. This world does follow the moral law under God. In the ultimate sense, good and evil are subsumed under the power of Brahman.

In concluding the offense against the Christian worldview, some of its presuppositions are shaky at best. The Bible claims to be God's revelation, but has both inconsistencies and contradictions in its theology. Its foundation of a personal God is irreconcilable with absolute perfection and incapable of addressing the problem of evil. On this shaky foundation, the explanation provided for the reality of the world and man, is less than convincing. Even granting the historical reality of Jesus Christ, the theological assertions of universal claims fall far short of a global appeal, in light of the particular redemption portrayed in the Christian gospel.

Christianity's Challenge

The above charges will receive a Christian response in the next chapter. There are many unique characteristics to Christianity that claim allegiance of all humanity. This section identifies some fundamental flaws in Advaita Vedanta that expose its precarious presuppositions, contrasted with the corresponding strengths of the Christian worldview.

Truth

Truth is the most important strength of the Christian worldview. Viewed biblically, Hinduism is a human attempt to grasp reality, while Christianity rests on God's true self-revelation to man. Man is neither God nor divine, even when made in the image of God. This image is further tarnished after the fall. Therefore God must reveal himself to man. This revelation becomes the basis of all understanding in the Christian worldview. The question is not whether one view is more appealing than another, but rather which one is true. Whether we like it or not, we must all live under that truth and

---

[8]Chandradhar Sharma, *A Critical Survey of Indian Philosophy* (London: Rider & Company, 1960), 192. The diverse states of valid and invalid knowledge, perception and cognition are examples of philosophical acuity.

[9]Raju, *The Philosophical Traditions of India*, 177-80. Maya is far from a silly illusion as sometimes caricatured, but its system is well developed to rationally address the observable reality.

be judged by that truth. This truth must cohere with other beliefs and correspond with the observed reality. It should likewise address good and evil, both within and without.[10]

Jesus made some explicit statements about the truth.[11] Krishna makes similar statements about himself.[12] How does one confirm the truth of one statement over the other? It is difficult for Vedanta to make ultimate truth claims which reach down into the current time and space. It lacks the metaphysical ground and epistemological basis in this world in order to trust its truth claims. Brahman, as the ground of being, is beyond reason and the world of time and space is a product of Maya which lacks causal connection with Brahman. Therefore no basis exists on which to trust any of its truth claims within time and space. There is no metaphysical ground for its truth quotient. There is no epistemological basis on which its claims have any validity whatsoever for the recipient.

> Unless something in the hearer stirs and goes out to receive a revelation it fails to make an impact . . . . So the best way to know a person is through his self-disclosure to us. On the other hand, we cannot have certain knowledge about God from his acts, because unless we know him, we cannot know with certainty which are his acts.[13]

In contrast, the Christian worldview makes truth claims on the basis of the God of truth who is true and acts in truth. Vedanta has no such ultimate grounds for its claims. When Krishna claims to be an avatar or incarnation of God, his action in time and space cannot be grounded in the ultimate Brahman with respect to truth. This basis is implicitly borrowed from the Christian worldview, by assuming a world governed by a true and rational God. Why must Krishna's statements about being the ultimate reality be true and on what basis is the validity of his statements evaluated? When ultimate reality has no distinctions – of good and evil, of distinct attributes, and ultimately of true and false statements, evaluation becomes impossible. Claims here are self-referentially incoherent.

One cannot dismiss the fundamental assumptions of Vedanta philosophy as simply a "different way of thinking." The identity of cause and effect, the immutability clause of perfection, and the excluded middle are some problematic issues for the Vedantin whose qualifications involve laborious arguments. Murty notes these arguments as logically fallacious and consequently at least some of their premises as untrue:

> (a) Eternal Scripture: The Mimamsa-Vedanta conception of an eternal scripture is absurd, because we can accept that truth has been disclosed to man only if there is someone who can do so.

---

[10]Harold A. Netland, *Dissonant Voices: Religious Pluralism and the Question of Truth* (Grand Rapids: Eerdmans, 1991), 182.

[11]John 8:32 says, "and you will know the truth, and the truth will set you free." John 14:6 notes: "Jesus said to him, 'I am the way, and the truth, and the life. No one comes to the Father except through me.'" In John 17:17 Jesus says, "Sanctify them in the truth; your word is truth."

[12]*The Bhagavad-Gita: Krishna's Counsel in Time of War*, trans. Barbara Stoler Miller (New York: Bantam Books, 1986), 9:18-39. Krishna states, "I am the way, sustainer, lord . . ." Krishna asserts, "I am Vishnu" and "I am gracious Shiva" and "I am the beginning, the middle, and the end of creations . . ." and finally, "I am the seed of all creatures; nothing animate or inanimate could exist without me." Krishna claims to be every incarnate god and assume attributes that Jesus Christ claims for himself. He asserts ultimate existence by saying, "Nothing is higher than I am" (ibid., 7:7).

[13]K. Satchidananda Murty, *Revelation and Reason in Advaita Vedānta* (Grand Rapids: Eerdmans Publishing Company, 1959), 320-21. Murty notes again: "A knowledge of God, in whatever way we may think we have arrived at, comes ultimately from God" (ibid., 321).

(b) Advaitavada: The Advaita Vedanta metaphysic cannot be true, because it is contrary to perception, and is logically refutable. Further, if Brahman is the one and sole reality, to speak of any revelation of Brahman is nonsense.[14]

In arguing for immutability, Brahman is rendered imperfect if having a goal, since purpose implies something lacking in Brahman, according to Advaita Vedanta. This position is upheld even when Brahman is the acknowledged material cause of the universe. A purposeless creation is deflected by making creation a play, without resolving the conflict. Instead of accepting a goal or denying it, play becomes the excluded middle. With contextual qualifications and compounded categories, the excluded middle for Brahman and his complement is invoked for the status of the world, violating self-evident logic. Likewise, an affirmation and its negation cannot both be true at the same time in the same sense, as in calling Maya and Isvara both real and unreal. The relation between cause and effect in creation is wrong, the effect being identified with the cause, and failing to distinguish between ontology and function. Logic is bent here to stake a metaphysical claim. This is not another valid way of thinking, it is error.[15]

Beyond metaphysical challenges, there are epistemological hurdles to believe any Vedanta truth claims, when the recipient of the claim is the Atman, distinct from the rational ego who receives spiritual knowledge. A strong divide between the metaphysical and empirical selves, questions the normative process of information gathering and processing, since there is no basis for trusting thought when the empirical actions are nothing but helpful fiction.[16] This obliges the over-evaluation of mystical experience since propositions cannot be relied to accurately transmit truth in the recipient.[17]

Historicity

A robust refutation of the Vedanta's claims comes from its poor historical validation. This further disconnects its metaphysical claims from reality on the ground.

Christianity claims truth in all aspects of its worldview – from its Scriptures as true history, to its characters as true individuals involved in true events that reflect the

---

[14]Ibid., 329.

[15]See the Advaitin view in Frederick F. Fost, "Playful Illusions: The Making of Worlds in Advaita Vedanta," *Philosophy East and West* 48 (1998). Fost says: "If Brahman created the world for a purpose, then there must have been some goal; Brahman must be lacking something. But if that were the case, then Brahman would not be perfect . . . . However . . . to act without purpose would not be acting at all" (ibid., 389). To avoid the world as an illusion, its appearance is said to be neither real nor unreal: "Appearance must therefore lie outside the supposedly exhaustive dichotomy of the Real and Unreal" (ibid., 393). The material cause and effect is seen in threads making the cloth. The cause is the thread, the effect the cloth. The cloth, however, is not the thread. The instrumental cause is similar to the potter making the clay. Brahman is both material and instrumental. See also James E. Taylor, *Introducing Apologetics: Cultivating Christian Commitment* (Grand Rapids: Baker Academic, 2006), 257-58.

[16]Eliot S. Deutsch, "Karma as a 'Convenient Fiction' in the Advaita Vedānta," *Philosophy East and West* 15 (1965): 7: "[K]arma is only a 'relative idea'; and it does not follow from the real nature of being. Its necessity is not logically implied by the metaphysical principles of the Advaita, and its denial does not lead to consequences which are self-contradictory."

[17]Francis-Vincent Anthony, Chris A. M. Hermans, and Carl Sterkens, "A Comparative Study of Mystical Experience among Christian, Muslim, and Hindu Students in Tamil Nadu, India," *Journal for the Scientific Study of Religion* 49 (2010): 274. Horizontal mysticism searches for the ultimate, for union of self with a wider reality as an experience of non-dualistic reality. The final state is a total loss of self.

true statements and actions of God. The Gita and the other Vedanta scriptures make lofty metaphysical claims, but fail to showcase truth in the historical dimension.

The historical facts of Christianity are validated by a mass of evidence for the Scriptures and Jesus Christ.[18] Contrariwise, Hinduism, whose fabled legends exhibit little historic verity, relies on insights underlying myths. The Hindu gods evolve from the Rig Veda to the Gita, with Hinduism transmuting from nature worship and polytheism to monotheism and pantheism, traversing intoxicated gods and phallus worship. Hindu gods change with time through their scriptures, until they are reinterpreted in Vedanta with cosmic significance. Vedanta cannot literally accept these early mythical gods.[19] A vast host of these early gods have no historic basis, while later gods like Rama and Krishna have only loose ties to any historical occasion from which their stories developed.

The insights from the propositional truths of Christianity are no less true than the historic events that convey them. Jesus was a historical individual. Adam and Eve are concrete individuals as are Abraham, Moses, David, Peter, and Paul. The crucifixion and resurrection of Jesus splits our history in ways such that one cannot calmly evaluate the teachings of Jesus apart from his historic birth, life, death, and resurrection.[20]

Given that Vedanta did not value literal historical facts in its scriptures, the assurance of truth from the mouth of Krishna is low. Krishna and his extant words are the

---

[18]See Craig L. Blomberg, *The Historical Reliability of the Gospels* (Downers Grove, IL: InterVarsity Press, 2007). Blomberg says: "Recent scholarship . . . has served to strengthen the view that the miracles are historical and that the Christian claim is true" (ibid., 151). A broad array of data is found in these works: Randall Price, *The Stones Cry Out: What Archeology Reveals About the Truth of the Bible* (Eugene, OR: Harvest House Publishers, 1997); Josh McDowell, *The New Evidence that Demands a Verdict: Evidence I & II Fully Updated in One Volume to Answer Questions Challenging Christians in the 21st Century* (Nashville: Thomas Nelson Publishers, 1999); Lee Strobel, *The Case for Christ: A Journalist's Personal Investigation of the Evidence for Jesus* (Grand Rapids: Zondervan, 1998). For a secular viewpoint see A. N. Sherwin-White, *Roman Society and Roman Law in the New Testament* (Oxford: Clarendon Press, 1963). This data is emphasized by Evidential apologetics, which has responded to centuries of attacks against the historic Christian truth. For Old Testament references see K. A. Kitchen, *Ancient Orient and Old Testament* (London: Tyndale Press, 1966); W. F. Albright, *The Bible after Twenty Years of Archeology: 1932-1952* (Pittsburgh: Biblical Colloquium, 1954); G. E. Wright, *The Bible and the Ancient Near East* (New York: Doubleday, 1961). For New Testament supports see, F. F. Bruce, *New Testament Documents: Are They Reliable?* (Radford, VA: Wilder Publications, 2009); *The Resurrection of Jesus: John Dominic Crossan and N. T. Wright in Dialogue*, ed. Robert B. Stewart (Minneapolis: Fortress, 2006); John A. T. Robinson, *Can We Trust the New Testament?* (Grand Rapids: Eerdmans, 1977); Gary R. Habermas, *The Historical Jesus: Ancient Evidence for the Life of Christ* (Joplin, MO: College Press, 1996); Michael Grant, *Jesus: An Historian's Review of the Gospels* (New York: Macmillan, 1977); *The Reliability of the New Testament: Bart D. Ehrman and Daniel B. Wallace in Dialogue*, ed. Robert B. Stewart (Minneapolis: Fortress, 2011); Paul Foster, "Who Wrote 2 Thessalonians? A Fresh Look at an Old Problem," *Journal for the Study of the New Testament* 35 (2012): 150-75. Jack Finegan, *Light from the Ancient Past: The Archeological Background of the Hebrew-Christian Religion* (Princeton: Princeton University Press, 1951).

[19]Zaehner, *Hinduism*, 9, 19, 22, 38. Varuna, Indra, Agni, Soma, Rudra, and Vishnu are early gods whose antics Vedanta would not prescribe as actual acts. Indra's mythological battles are variously interpreted, while most stories clearly reflect social conditions of the times, including caste conflicts. Magic rituals get reinterpreted into the identity of Brahman and Atman, as seers move from the scandalous plurality of gods to the unifying principle of the universe. Sankara himself symbolically interprets those scriptures which contradict reason in their plain reading.

[20]I. Howard Marshall, "Raised for Our Justification," in *Tough-Minded Christianity: Honoring the Legacy of John Warwick Montgomery*, ed. William Dembski and Thomas Schirrmacher (Nashville: B&H Academic, 2008), 245. See also F. F. Bruce, *The Books and the Parchments* (Grand Rapids: Fleming Revell, 1984).

product of an uncertain Vyasa, the author or compiler of the Mahabharata. The actions of Vyasa recorded in the Mahabharata give little credence to trust his works and ethics. If he was the author, then it contradicts the understanding that he wrote the book later than the actual events. If he is a compiler, he gratuitously adds his namesake into the story. Disregarding these anomalies, his actions show selfish pettiness.[21]

The Bhagavad Gita is inserted at a later period, disconnected with the rest of the Mahabharata. The Bhagavad Gita's historicity is not taken seriously even by Hindu proponents like Vivekananda, who values its teaching when conceding its inauthenticity. The Gita is also inconsistent and hard to interpret.[22] Metaphysical claims in these texts lose credence when their origin and record of events are historically dubious.[23]

Best Explanation

Christianity provides the best explanation for all our observation. It provides the finest clarification for why humanity has such a capacity for both greatness and smallness within. Humans can tend to extreme acts of goodness and evil. The image of God in man represents God's character, but his fallen nature displays the depths of his depravity. The world as a creation of God showcases the ordered beauty that reflects its creator. Reason has a basis in God who is a rational person. Many other fundamental aspects of life, from meaning to *teleos*, find significance in the Christian God.[24]

> Given theism, we'd expect that God would have created the self in question in such a way that her beliefs, at least in many areas, would be for the most part true. But given naturalism, there isn't, of course, any God who designs us so as to resemble him in holding true beliefs.[25]

Hinduism does not need to prove the mystery, but it must be able to answer objections and back up its claims for Brahman and the observed world.

It should be clearly noted that when it is said that knowledge of God, or Incarnation (if there had been one) is not contradicted by reason, it does not mean that they can

---

[21]Vyasa lies with his dead brothers' wives, but curses their offspring to blindness and anemia due to their mothers' shyness and fear before him. These children play key roles in the Mahabharata. If Vyasa was a later compiler, these events in the book are false. If he was the author, then the book is recent and the war does not correspond to any historical events of the time. Further, the lack of ethical and moral righteousness is not represented as reprehensible, making it untrustworthy.

[22]Zaehner, *Hinduism*, 93. See also Swami Vivekananda, *The Complete Works of Swami Vivekananda* (Madras: Vedanta Press, 1947) [on-line]; accessed 27 January 2013; available from http://en.wikisource.org/wiki/The_Complete_Works_of_Swami_Vivekananda/Volume_4/ Lectures_and_Discourses/Thoughts_on_the_Gita; Internet.

[23]Alain Danielou, *A Brief History of India* (Rochester, VT: Inner Traditions, 2003), 24, 46. The Mahabharata refers to past events, rewritten and adapted, while "most of the critical work required to separate the original elements from later additions still remains to be done" (ibid., 24). Its current version was written around 500 B.C. The seed of these events could be anywhere from 1000 B.C. to 3000 B.C. The Bhagavad Gita is "inserted into the Mahabharata at a later date," possibly around 400-100 B.C. (ibid., 46). Vivekananda's thoughts on the Gita also candidly admit the lack of historical validity.

[24]Harold A. Netland, *Encountering Religious Pluralism: The Challenge to Christian Faith & Mission* (Downers Grove, IL: Intervarsity Press, 2001), 311, 315. This apologetic is drawn out from the Classical and Reformed perspectives.

[25]Alvin Plantinga and Michael Tooley, *Knowledge of God* (Malden, MA: Blackwell Publishing, 2008), 51. What is said of naturalism here applies directly to Brahman in Vedanta.

be comprehended, or that they can be proved. Even the most concentrated exercise of reason cannot completely elucidate the mystery of God . . . . Here the position of Advaita Vedanta is fundamentally sound, for it holds that Brahman cannot be proved, but at the same time it maintains (i) that what is said about Brahman is not meaningless, or as Leibniz says the terms employed must not be *sine mente soni*, words meaning nothing; and (ii) that the objections of opponents must be capable of being answered. The knowledge of God, theists maintain, is based on the consciousness that God has revealed himself. It is for the opponent to prove that this belief is unjustified.[26]

Vedanta does not provide that compelling reason to explain observed reality, as it posits a "Lessing's Ditch" between the inferential observation of our natural faculties and the ultimately real state of affairs. The greatness and smallness of humanity cannot be attributed to ignorance.[27]

If the Atman is fully aware and the ego is evil to the degree that it fails to identify itself as Atman, evil is graduated on its degree of inner knowledge. However, with no ethical ground in Brahman and Atman, the actions or knowledge of the ego cannot be judged until it is fully merged with the Atman, when it is presumably perfect. Until then, there are two entities, the ego and Atman. The Atman cannot sin. If the ego sins, it has no basis for evaluation whether in knowledge or action, since there is no ultimate standard for both in relation to partial knowledge or specific wrongs. Likewise, the temporal injunctions of karma and dharma find no final setting in Brahman.

In contrast, a person who acts worthily, either unaware of or willfully rejecting the Atman, lacks qualification in Vedanta. Assuming perfection, the Atman can account for greatness. This Atman is disconnected from the actions of the ego. The ego finally transcends physical reality when in touch with one's inner reality. Such transcendent persons, who excel in good works, as is commonly understood, seem lacking. In the temporal plane, its good deeds lack true ethical standards. Vedanta cannot provide a final justification for the moral and immoral acts of men, with a neutral Atman internally and an amoral Brahman over all.

Further, man's sinfulness cannot be attributed to Maya. The evil has no other objective referent than Maya, which being the power of Brahman, cannot be deflected from Brahman. By denying good and evil in Brahman, that norm must cascade all the way down to the ego, losing moral categories in humanity. This can be avoided by giving Maya an independent reality outside of Brahman, which Vedanta disallows. People intuitively understand good and evil. The denial of the absolute morals and relegating it to a temporary but convenient fiction fails to correspond to a universally true reality.

Rationality has no basis in this universe if Brahman is its ground of being. A host of questions within Advaita end in mystery: Why must Maya create a rational universe? How can we trust in reason when discoursing on metaphysics, or living life on a daily basis, when reason is untethered from the absolute? Even by calling Brahman super-rational, one cannot justify why Maya produces a reasonable universe. If the

---

[26]Murty, *Revelation and Reason in Advaita Vedānta*, 323-24.

[27]See Miller, *The Bhagavad-Gita*, 7:15, where Krishna says: "The evil doers, the ignorant, the lowest persons who are attached to demonic nature, and whose power of discrimination has been taken away by divine illusive power (Maya) do not worship or seek Me." Assigning evil ultimately to ignorance alone ignores a vast array of contributory sources to sin. The existence of evil is obvious. Attributing it to ignorance is an error.

Atman is super-rational, why is the ego not the same or even worse, irrational, rather than rational? The ignorance of Maya does not explain the logic governing the current state of affairs. To explain the basis of rational selves and creation, there is no reason in Advaita.

Personality

Finally, in contrast to Vedanta, Christianity is eminently personal. Humans are persons. They are made in God's image as persons. God revealed himself as a person, especially in Jesus Christ. People know God as a person in a relationship. While the term "personal" carries some baggage, especially with petty gods pursuing personal interests, the God of the Bible is supremely personal. He is also revealed as holy in his personality. Everyone understands life personally. Human laws and principles are understood in the context of personal law givers and personal authorities. Natural laws are set in place by a personal God. To obscure the Person behind the orderly laws does not transcend truth, but obfuscates it, stopping short of honoring the personal God behind nature.[28]

Hinduism is rampant with repulsive rather than respectable gods. Setting aside the selfishness of the minor gods like Indra, Varuna, and Agni, even the revered gods are unattractive. It seems ironic that the gods of Hinduism eminently portray the pettiness of human error, often lacking common moral sense. It is historically shown how Hinduism transmutes from the worship of nature to better defined deities, from performances of sacrifices to a philosophy of life.[29] They often major in one virtue only to exclude another. In elevating justice, Kali violates temperance. Elevating social reputation, Rama lacks spousal responsibility. In assuming the divine, Krishna flaunts moral distinctions. The development of the polytheistic gods and their absorption into the Vedantic pantheon indicates a force fit of diverse gods into deities contending for Isvara. Later, Trimurti has Brahma as creator, Vishnu as preserver, and Siva as destroyer, in order to reconcile Siva and Vishnu.[30] Krishna claims to be all of them as Brahman in the Gita.

Advaita minimizes the personal in order to exalt the transcendent Brahman. It seems to reject the personal in order to jettison the errors of these former deities, just as Buddhism rejected Vedic rituals. As Socrates rejected the petty Greek gods for the ideal, Vedanta corrects one error by falling into another. By bartering the personality of the ultimate reality for impersonality, Vedanta devalues human nature. It cannot ground any true virtue or reason, especially the necessity placed upon persons to act as they "ought."

Physical forces can limit humans to its impersonal laws. What law binds man to follow moral, ethical, and rational choices? No such law is impervious, since people violate these laws and makes poor choices every day. For justice, karma provides the fair consequence of every cause. Karma invokes duty requiring the "ought," but it is in

---

[28]Alvin Plantinga, *Warranted Christian Belief* (New York: Oxford University Press, 2000), 170, 181. The personal nature of God in relation to people is well argued by Fideistic apologetics. See also Vern Sheridan Poythress, "Why Scientists Must Believe in God," *Journal of the Evangelical Society* 46 (2003) [on-line]; accessed 27 January 2013; available from http://www.frame-poythress.org/why-scientists-must-believe-in-god/; Internet. See Peter J. Bussey, "Physical Infinities: A Substitute for God?" *Science & Christian Belief* 18 (2006): 133-50. Against a vast universe God having personal interest in human beings seems tough. The Christian response is that not a sparrow falls to the ground without God knowing about it. Every electron in the universe is identical and God knows all details, small and large.

[29]Danielou, *A Brief History of India*, 8, 28, 48. The evolving moral issues with the Hindu gods were discussed in the earlier section.

[30]Zaehner, *Hinduism*, 86.

discord with moral values. Also, Arjuna yields to Krishna as his personal Lord. If Krishna is ultimately the impersonal Brahman, Arjuna owes no allegiance to Brahman in order to act honorably. Further, Krishna's own actions fail to obtain moral justification.

The honorable Yudhishthira misses the mark for upholding the moral law in contrast to his religious duty. He sees the wicked Duryodhana in heaven for fulfilling his duty as a warrior, while his more righteous wife and brothers are in hell. He is deceived by the gods in apparent tests. "He is forced [by duty and Krishna] against his will and his better judgment to do things he knows to be wrong."[31] The Vedanta option to trust in deceptive gods or an amoral Brahman is unnecessary. The personal God of the Bible is good and trustworthy, setting the personal standard and the mandate for good action.

The Christian worldview comprehensively addresses what Vedanta lacks. It has been shown that Vedanta cannot function in the real world in the areas of truth, reason, and morals – what Van Til calls, "the impossibility of contrary," or the self-implosion of a worldview lived purely on its own terms. Only by implicitly borrowing from the Christian worldview can the Hindu live in God's world. Vedanta's injunctions are inconsistent with the nature of Brahman. The moral argument finds a basis for morality in Christianity and lacks an answer in Vedanta Hinduism. The design argument finds an intelligent designer of order and beauty in a Christian worldview, vital traits missing in Brahman.

Overall Vedanta's presuppositions of their scriptures and Brahman are flawed. The Vedanta scriptures fail the test of temporal truth and cannot sustain their claims of eternality. The presentation of Brahman has philosophical issues with ontology and communication. The lack of the moral dimension is severely problematic for the gods who represent Brahman, especially Krishna, the most popular object of devotion.

The Vedanta superstructure of Atman, the world, and liberation fails to correspond with reality. Maya shrouds the connection between the ineffable Brahman and the distinctive world. Its analogical explanations do not present a compelling picture, as it fails to provide a simple philosophical basis for observed reality. The disconnected Atman and ego of man cannot be overcome by its proposals. The world finds poor cause in Brahman and its existence cannot be justified by Brahman. Its operations have little grounding, but are simply assumed by Maya and the gods. The gods fail to represent the absolute Brahman, recognizable in any fashion as good. The life and liberation of humans find no stable floor in Brahman on which to stand. The entire system, while being put together elaborately, has severe flaws. These occasion the extreme renunciation of Advaita with which Ramanuja and Madhva charge Sankara within Vedanta. The specific arguments are not provided for want of space but their general thrusts are employed.

Apologetic Review

From a vast scope of material, some apologetic content was targeted for this particular encounter. This review examines the choice and effective use of this content, along with the Christian sanctification through the encounter. The review begins by evaluating the apologetic application against the theory of Worldview apologetics.

With regards to theory and practice, this apologetic utilized a proper worldview offense. For the most part, both Advaita and Christianity targeted areas of

---

[31]Ibid., 11. Krishna makes him deceive Drona and Indra tempts him at the door of heaven and in hell.

weakness in the worldview that were internally lacking in consistency, coherence, or correspondence. The philosophical arguments against Advaita were framed against the corresponding strengths in the Christian worldview. This included a broad array of data from the Advaitin worldview often well contrasted with other data within that worldview.

These offensive forays targeted key foundations on which the worldviews were structured, exposing their presuppositions. The detailed engagement with each viewpoint was properly engaged within the worldview and then contrasted using the alternative standpoint. Logic and reason, intuition and commonsense were used without elevating any of them as the fundamental ground upon which the worldview must live or die.

The Vedanta worldview had its weakness highlighted. This was done in a manner to showcase how the deficiencies of that worldview were addressed in the Christian worldview, without simply judging the failure of one worldview to meet any unrealistic or unnatural expectations of the other worldview. These arguments could be disputed, not for setting up and destroying straw-men, but for their degree of potency.

Finally, the presentation of these charges must be made with some humility, which is not evident in the language employed. While the Christian is fully convinced of the truth of the Christian worldview, he cannot be an expert on Advaita by any stretch of the imagination. His knowledge of the system is necessarily limited, especially as the arguments go further into the recesses of that worldview. The offense is presented in a person-centric way, in order that those areas which strike a chord with the particular individual can be taken further, to expose the issues with Vedanta. Gentleness does not minimize the presentation of the true Christian worldview with conviction and power.[32]

Interpersonal Honesty

Any Christian due to his particular propensity and background may find something appealing in the Vedanta worldview. Intellectual honesty requires admission of those areas of attraction to what may ultimately be false, but is currently convincing, albeit superficially.[33]

As an example, if the impersonal seems broader than the personal, it is honest to admit it and explore why this may be so. However, this concession must be done in the context of Worldview apologetics where the revelation of God supersedes humanity's inclinations. It is fine to concede that the impersonal laws seem better than a personal lawgiver and enforcer. However, as this thread is tracked further down, the charge against the fickleness of the personal enforcer must be forced against the wall of necessity – why must any impersonal law exist? The resulting conclusion will find that the Christian God is not fickle. It is good to admit the struggle for sinful humanity to comprehend a righteously jealous God. For the Christian who acknowledges God's character, the context is obvious, but it may not be so for the unbeliever. God establishes the laws and upholds the universe by his trustworthy character. The natural laws themselves may be attractive due to *imago dei*, but they fall short as a final explanation for our universe.

---

[32] 2 Cor 10:3-5 says, "For though we walk in the flesh, we are not waging war according to the flesh. For the weapons of our warfare are not of the flesh but have divine power to destroy strongholds. We destroy arguments and every lofty opinion raised against the knowledge of God, and take every thought captive to obey Christ." The charge of gentleness and humility largely follows the apologetic mandate.

[33] John G. Stackhouse Jr., *Humble Apologetics: Defending the Faith Today* (New York: Oxford University Press, 2002), 150.

Alternatively, if change really seems less attractive than immutability, then it is fine to admit this and examine the troubling contexts of change in the Christian God. It should produce an incentive to explore the essential attributes of God, especially his eternal nature and counsel, in order to understand the personal relation of God with his creation and examine whether this detracts from or adds to our imperfect knowledge of the one who is wholly other.[34] Christianity rests on the revelation of God that changes the minds of sinful individuals, including Christians. Thus individual preferences are held tentatively and not overindulged to drown out God's revelation with human thought.

Christian Integrity to God

While being honest with the questions from the unbeliever and oneself, one must above all, be honest with God. The doubt introduced or the problems faced, must always be within the context of the faith. One who is weak in his faith and does not understand the grounding of the truth in the Scriptures can only go as far as his faith and intellect would permit. So, a brand new Christian with a limited knowledge of the Scriptures could provide gospel-centered scriptural data and admit that his own knowledge and understanding would not allow him to journey any further yet.

The range of human finitude obligates each person to reach a point where his intellectual prowess fails. Those without a genuine faith cannot resist the offensive intellectual assaults. It would only be honest for them to admit that they can no longer hold their Christian belief system. Such admission is not a loss of faith, but an acknowledgement that genuine faith was not theirs at the beginning. Their true state is now exposed through further study; as such an affinity now becomes a part of one's core beliefs. Michael Sudduth's conversion to Hinduism is one such example.[35]

The Christian, however, cannot be in this position. His tie to God is not easily severable. His allegiance to God and his self-awareness require him, first and foremost, to be honest with God. In such honesty, he has a spiritual and intellectual conviction that cannot be shaken. Thus, all his doubts and problems find a context to rest within his broader worldview, even if it does not get completely resolved on this side of eternity.[36]

While such an attitude may seem to stack the cards against other worldviews, such is the nature of true faith. The Christian can be honest with the Vedanta Hindu about this position. While acknowledging the areas of doubts, no doubt is examined neutrally, as in judging the evidence for and against his faith. Rather than retract his position, he would restate his stance and the specific areas troubling him, from within his broader worldview.[37]

---

[34]Grant, "Contemporary Relevance of Advaita," 160-63. Grant considers the Advaitic framework to develop a knowledge of the ultimate as deep calls to Deep.

[35]Bede Griffiths, *Vedanta and Christian Faith* (Los Angeles: The Dawn Horse Press, 1973), 41, 52, 80-81. Griffiths' level of identification with Vedanta diminishes Christian core claims. See also Corduan On Sudduth [on-line]; accessed 29 March 2013; available from http://triablogue.blogspot.com/2012/01/corduan-on-sudduth.html; Internet: "I find the conversion of someone to [Hinduism], essentially a 'dog-bites-man' story. He is neither the first, nor will he be the last, I'm afraid, who finds an idolatrous Eastern religion preferable to salvation from sin in Christ."

[36]Richard B. Ramsay, *The Certainty of the Faith: Apologetics in an Uncertain World* (Phillipsburg, NJ: P&R Publishing, 2007), 100, 144-49.

[37]K. Scott Oliphint, *The Battle Belongs to the Lord: The Power of Scripture for Defending Our Faith* (Phillipsburg, NJ: P&R Publishing, 2003), 166-67.

The Christian's overall confidence is that God is true. The Christian can be honest with the unbeliever while trusting God. Worldview apologetics does not attempt to coerce the conversion of an unbeliever with presumably perfect bullet-proof arguments. Rather, it presents the truth as best as any finite, sinful human being can. The Christian can humbly admit where the argument or evidence is unclear or insufficient, but always rest on the truth of the infallible Scriptures.

Conclusion

Having provided an offense from each worldview, these attacks will need to be defended both in the areas of weakness and also to make the final presentation of each system. This will conclude the apologetic engagement and therefore the strongest answers will now be furnished from within the Advaitin and Christian worldviews.

CHAPTER 6
DEFENSE: RESPONDING TO CHARGES

The last section in apologetics is defense. Both the Christian and the Hindu recognize the perceived weaknesses in their own system. Reasonable responses are provided from each worldview, augmented with positive data that better presents new facets that account for any fundamental problems or misunderstandings of the system.[1]

Vedanta's Defense

The specific charges leveled against Vedanta are first responded to using the categories from the previous chapter. Key presuppositions are then made explicit in order to demonstrate why certain charges become invalid in this worldview.

Truth and Trust

First, the category of truth is defended. The sayings of Lord Krishna have been charged with a lack of trustworthiness. The ground to trust in the giver of truth was challenged if Brahman is beyond values and the world is created by Maya. The objector fails to recognize that Maya is the power of Isvara. As God, all truth and goodness cohere in him. Isvara cannot be separated from Brahman, who is the ultimate ground.

The concepts of Indian philosophy have been claimed to be less than logical. This included the identity of cause and effect, the need for absolute immutability for perfection, the law of excluded middle, and the dichotomy of the Atman and ego as the recipient of truth. The charges here have been made from the perspective of the Christian worldview, failing to understand the context of Vedanta. The identity of cause and effect had shown the difference between Christianity and Vedanta in the agency of instrumental and material causation. Lacking this knowledge, Christians do not delve deeper into the true nature of both God and creation, since their causation is necessarily restricted by distinctions. Just as Brahman and Isvara are related in mystery, so also is the Atman and ego related in ways that cannot be rationalized by finite individuals.

---

[1]John M. Frame, *Apologetics for the Glory of God: An Introduction* (Phillipsburg, NJ: P&R Publishing, 1994), 149.

Historical Evidences

Second, the historicity of Vedanta is debated. It has been claimed that Vedanta is a human attempt rather than divine. This is an unsubstantiated charge, which can equally be made against Christianity, as has been done by higher critical scholars.

The charge has been leveled that the Hindu scriptures are unhistorical and based on myths. The stories, especially relating to Krishna and Vyasa, are claimed to be legends from the Vedas and the Baghavad Gita. It is true that Hinduism does not weigh the written word as heavily on as it does oral tradition. Temporal-spatial data is granted less importance in light of its subordinate existence in Vedanta. However, the lack of data is not the same as false data. Research on historical evidences has been slow and some earlier claims on the dating of events will be revisited. However, foisting the entire worldview as a human innovation is a strong assertion lacking adequate justification.

Best Explanation

Third, Vedanta is actually the best explanation. Vedanta is charged with being disconnected from reality for its inability to explain the greatness and smallness of humans, Maya's relation to evil in the world, and its cause in Brahman. The objector fails to realize that this world needs no ultimate ground. As a projection of Maya, everything needed for explicating life is provided in Isvara. What truly needs grounding in Brahman is the Atman which ought to be the focus of the one seeking spiritual growth.

The creation of the world by Maya is claimed to be fallacious and shrouded in mystery because of failing to cohere within the Vedanta worldview. The issue here is twofold. A finite human under the thrall of Maya cannot expect to understand the mystery which becomes self-evident to the enlightened. The Christian seems to struggle with his dualism, where he sees the world as essentially different from its creator which necessitates an explanation. Vedanta does not see any concern with the essential monism that unifies Brahman and the world. Isvara is the organizing principle of the universe, while acting as the face of Brahman toward creation.

Christians reject sin defined as man shrouded in ignorance, failing to fathom his epistemic state. This unsupported statement argues against Vedanta using Christian presuppositions. It can be argued in response that the Christian sin results from a type of ignorance – an ignorance of God, by ignoring or suppressing the knowledge of God.

The proofs for causality, design, and morality are claimed to refute an amoral and impersonal Brahman for a good and personal God. This argument ignores the role of the personal Isvara who exemplifies everything that the Christian God does, except in a different context and language. The moral standard of Isvara is higher, to which humanity is drawn by valuing divine canons over the ethical.

Impersonal Absolute

Finally, the impersonal nature of reality is defended. An Enlightenment indictment was leveled in the historical evolution of petty gods in Hinduism. The understanding of God in the Christian worldview is not very different. God reveals himself in the Old Testament differently than in the New Testament, which is not easily reconciled by the uninitiated. Likewise, the early Vedic legends convey some direct content to their early recipients which is better understood by humanity in its progress toward Brahman. These gods no longer have a central place in the minds of those who espouse Vedanta. However, they still serve those who are in spiritual darkness in order to draw them that much closer toward Brahman.

The deeper issues underlying karma, dharma, and submission to a personal Lord beyond moral categories was challenged. Isvara completely satisfies the personal need for the seeker after truth. Moral categories are vital on this side of liberation and find their basis in a qualified but supernal Isvara. Humans do submit to a higher personal authority, but those who grasp Advaita Vedanta can scale the higher cliffs that are impossible for the dilettante. As regards karma and dharma, this operation of samsara governs our plane of our existence until the Atman is liberated from the karmic cycle.

The Hindu gods are depreciated as idols, denigrating the religion as a superstition. As noted earlier, some deities meet individual persons at various states on their spiritual journey. However, these gods are not ultimate as Advaita Vedanta teaches the underlying reality behind these gods. Sankara approved idols as a means of directing devotion to Isvara. Truly, any positive action can turn into a heartless and mundane superstition. While Christian superstition as seen in Catholicism is reckoned hopeless, the Hindu superstitions provide an intermediate stage until a full liberation in the future.

Experience

The strongest defense of the Hindu worldview is experience. Metaphysical, epistemological, and ethical philosophical arguments can quickly become sophisticated. One's conviction ultimately reposes on the experience of those who have climbed the pinnacle of being and attested to the genuineness of that experience.[2] In one sense no one can dispute the claimed experience since only the individual subjectively experiences this truth. In another sense, the similarity of such experiences among multiple individuals further attests its truth. Finally, the life of these transformed individuals speaks volumes as to what their experience achieved both for them and those around them.

Those who have not reached the pinnacle, still have experiences that get progressively richer. The path is thus confirmed through their stages of validating what they have seen or heard from others, who have reached the top and come back down to aid the rest. As those who refute the weakness of written documents, the need for such scriptures diminishes in this worldview. The authority shifts significantly toward those who have validated this truth through their lives.[3]

Epistemology

Trusting in the experiences of others' and one's own does not mean that Hinduism is epistemologically flawed. It is not irrational, but supra-rational. It meets and exceeds rationality. For those disputing the illusory nature of reality, there are sufficient evidences why it need not be a problem. For example, the fact that we dream is not annulled by the counter-fact that we cannot explain its nature completely. The dream is

---

[2]Chandradhar Sharma, *A Critical Survey of Indian Philosophy* (London: Rider & Company, 1960), 287-89. Ramakrishna Paramahamsa and Chaitanya are good examples of experienced souls.

[3]See also, Mahendranath Gupta, *The Gospel of Sri Ramakrishna*, trans. Swami Nikhilananda (New York: Ramakrishna-Vivekananda Center, 1942), 257: "A man should reach the *Nitya*, the Absolute, by following the trail of the *Lila*, the Relative. It is like reaching the roof by the stairs. After realizing the Absolute, he should climb down to the Relative and live on that plane in the company of devotees, charging his mind with the love of God."

real to the sleeping person, even when waking up to understand the dream's content as ultimately unreal. Vedanta epistemology delves deeper into the human psyche in presenting the various levels of consciousness, including the appearance of a rope as a snake in the dark. Reality and its appearance are both cognitively real at various states of the observer.[4] In transcending the darkness what appears real is revealed as mere appearance.

Coherence

This deeper understanding provides a more fundamental level of coherence between the various aspects of Vedanta philosophy and its worldview. While Christianity broadly explains its system of beliefs, Vedanta actually does greater justice to the minutiae, tying up loose ends in the monistic context. Those who find Maya troubling need only look at the world-facing aspect of Brahman to understand how this manifestation of Brahman is logically dealt with. Those who think this illusory world should be meaningless, need only to look at the Atman's place in the world, as Brahman's eternal counterpart, able to live within the confines of samsara and to provide the escape clause out of it, in pure identification with Brahman. This distinction of Brahman causing the world from itself is often misunderstood and misrepresented.[5]

Correspondence (Problem of Evil)

The biggest challenge for those viewing Vedanta from the outside is the correspondence of the worldview with the physical universe. The verification principle poses the same false challenge to both Hindus and Christians. Spiritual verities are a superset and not a subset of physicality to be defended scientifically. The monist does not reject any of the physical laws as is often claimed by his detractors. Can those who realize the laws underlying nature, actually transcend it? That is precisely the experience of sanyasins who perform extraordinary feats. This is evident even in the life of Jesus and his disciples as miracles. Yet, those who have not yet attained such experiences are under the constraints of the physical realm and must obey it, as must anyone ignorant of the Vedanta system. However, the Hindu view of correspondence does not purely defend what appears disconnected for outsiders. Rather, it provides the strongest correspondence in the varying levels of lived and experienced reality.[6] It explains why Christians ignorant of Brahman can freely follow Jesus at this stage of their lifecycle. It explains the poor villager who worships his village deity seeking temporal gains. It explains the foolish merchant who profits at the expense of his soul, regressing further in samsara. Evil is worked through the karmic cycle as the Atman seeks liberation in Brahman. The overall picture of the universe fits far better than any other worldview can ever present it.

---

[4]P. V. Joshi, *Introduction to Sankara's Advaitism* (Delhi: Motilal Banarsidass Publishers, 2006), 76-84, 122-26, 138-43.

[5]Sarvepalli Radhakrishnan and Charles E. Moore, eds., *A Source Book in Indian Philosophy* (Princeton: Princeton University Press, 1957), 509-12.

[6]K. Satchidananda Murty, *Revelation and Reason in Advaita Vedānta* (Grand Rapids: Eerdmans Publishing Company, 1959), 329-32.

Christianity's Defense

Specific charges leveled against Christianity are addressed from within the Christian framework. Key underlying presuppositions are made explicit in order to demonstrate the invalidity of these charges and to broaden the presentation of the Christian worldview.

Plurality and Monism

Firstly, Christianity's refutation of monism is charged with inconsistencies. If the world and humans are created in time, they are accused of being less than real. The issue actually has to do with the definition of "real." The world has a temporal existence and is made for people to enjoy in time and space. The Christian worldview made no claim for the substance to be real in any independent sense. However, physical matter is created out of nothing to be given a substantive existence under God's governance. The universe is not a rope in the appearance of a snake. This projection is a poor analogy even for ultimate dependency, since the universe is ontologically real and epistemologically perceived accurately. The world is not metaphysically self-sufficient. It needs to be preserved by its creator God. Christians see the world as given to man by a powerful and benevolent God, who is completely different from the world and from all humanity.

Man is made in the image of God but is not God. This truth is faulted with obscurity. Man is able to live through eternity due to God's spirit, enjoying God's gift of eternal life or paying the penalty of eternal death. In having the image of God, man has an inherent value that does not perish. However, God intentionally fashioned humans' duality of spirit and matter. The physical body perishes like all matter. God promises a new body to host man's soul for eternity. Christians foretaste this in the resurrected body of Jesus Christ. God's image in humans remains just that – an image reflecting God's attributes and can never be the actual entity, as God is only reflected in his creation.[7]

Plurality is not inconsistent when the relationship between the various objects is satisfactorily explained. Instead of being a hindrance to understand Vedanta's monism, Christianity employs a common sense rejection of a false unity. The perceived complexity of the Christian explanation is a problem with the recipient's epistemology – without eyes to see or a will to acknowledge, the truth remains dissatisfactory. The duality of God and creation are simply understood in a causal relationship. Man is distinct from the rest of creation with the unique image of God in him. The plurality of existence in the world showcases God's creativity in the diversity of everything made.

The western world has rejected the god-of-the-gaps to explain the unknown. This materialist critique is invalid since the awareness of a process does not explain the existence of the process itself. It is perfectly logical for God to set laws in place that humans discover to better understand the observed universe. It makes better sense for a personal God to order the universe using these regular laws. Man's noetic equipment is fitted to reflect the mind of God in order to discern these underlying laws. An invisible Brahman operating under the observed reality fails to explain the ordered universe.

---

[7]See also, Thomas Joseph Walshe, *The Principles of Christian Apologetics: An Exposition of the Intellectual Basis of the Christian Religion, Specially Written for Senior Students* (New York: Longmans, Green and Co., 1919), 114: "Our intimate sense attests that we do not naturally share in the Divine Nature."

Personality and the Impersonal

Secondly, personality in God is claimed to be deficient. The trend of those preferring an impersonal force over a personal God does not validate Brahman, any more than the rising tide of crime and mass shootings validates senseless killings. The apparent limitations of a personal God are projections of human failure, not different from the projections Sankara claims of the illusory views that plague humanity. The standard of perfection is questioned for personality. God is the standard for perfection and human measures of limited goodness draw upon God as the absolute good. What Vedanta considers as lacking in a personal God are faulty standards of an impersonal perfection. These have no warrant except in the defective intellect of a spiritually fallen human.

Paradoxically, a fundamental biblical presupposition of the personal nature of God is attacked by claiming the Christian God as a projection of humanity's perfect ideal. The Christian God is charged not just with paradoxes, but with contradictions. These include the lack of immutability especially manifest in the choices of God to love and reject, in changing his mind, in responding to prayer even when decreeing his pre-ordained plan. The kind of immutability expected by Vedantins is unrealistic. Such a being corresponds more with nothing rather than everything. God is immutable in his being and character – God does not change arbitrarily, but remains true to his goodness.[8]

This aspect of immutability does not conflict with God's choices and responses. God can freely choose in accordance with his will and pleasure. Such choices may be inscrutable to us, but as actions of grace, they are supererogatory rather than bound by some law of impartiality. God's justice in recompensing evil does not conflict with his love upon those made holy by the work of Jesus Christ. God's response to prayer is not outside of God's sovereign decree, but manifests his character of love in an intimate relationship primarily by his initiation and secondarily in response to his people. God's eternal decree accounts for his response to prayer.[9] There is no contradiction but perfection as its pinnacle in the personal God of the Bible.

Exclusivity and Universality

Thirdly, the Christian lack of inclusivity is arraigned. The fact that the larger mass of humanity does not find God's favor seems heartless for a good God. God is under no obligation to rescue anyone after the fall of the first man who represented all humanity in sin. Thus the question is not why God does not save everyone, but why God graciously saves anyone.

---

[8] John Frame, *The Doctrine of God: A Theology of Lordship* (Phillipsburg, NJ: P&R Publishing, 2002), 568-70. Frame notes: "the unchanging character of God's covenant is vitally important to the biblical doctrine of salvation" (ibid., 570). Immutability in character is different from immobility in action: "Since God knows all things in all times, from all eternity, his knowledge neither increases nor decreases. Nor does his power change, for . . . God is omnipotent, and there are no degrees of omnipotence. The same must surely be said of God's goodness and truth, for, as we have seen, God is supremely perfect in these attributes – indeed, he is the standard for the corresponding attributes in human beings" (ibid., 570).

[9] Origen, *Origen On Prayer,* 13 [on-line]; accessed 27 January 2013; available from http://www.ccel.org/ccel/origen/prayer.v.html; Internet: "In His arrangement it will accordingly have been ordained somewhat after this wise: This man I will hear for the sake of the prayer that he will pray, because he will pray wisely: but that man I will not hear, either because he will be unworthy of being heard, or because his prayer will be for things neither profitable for the suppliant to receive nor becoming me to bestow."

Independent righteous acts recognized by God seem paradoxical, contrary to the implication of a majority of the Scriptures. In context, these righteous acts are qualified as done by those upon whom God places his special favor. Some acts are good in the human sphere, which are morally good before God. Yet, no good action is capable of meriting God's absolute approval, since all actions are tainted with sin and no good deed is capable of compensating sin. Only in the perfect work of Jesus Christ can anyone find grace and mercy to cover all sin and to enter God's presence.

Just one lifetime seems to unnecessarily limit the hope of humanity. In response, what right has the clay to interrogate the potter? God decreed one lifetime to respond to his gift of Jesus Christ. God also decreed reward and retribution to satisfy justice in love at the end of each life. This is God's standard and not man's. Is man's fallen character or the perfect character of God a better judge of what is good? For sinful beings, redemption is not an issue of quantity but quality. A million years cannot transform the sinful heart, but God changes it in a moment by his grace. One lifetime of sin is a merciful limitation in relation to the retribution for millennia of compounded sin.

The eternal Vedas are contrasted against the biblical Scriptures as the better authority to trust in. What is eternal is truly to be valued over what is temporal. However, the Christian disputes the truth claims of an eternal Veda, which is also demonstrably inaccurate in its transmission. The extant document with its flaws is the actual source of authority, despite its presumed eternal origins. The inherent contradictions of the Vedas require a host of commentators to reconcile these diverse texts, resulting in great diversity relative to Christianity. Even Vedanta has sharp disagreements on the nature of Brahman and the world, among the most foundational of its beliefs. While the Bible has been given to man in time, not over four thousand years ago, the men who wrote were guided by God and encapsulated the eternal Word of God in human words. Jesus is the embodiment of God's revelation to us and he remains eternally God's Word. The transmission of this document has been shown to be accurate and it is without contradictions.[10]

Evil and Reason

Christian rationality is questioned over the problem of evil. Theodicy has been a perennially troubling question, claiming that a good and powerful God should not allow evil and pain in his created universe. Christians attempt to justify the sore reality by various suggestions, including the best of all possible worlds, the necessary result of granting freewill, and essential goodness-making properties. A better reply constrains itself to the premises which God, the physician of the suffering, provides in the Scripture.

The biblical worldview adequately explains the introduction of evil and suffering in the world. Man was created with the potential to obey or disobey God – in his free choice, he plunged the universe into suffering. God was not obligated to aid the children of Adam, but freely graced some through his sovereign grace. This grace was not given to the devil who rebelled against God. Ultimately, some specific cases of gratuitous and heartbreaking suffering are impossible for finite humans to reconcile. Instead of charging God with injustice or inability, what is required in this fallen universe, is to trust in the character of the omnibenevolent and omnipotent God.

---

[10]Jesus Christ is the complete revelation of God as the eternal Word. Jesus takes on flesh and lives among men as a visible demonstration of God. In Scripture, the truth of God's Word is communicated to man. The Word became flesh in Jesus and took on Greek letters as God's revelation to man in Scripture.

This trust is impossible without being a recipient of God's free gift in Jesus Christ. This may not satisfy the unbeliever, but the Christian can provide no further answer than God's own response to evil. The greatest evil is the unjust killing of Jesus Christ by sinful humanity. Yet in that very act, God sovereignly ordains the salvation of many. God's purposes and rewards in and through suffering in this fallen world showcase how God works all things for good.[11] Suffering draws humanity to its remedy in God and purifies those who trust in God with greater degrees of faith and holiness.

Experience

The Christian faith is similar to the Hindu experience in the sense that it is not purely propositional or only logical in nature. The demons believe certain truths, but it does not profit them anything. Rather, the Christian belief is existential. The Christian encounters God through the Scriptures and his life becomes a living testimony to the power and veracity of God. Each Christian's life is transformed individually. It demonstrates the truth of what Christians believe. It is true that there are problems here – some claim to be Christians, but cannot demonstrate their claims in their lived out life. Even excluding the charlatans who falsely profess belief, there are genuine Christians who seem to plod along morally no better than Hindus, and sometimes worse. However, in examining each individual under the lens of the biblical worldview, one will see the wholesome progress of sanctification within the sphere of this world. Some progress fast and others slow, but they will ultimately reach the state of glory, culminating in heavenly perfection what begins in weakness here.[12] Christians experience the joy of fellowship with God in the Holy Spirit, which subjectively affirms the objective scriptural truth.

Epistemology

Christian epistemology is simple. God made man in his image and able to communicate with him. The fall has caused a breaking of his spiritual antennae. Regeneration restores the antennae. Those with broken antennae can still perceive the reality sufficiently to recognize truth but their sinful framework suppresses their knowledge of God in ambiguity and vagueness.[13] Christians give the gospel which God uses instrumentally to convict and transform sinners. The knowledge of God is not obtained by just dispelling mental ignorance, but by the work of the Holy Spirit in transforming the will of humans. This occurs when the one is born again.

Coherence

The Christian worldview claims ultimate coherence. While there are many Christian sects, genuine Christians' worldview coheres around the central truths of Christianity. There can be no divergence on fundamental aspects of reality. This is unlike

---

[11]Rom 8:28 says, "We know that for those who love God all things work together for good, for those who are called according to his purpose." Job's suffering provides an example of God's rule over the unmerited suffering. 1 Peter and other scriptures provide the salutary effects of suffering in God's people.

[12]Frame, *The Doctrine of God*, 75. Rom 1:19-20 says that natural revelation is plain and clear.

[13]John M. Frame, *Salvation Belongs to the Lord: An Introduction to Systematic Theology* (Phillipsburg, NJ: P&R Publishing, 2006), 90; idem., *The Doctrine of the Knowledge of God* (Phillipsburg, NJ: P&R Publishing, 1987), 58; Alvin Plantinga, *Warranted Christian Belief* (New York: Oxford University Press, 2000), 59.

the Hindu monists where Ramanuja finds severe discrepancy in Sankara, in seeing Brahman with qualifications and the universe as Brahman's body. The orthodox churches concur on matters pertaining to God, creation, man, and Jesus Christ. This is because none of the truth of Scripture can contradict itself It must be conceded that there are heretical sects that do differ on the divinity of Jesus Christ and the Trinity, but that exhibits a rejection of central truths from the Scriptures. Also, the Christian worldview admits mystery, being supra-rational, as the transcendence of God necessarily exceeds the finitude of humanity. However, the worldview exhibits no internal contradiction.[14]

Correspondence (Problem of Evil)

The Christian worldview is compulsively attractive in its correspondence. From physical reality to humanity's moral state, Christianity provides the best explanation of the observable universe. It explains the heights and depths of creation, the problem of man as it really is and the means for salvation from his desperate estate. Even those who reject it acknowledge sin – man's most empirically verifiable truth. Those who seek alternate wellsprings are on a futile endeavor, living in quiet desperation or false comfort. The Christian system contrasts both with the right means to approach God.[15]

The Christian apologetic boldly admits that the universe in one sense is transitory like the Hindu creation, but in a radically different sense. Apart from God, the universe has no existence since it is a contingent creation. Yet what has been made is real in the simple use of the term, different from and sustained by God in the present. Its creation and dissolution are accomplished within the context of God's divine order.[16]

Apologetic Review

The formal engagement of the Advaita Vedanta and Christian worldviews concludes with an intentional application of Worldview apologetics. At this point, a reflexive examination of the apologetic method within the larger Christian worldview is attempted. The review focuses on faithfulness of the apologist to his cognitive understanding of both worldviews and personally to God and the unbeliever.

Apologetic faithfulness

The apologetic encounter could have been engaged deeper by more skilled apologists or more superficially by those less skilled. The apologetic encounter is reviewed on the faithfulness to the content that the apologists were aware of. The Worldview apologetic encounter as an ongoing dialogue must grow in greater depth on the specific disagreements within the broader framework. In evaluating the current engagement, the apologists should not be afraid of conceding internal difficulties.

While both apologists remain committed to their respective worldviews, those questions in the offense section were engaged as directly as possible. There were

---

[14]Frame, *The Doctrine of the Knowledge of God*, 21.

[15]Plantinga, *Warranted Christian Belief*, 59-62. Alister E. McGrath, *Intellectuals Don't Need God & Other Modern Myths: Building Bridges to Faith through Apologetics* (Grand Rapids: Zondervan Publishing House, 1993), 43.

[16]See also, Frame, *The Doctrine of God*, 279: "To say that God metaphysically preserves the world is simply to say that the world is radically contingent. It depends on God for everything, and without his permission it could not continue to exist."

concessions on the points of difficulty, whether relating to the historicity of the Vedanta scriptures or theodicy in Christianity.

Queries like these were adequately qualified by the broader perspective of the worldview to address specific questions. Areas misconstrued by the opposing worldview were responded with additional content that redirected the inquirer in the right course. Theological foundations were supported by philosophically sound argumentation, rigorously defending the consistency, coherence, and correspondence of the worldview.

The apologists clearly held to the superiority of their own worldview. Vedanta claimed that Christianity was a subset of its own, while Christianity argued that the other worldview was incapable of sustaining itself by its own terms. The argumentation is persuasive to the individual committed to each corresponding worldview.

Faithfulness to God

The Christian engaged the Vedanta worldview within the bounds of biblical fidelity. The Reformed theological framework adequately supported the argumentation that was executed. The content of the apologetic was biblically based and the tone of the engagement was not lacking in force in its categorical statements. It was clear in its presentation and defense of its worldview and civil in its offensive against Vedanta. Most charges were taken up in additional detail and given a thoroughly biblical answer which would honor Christ, in keeping with the biblical mandate.

Frankness with Unbelievers

The Christian defense was open to admit points of concern for unbelievers, such as theodicy. After a gospel-centered response, the inability of humans to understand the reason was qualified by the need to trust God. It also properly qualified the inability of unbelievers to accomplish both tasks without God's grace. Far from being a philosophical white-flag, this presents the response within the Christian worldview, honestly acknowledging the difficulty for a conversation on the unbeliever's terms.

The admissions extended to the area of epistemology, which used the analogy of broken antennae and with experience, where it volunteered data on how some Christians may appear less sanctified than a Hindu. This genuinely presented any pertinent data that came up in the encounter. The Christian is not ashamed of the difficulties in Christianity, but represented it within the context of the biblical worldview. The Christian has a joyful confidence in the ability of truth to address the data that may not have been understood or reconciled yet, in contrast to unbelieving worldviews.

Conclusion

Worldview apologetics included several comprehensive approaches in critiquing the opposing worldview. The apologetic was worldview-oriented rather than piece-meal. The entire argumentation was built on a Reformed apologetic framework with support from the Classical and Evidential methods. While some Fideistic overtones crept in, that element of apologetics will be covered separately in a subsequent chapter.

In the past three chapters, a practical demonstration of Worldview apologetics with Vedanta was completed. This laid out the Christian arguments and responded with a biblical defense against attacks. A formal philosophical review of this engagement will be attempted in the next chapter.

CHAPTER 7
APOLOGETIC REVIEW

The apologetic encounter between Vedanta and Christianity has progressed through the stages of proof, offense, and defense. Each stage was reviewed in terms of fidelity to the apologetic method, using the guidelines of success and failure in relation to God, the unbeliever, and the conscience of the apologist. The philosophical differences in the worldviews are now categorized in order to sharpen the dialogue content when it resumes. The traditional classifications of metaphysics, epistemology, and ethics are employed to sort through these worldview dissimilarities from a Christian perspective.

The Christian statements and axioms are reliable for truthfulness, to the extent that they cohere with God's Word. Objective truth must be uncompromisingly held. Yet the subjective understanding of that truth is not without error. This error ranges from the interpretation of Scriptures to one's ability to communicate clearly. The propositions extend to matters such as the nature of God, the spiritual problem plaguing humanity, the mystery of sovereignty and responsibility, the nature of glorification, and eternity.[1] These doctrines have been honed against other philosophical perspectives in the past.

Historical Christian arguments toward other false worldviews are adaptable to the Vedanta worldview. Arguments toward Vedanta will be evaluated against two major recipients of Christian apologetics: philosophical Naturalism and Gnosticism. This is done within the porous philosophical containers of metaphysics, epistemology, and ethics.

Metaphysics

Metaphysical questions primarily deal with ontology. Ontological validity was debated in the apologetic encounter to identify the objective truth of being. The Christian and Advaita Vedanta worldviews defined reality on radically different terms. Statements on ontological reality are evaluated here through the Christian worldview. Each worldview proponent believed his own understanding of reality, with no neutral arbiter of truth other than God alone. The self-authenticating Word of God represents God, even if

---

[1]Paul Helm, *Faith and Understanding* (Grand Rapids: Eerdmans Publishing Company, 1997), 5-13. The issues mentioned sample the fundamental divide between Christianity and Vedanta. Helm does an excellent job of distinguishing the objective and subjective dimensions of apologetics. See also Rick Wade, "The History of Apologetics: Four 20th-Century Apologists: E. J. Carnell, Cornelius Van Til, Gordon Clark, Norman Geisler," *Areopagus Journal* (2008): 29-30.

the Hindu rejects its ultimate authority. This section focuses on objective verity showcasing the actuality of the ultimate reality with supportive data.[2]

Vedanta and Philosophical Naturalism

Philosophical Naturalism tends to be reductionist as it conflates the universal reality to a materialistic ontology. In doing so, it fails to address the ontological existence of God, along with the spirit of man. It also cannot adequately account for the existence of the universe, particularly its origin. Naturalism is further challenged in its attempts to ground immaterial values such as morality, justice, love, and necessity.

Little common ground exists between Vedanta and Naturalism as they are on opposite ends of the spectrum on the material-immaterial bandwidth. However, Vedanta fails to ground ontology in some ways not very different from Naturalism. The Christian arguments used in the earlier chapters can be mapped with those used against Naturalism. This exercise intends to highlight the versatility of these arguments and also to identify those areas where the argument against Vedanta can be further developed.

Christian Worldview apologetics to Naturalism or Vedanta come from within the viewpoint of scriptural presuppositions. Thus there is no radical difference in the basic apologetic approach used toward both worldviews.

Grounding values. The arguments against Naturalism were tailored earlier for Vedanta. In regards to grounding values, Brahman failed to satisfy, even as Naturalism could not find a definitive basis for values beyond humanity's cultural or evolutionary contexts. This charge against Naturalism is vigorously used against Vedanta. However, Vedanta was able to deflect the full force of the argument by positing Isvara as a determinate God presenting the face of Brahman to the world. The lack of ultimacy in Isvara and the mystery of Maya to conjoin Brahman and Isvara, expose its shaky ontological grounding. In stark contrast, these values find a solid source in the Christian God. Vedanta's mystical claims can bridge the gap for ineffable verities, but such experiential claims are necessarily imbued in skepticism when they lack universality. This claim is further engaged in the epistemological review.[3]

Origins. The origin and nature of the universe is a conundrum that neither Naturalism nor Advaita Vedanta can satisfactorily address. Naturalism attempts to avoid a philosophical contradiction in positing the origination of something from nothing. It devolves into a speculative enterprise by expecting science to resolve the issue with alternate universes or alien sources. These theories merely kick the proverbial can further down the road, or in this case, space and time. Vedanta does ground the universe in the being of Brahman, but fails to account for its origin since Brahman lacks the purposeful intent necessary for creation. It changes creation into a purposeless play. It invokes the excluded middle for Brahman to avoid creation and its complement. It transfers the actual creation to the task of Isvara, operating under Maya. Maya's repetitive enigmas raise

---

[2]John M. Frame, *Apologetics for the Glory of God: An Introduction* (Phillipsburg, NJ: P&R Publishing, 1994), 122. K. Scott Oliphint, *The Battle Belongs to the Lord: The Power of Scripture for Defending Our Faith* (Phillipsburg, NJ: P&R Publishing, 2003), 175.

[3]Paul Copan, *When God Goes to Starbucks: A Guide to Everyday Apologetics* (Grand Rapids: Baker Books, 2008), 69. Mystical experiences lend themselves to be easily over-reported.

concerns about its complicated explanations for the origin of an apparently accidental universe. The reason for creation is difficult for Sankara whose Brahman lacks desire. However, the Bible speaks of God desiring his glory through creation. Immutability as conceived by the Vedantins is philosophically and theologically unnecessary.

Nature. The nature of the material universe has a much more satisfactory explanation in Naturalism than Vedanta, only because Naturalism does not attempt to qualify the reality of matter any further than its physical existence. Vedanta attempts to justify its earlier statement of grounding all reality in an unqualified Brahman and loses the ontological validity of matter that is preserved in Naturalism. Its subordinate reality fails to grant the necessary metaphysical heft for a substantive universe. At the other end of the spectrum, Vedanta rightly recognizes that the universe must be seen in its dependent relation to something else. Thus the transitory nature of the universe is better represented by Vedanta. Vedanta additionally attempts to explain spiritual realities. The interweaving of spirituality and transience, the real and the less-than-real, fails to account for the true ontology of material and spiritual being, given the attribute-less Brahman.

Governance. The governance of the universe is another problem for both worldviews. As Naturalism rejects design or purpose in the progress of evolution, so also Vedanta cannot have Brahman orchestrating the movement of history. Vedanta again deflects the blow with the operations of karma and dharma. However, these concepts have only an intermediate resolution in Isvara, lacking a final base. Ontologically, the universe suffers from a less-than-fully-real nature and misses a purposeful *teleos*. Despite its conflicting sources in the Vedas, the karmic cycle is grounded ultimately in Brahman. It is therefore impersonal, not dissimilar from the laws of Naturalism. These laws of governance have no explanation other than that they exist. Karma cannot provide the true ontological basis upon which a personal and purposeful life subsists.

Personality. Both Naturalism and Vedanta rest their perceived perfection on the impersonal base of matter and spirit, respectively. The ontology of impersonal forces and being lacks the fundamental agency necessary for causation, governance, and dissolution. Naturalism postulates that final causation and dissolution, if valid, may be unknown today. It believes science can understand the operations of nature with the continual progress of humanity. Vedanta advances an existence beyond matter, but Brahman shares in the same impersonal nature which is admittedly incapable of causation, governance, or dissolution. Vedanta again slips the hoop by deferring these functions to Isvara under the mysterious operation of Maya. The personal Isvara is subordinate to an impersonal Brahman. The ontological state of this ultimate being is deficient with regards to causation. The personal God of the Bible adequately addresses causation in keeping with his sovereign will and power. Both governance and dissolution are within the purview of a personal God in relation with his creation. This God executes all actions in accordance with his benevolent and just character. The historic actions of redemption in the person of Jesus Christ provide a substantive representation of this Triune God in time and space, providing a satisfactory ontology for all of reality.

Vedanta, Gnosticism, and New Age

The ancient false religion of Gnosticism tried to make inroads into the early Christian faith. It has made a recent comeback and shares some of its beliefs with the modern New Age spirituality, which is more monistic than the qualified monism of Gnosticism.[4] Vedanta predates both these beliefs which share some of its presuppositions. The documented responses of early Christian apologists from Irenaeus to Tertullian are just as valid against Vedanta as they were against ancient Gnosticism. Gnosticism can be used as a foil to look at the ontological concerns in Vedanta from an alternate viewpoint.

Creation and creator. Gnosticism finds creation problematic. It claims that the creator of the material universe is deficient, since matter is inherently inferior to spirit. To resolve this problem, a progression of beings exists from the Supreme Being to the creator god, who is neither ultimate nor good. Vedanta cannot connect Brahman directly with creation and finds its alternate creator in Isvara through Maya. This intends to avoid tainting Brahman with change, intent, and relation to the transient world. The ontological incapacity of Brahman, far from being a source of perfection, tends to highlight its deficiency.

The ontology of the Gnostic universe is falsely construed, failing to recognize evil as an aberration of a good creation, rather than a property inherent in created matter. Irenaeus spoke of the value of matter and the revelation of God. Matter is not intrinsically evil, as neither the creator God nor created matter inherently suffers any flaw. It is in the corruption of creation that the problem of evil lies and must be dealt with. By positing the failure within creation, the Gnostics and the Advaitins generate a philosophical problem which they cannot resolve.

But nature also testifies of God. It is the work of his hand, and in itself good; not as the Gnostics taught, a product of matter, or of the devil, and intrinsically bad. Except as he reveals himself, God is, according to Irenaeus, absolutely hidden and incomprehensible. But in creation and redemption he has communicated himself, and can, therefore, not remain entirely concealed from any man.[5]

Matter and spirit. This false dichotomy of matter and spirit are inherent in

---

[4]L. Russ Bush, "Christ in the New Age," in *Passionate Conviction: Contemporary Discourses on Christian Apologetics*, ed. Paul Copan and William Lane Craig (Nashville: B&H Academic, 2007), 175-80. Don Cupitt, *Mysticism after Modernity* (Malden, MA: Blackwell Publishers, 1998), 116.

[5]E. Wilhelm Moeller, "God and the Creation," in *History of the Christian Church,* vol. 2, *Ante-Nicene Christianity A.D. 100-325*, ed. Philip Schaff (Grand Rapids: B. Eerdmans Publishing, 1994), 2 [online]; accessed 10 January 2013; available from http://www.ccel.org/ccel/schaff/hcc2.v.xiv.vi.html; Internet. The church fathers spoke clearly of creation and redemption in the will of God: "As to creation: Irenaeus and Tertullian most firmly rejected the hylozoic and demiurgic views of paganism and Gnosticism, and taught, according to the book of Genesis, that God made the world, including matter, not, of course, out of any material, but out of nothing or, to express it positively, out of his free, almighty will, by his word. This free will of God, a will of love, is the supreme, absolutely unconditioned, and all-conditioning cause and final reason of all existence, precluding every idea of physical force or of emanation. Every creature, since it proceeds from the good and holy God, is in itself, as to its essence, good. Evil, therefore, is not an original and substantial entity, but a corruption of nature, and hence can be destroyed by the power of redemption. Without a correct doctrine of creation there can be no true doctrine of redemption, as all the Gnostic systems show." See also Moeller, "God and the Creation," 2 [on-line]; accessed 10 January 2013; available from http://www.ccel.org/ccel/schaff/hcc2.v.xiii.vi.html; Internet. The ideal world Pleroma is contrasted with Kenoma, the material world of emptiness.

both Gnosticism and Vedanta, even if the hostility to creation is rather veiled and more sophisticated in the latter. Losing any substantive ontological goodness in creation, Vedanta cannot justify, in any ultimate sense, living life on earth without fictional qualifications. Likewise it places a much greater emphasis on enlightenment for liberation even as Gnosticism extols special knowledge. Consequently the moral imperative of truth and falsehood, good and evil lived out in practical life lacks a genuine hold upon the enlightened. While Sankara enjoins the enlightened to continue with karmic works, that injunction loses significance in light of the ontological reality of the absolute contrasted with the fictional qualities of the relative. Even as the Gnostics were ambivalent in their various attitudes to sin – whether limited to the body, incapable to touching the spirit, or with no impact for the enlightened – so also the Vedantin cannot ground moral values in the ontology of an unqualified Brahman for a transitory universe.

Metaphysical Failure

The metaphysical assertions of Vedanta are philosophically difficult to substantiate. Naturalism limits itself to the material universe and attempts to explain all of reality in a reductionist way. Gnosticism identifies the spirit as the metaphysical ideal. Vedanta makes similar expansive claims that defy its own ontological statements: Its accounts on the ontological reality of Brahman and Maya are contradictory. Brahman is said to be the only reality without a complement. Yet substances exist through Maya that cannot be identified either with Brahman or something different than Brahman. While Ramanuja and Madhva avoid this conundrum by speaking of the world as the body or creation of Brahman, Sankara's Advaita cannot satisfactorily defend its monistic claims in the extant face of plurality. "Maya, as expounded by the Advaitins, is self-contradictory and false."[6] Maya is neither real nor unreal. As the weighty load-bearer of every interface from creation to Isvara and the Atman, the lynchpin of Advaita fails the law of non-contradiction.

The excluded middle is further invoked to explain the nature of the world and humanity. They share their existence in Brahman, but are neither real nor unreal. The problem is not merely epistemological despite the many projection analogies given. The universally perceived reality is claimed to be entirely a product of Maya, mainly because the mind does not always associate its dependency upon Brahman. However, everything from the human body, to the inanimate substance, to the core values of life, can neither find identity with Brahman for its ontology nor be different from Brahman. Despite the much vaunted identity of cause and effect, the essence of Brahman in persons is purely the Atman, while his ego neither shares in Brahman nor is different from Brahman. Metaphysically, Advaita has created an unrealistic ideal for Brahman and thereby diminished the existence of people and the world in a manner that cannot be philosophically sustained. Casserley provides a simple response to the issues pertinent to this unrealistic ideal as they fail the test of correspondence with the real world.

> [T]here are philosophies that protest that there are no really separate things at all, and that ultimate reality is seamless . . . . All these philosophies are subtle and

---

[6]P. T. Raju, *The Philosophical Traditions of India* (London: George Allen & Unwin, 1971), 190. Ramanuja demonstrates ignorance as a property. Maya cannot fail to sully Brahman given the Advaitin definition of avidya in Brahman to create.

sophisticated simplifications of reality that must be rejected from the very outset. Our world contains both material and mental realities, so that neither materialism nor idealism is acceptable. Similarly, in a world in which there are subjects there must always be objects, just as in a world in which there are objects there must always be subjects . . . we are therefore compelled to be equally realistic about objectivity and subjectivity and to do equal justice to the validity of both.[7]

The presupposition of Brahman as the base of all reality fits only with the Christian theistic understanding of God. Sankara's philosophical base for monism requires a speculative idealism where action is meaningless with nothing to truly act upon.[8]

Epistemology

Epistemology deals with the source and authority of our knowledge. It also addresses our subjective understanding of this information.[9] Each system's self-acknowledged authority is used to evaluate its basic presuppositions. These underlying basic beliefs which implicitly guided the superstructure of the worldview are examined.

Vedanta and Philosophical Naturalism

Vedanta and Naturalism do not share a common epistemological background. Naturalism claims to rely on reason and science, while Vedanta places a higher authority on scriptures, reason, and intuition. Vedanta exalts the individual's cosmic experience even as Naturalism elevates reason; Vedanta values scriptures even as Naturalism looks to science. These epistemological bases are reviewed for their philosophical validity.

Presuppositions. In examining epistemic authority, the basic presuppositions needed to be honestly evaluated and examined. Since they are foundational, they could not be proved or disproved, but instead of implicitly guiding the superstructure, they develop a more informed role in the process. The Christian presuppositions of biblical authority or subsequent teachings of Christian doctrine are drawn out to show how they influence the Christian understanding of the world in a coherent manner.[10]

Epistemological transgressions in the source of knowledge are difficult to question when Scriptures are given primacy. Also, intuition, natural revelation, and spiritual experience must be guarded against presuming more than can be truthfully affirmed. The subjective understanding of this knowledge is a potential source of error as Christian theology admits even in redeemed persons.[11]

---

[7]J. V. Langmead Casserley, *Apologetics and Evangelism* (Philadelphia: The Westminster Press, 1962), 181.

[8]Karl H. Potter, *Presuppositions of India's Philosophies* (Englewood Cliffs, NJ: Prentice-Hall Inc., 1963), 44.

[9]Arthur F. Holmes, *Contours of a World View* (Grand Rapids: William B. Eerdmans Publishing Company, 1985), 46. We have metaphysical objectivity and epistemological subjectivity.

[10]Michael S. Horton, "Consistently Reformed: The Inheritance and Legacy of Van Til's Apologetic," in *Revelation and Reason: New Essays in Reformed Apologetics*, ed. K. Scott Oliphint and Lane G. Tipton (Phillipsburg, NJ: P&R Publishing, 2007), 147.

[11]Ibid., 138.

Reliability. The objective claims of Vedanta are first critiqued. The Naturalist suffers from the tentativeness necessary in merely holding on to science, along with its limitation in areas beyond the physical. Naturalism has leveraged and over-extended science to make strong epistemological claims on all of life. Just as science cannot claim ultimate submission, the central dilemma for the Vedantin is the reliability of their scriptures. From the Vedas to the Gita, the documents are not only self-contradictory, but have an unreliable transmission, not to mention provenance. The inherent problems in these scriptures have led to radically diverse interpretations, even within the Vedanta camp as reviewed for "Tat twam asi." Far from being the eternal scriptures, reason had been employed to bring into these texts what each school considered critical, by integrating texts that in many cases are impossible to reconcile.[12] One cannot fail to see that even as Naturalism suffers from its stake of faith in science, Vedanta trusts a shaky foundation upon which its entire system has been astutely built and fervently articulated.

Personality. Naturalism seeks to discover the impersonal laws of nature in order to understand life. Vedanta seeks to discover the impersonal ground of life to intuit reality. Christianity makes it clear that what lies beyond is not just an impersonal law or Brahman, but the personal God of the Bible. Epistemologically, revelation is impossible for a being that is impersonal and immutable.[13] It is through personal communication that humans, who are eminently persons, can grasp the intelligent information from a superior being. "A cognition" is unsuccessful to thwart this obvious error.[14] The epistemological base is severely lacking in any impersonal law of Naturalism or the impersonal ground of Brahman in Vedanta.

Vedanta, Gnosticism, and New Age

The subjective element of epistemology cannot be ignored. Even as there is an external basis of knowledge and understanding, there also exists an internal mechanism within humans that enable them to grasp the external realities through correspondence.

Dichotomy. Gnosticism posits a deep divide between spirit and matter. Vedanta creates a sharper schism between Atman and the ego. Christianity claims that the soul of man retains the image of God. It does not diminish the corporeal component of humans as superfluous, especially since it gets recreated in splendor for eternity.

---

[12]A good example is the polytheistic universe of the Vedas and the vulgar setting of the Mahabharata, in contrast to the abstruse teachings of monist Vedanta and the Bhagavad Gita.

[13]Sarvepalli Radhakrishnan and Charles E. Moore, eds., *A Source Book in Indian Philosophy* (Princeton: Princeton University Press, 1957), 543-48. It is further noted: "Proof of such a substance, for all means of right knowledge have for their object things affected with difference" (ibid., 48).

[14]J. N. Mohanty, "A History of Indian Philosophy," in *A Companion to World Philosophies*, ed. Eliot Deutsch and Ron Bontekoe (Malden, MA: Blackwell Publishers, 1997), 36-37. Mohanty notes: "*A cognition* is manifested directly by the witness-consciousness; the latter manifests itself. The qualifier 'directly' is added because while all objects are also manifested by the witness-consciousness, they need the mediation of a cognitive state, but *a cognition* is manifested by the witness-consciousness without the mediation of another cognition. On this theory, then, to say that *a cognition* is self-revealing is to say that by its very occurrence it becomes directly manifested by the witness-consciousness. The witness-consciousness, however, is self-revealing in the strictest sense" (ibid., 37).

Nature of humans. Epistemologically, the creation of man by God and the image of God in humans explain the "sense of the divine" that all humanity experiences, whether to acknowledge or reject. Vedanta claims that the Atman seeks to transcend the physical to be united with Brahman, while it mysteriously controls the individual through Maya. If the Atman shares the essence of Brahman, then it lacks attributes to act upon the world. If the ego is thus disconnected from the Atman, then the ego has no epistemological basis upon which to understand or reach out to Brahman. All that remains is a finely woven system missing an epistemic foundation.[15]

The conscious witness-self lacks any distinction between truth and falsehood. Its non-conscious inner sense is modified to predicate knowledge of truth. This knowledge is empirical in contrast to the metaphysical and epistemological transcendent verity. The claim of devout meditation upon Brahman for release of the Atman is an error, rather than a mystery, since by definition neither the Atman nor the Brahman provide any epistemological hooks for understanding and rising up beyond the ignorance of the ego.[16]

Intuition. Gnosticism elevates special knowledge while New Age movements value intuition. Vedanta values pure consciousness. Here the finite self divests itself of its ignorance of seeing reality relationally. The Bible speaks of the image of God in man as something that God has given humans in order to recognize God, even when observing nature as God's creation. Calvin and Plantinga speak of Sensus Divinitatis, corresponding to the intuition that Vedanta claims. However, the reason that intuition can work is

---

[15]See also, Arindam Chakrabarti, "Rationality in Indian Philosophy," in *A Companion to World Philosophies*, ed. Eliot Deutsch and Ron Bontekoe (Malden, MA: Blackwell Publishers, 1997), 271: "Mohanty, on the other hand, is not baffled by this apparent lack of interest in purely formal necessity/possibility on the part of the Indian logicians. Since Indian logic arose out of two different contexts – namely, as a science of adjudication of actually happening debates and disputations, and as part of a general epistemology in which inferential cogitation as a form of veridical awareness had to be normally thematized – it was natural that component sentences of a valid argument were usually confined to those which were materially true. Soundness was more important than mere validity."

[16]See also, Amita Chatterjee, "Truth in Indian Philosophy," in *A Companion to World Philosophies*, ed. Eliot Deutsch and Ron Bontekoe (Malden, MA: Blackwell Publishers, 1997), 338-39: "The Advaita Vedanta theory of truth . . . can be understood only in the light of the Advaita metaphysics and the Advaita conception of knowledge. It is well known that the Advaitins admit two levels of reality – the transcendental (paramarthika) and the empirical (vyavaharika) – and accordingly they admit two kinds of truth. There are four candidates for the position of truth-bearer in Advaita philosophy. Of these, the ultimate reality, which is the pure undifferentiated consciousness, is beyond the knower-known distinction. The witness self (saksin) is the knower *par excellence*, for it can never be the object of any knowledge. It is also consciousness and hence self-revealing. It even reveals ignorance and is not opposed to it. Of the witness self, therefore, truth or falsity cannot be ascribed, although its grasp of the object is characterized by immediacy. So knowledge of which truth can be predicated is, according to the Advaitins, the modification of the inner sense (antahkarana). Whenever antahkarana is modified (that is, a particular relation is established between an object on the one hand and antahkarana on the other), the self gets reflected in it. The modification of antahkarana may, therefore, be taken to be knowledge. But antahkarana in the Vedanta ontology is material (jada), hence non-conscious, and reveals itself only with the help of the witness self. So in the fitness of things consciousness delimited by a modification of the inner sense should be regarded as knowledge. Knowledge, when understood in either of the last two senses is of the empirical variety. So it is evident that truth or falsity is ascribable only in the empirical realm. The Advaita theory is svatah-pramanyavada with respect to the origination as well as the apprehension of truth because the Advaitins hold that: (1) the originating conditions of a cognition together with the absence of any vitiating factor are sufficient for generating its truth; and (2) the same witness self through which a cognition is apprehended also apprehends its truth."

because God places that equipment in man which clearly corresponds to the knowledge of God and his works in creation. Vedanta fails to account for this sense with Brahman and Atman. These are by definition neither relational nor qualified to correspond to the external observation made by humans. Rose Ann Christian claims that for Advaita Vedanta, human knowers could be metaphysically constituted with something like a Sensus Divinitatis that can comprehend reality.[17] However, what Vedanta asks of humans with intuition is impossible in the Advaita framework, given the large divide between the immutable ideal and the mundane life disconnected from it. This becomes an impassable Lessing's Ditch. However, the true correspondence makes perfect sense in Christianity.

Epistemological Failure

The Vedanta worldview cannot account for how humanity understands truth. Corduan exposes the conflict in the epistemological claims of Vedanta.[18]

In one sense, all knowledge is revelation, since we find facts and do not make them. Religious faith cannot be of the absurd. Vedanta cannot claim eternal scriptures since revelation needs a revealer and a receiver. The eternal Christian Word subsists in Christ, but takes on words in time. Murty claims that Advaita is untrue, being contradictory to perception and logically refutable. If Brahman is the only reality, revelation of Brahman is unintelligible. Humans have an immediate awareness of God, but also a mediate role in receiving and interpreting it. Propositions are admittedly false for an inconsistent system like the Hindu scriptures, unlike the Christian Scriptures. Hindu pluralism with the concept of absolute but lacking universal norm is problematic, as truth must necessarily be both absolute and universal. The cognitive element of revelation undergirds faith and feeling. Murty excellently refutes the notion that theological statements are outmoded and just poetic, elevating the rigorous hermeneutic used to glean theological knowledge from the scriptures.[19] Thus,

---

[17]Rose Anne Christian, "Plantinga, Epistemic Permissiveness, and Metaphysical Pluralism," *Religious Studies* 28 (1992): 568-69, quoted in James Beilby, "Plantinga's Model of Warranted Christian Belief," in *Alvin Plantinga*, ed. Deane-Peter Baker (Cambridge: Cambridge University Press, 2007), 125-65.

[18]See also, Winfried Corduan, "Hinduism: Empty Diversion," *Eastern Religions* (2009): 13: "The finite part of you does not know that it is infinite because the finite is not infinite; it is not even truly real. But then the question arises, who exactly it could be that could quite possibly be spending a lifetime in pursuit of the spiritual goal of knowing that he is infinite? We just ruled out the finite person because the finite is finite and will never be infinite. Neither can it be the infinite that is spending a lifetime learning that it is infinite because the infinite certainly cannot have forgotten that it is infinite and now be in the process of learning of its infinity through meditation and yoga. The infinite must know that it is infinite or it would not be infinite, so there is hardly any deep spiritual meaning in declaring that the infinite is finite. Conversely, of course the finite can learn that the infinite is infinite, but there's nothing particularly new and startling about such an assertion either. This scheme would be meaningful only on the condition that something finite can also be infinite, an idea that Vedanta itself rejects. In short, even though Vedantic Hinduism has had a strong appeal to people who are trying to find fulfillment in a non-Western religion, it ultimately suffers from a logical breakdown from which it cannot recover."

[19]K. Satchidananda Murty, *Revelation and Reason in Advaita Vedānta* (New York: Columbia University Press, 1959), 314-26.

The task of a theologian, who has soaked himself in the tradition, must be to study critically these linguistic expressions and to see whether they can be more adequately formulated in terms of current forms of thought and language.[20]

Each individual will continually grow in knowledge, but objectively we have a completely sufficient and once-for-all delivered revelation of Scripture. The Advaitins' view of relationship between religious language and Brahman needs consistent adherence to the internal logic of that language. Thus, the Christian Worldview apologetic addressed internal inconsistencies to demonstrate invalid propositions of Vedanta.

Murty decries objective proof in religious revelation which needs subjective belief and has no external neutral manner to judge it. This coheres with Plantinga's Reformed epistemology, which requires Sensus Divinitatis to be activated by God before what is true becomes internally evident for warranted belief.[21] Until that occurs, each man is responsible to examine what is claimed and is judged by his response to the truth.

Advaitins' adhere strongly to the scriptures and use exegetical principles that attempt to bring out the authorial intent. Their primary problem is in their presuppositions used to variously interpret the scriptures. The Hindu texts permit varied interpretations, being a diverse body of literature. Self-acknowledged as not historically objective and self-contradictory, these learned men seek to unify it. Within the Christian Bible, this unity is already inherent making the exegete's task simpler. Any preconceptions that are brought in can be more readily weighed against the Scripture's self-evidence, even as the task of maintaining biblically coherent presuppositions is just as crucial.

The secret things belong to God, thus religious truth can never be fully comprehended but what is understood cannot be irrational. Thus reason helps distinguish invalid interpretations of Scripture that run contrary to truth, but it cannot become the basis to establish revelation. The existence of God and moral principles are self-evident to man made in God's image. Reason confirms the truth of God's existence internally.[22]

Vedanta fails to provide a strong reason either in Brahman or in man to trust in the knowledge gained and processed. Through Maya, man's sensory faculties are connected mysteriously with his spiritual Atman. Likewise, Brahman is mysteriously connected with the world we live in. Both in the physical and spiritual realms, there is no direct cognitive basis upon which anyone can rely upon the information that Vedanta posits. It is in light of this idealism that the proposed means of cognition in Vedanta are excessively complicated, being skeptical of empirical knowledge and focusing inordinately upon the deceptive nature of memory and perception. The Christian worldview acknowledges error, but the error is not in God or the creation, but in the fallen nature of man, who is called to evaluate the deliverances of his physical and spiritual senses in light of the true Scriptures.

---

[20]Ibid., 326.

[21]Alvin Plantinga, *Warranted Christian Belief* (New York: Oxford University Press, 2000), xi.

[22]Murty, *Revelation and Reason in Advaita Vedānta*, 329-32. Sensus Divinitatis corresponds to general revelation. Since the "antenna" is broken, it must be first fixed or activated by God.

Ethics

The ethical failure of Vedanta lies in its inability to philosophically ground ethics in Brahman. It also has practical ramifications which are similar to the situational ethics of modernity. Christianity, by contrast, grounds its daily ethics in a holy God.

Vedanta and Philosophical Naturalism

Philosophical Naturalism has found it difficult to ground morality and ethical action. Among its various solutions include deontological ethics, teleological ethics, or relativistic ethics for symbiotic group behavior, minimizing pain, or maximizing happiness for the individual or the group.[23] Given the materialistic universe, these theories are developed to fit the broader framework of evolution, revered as the best current scientific explanation of life. Vedanta, despite its deeply spiritual base, finds itself in a very similar conundrum of lacking a solid platform for ethics.

Fictional ethics. Brahman lacks any differentiation, either to approve good over evil or to provide a standard for the ethical norm. The subsidiary life on earth can only be given a fictional standard to satisfy the temporal existence, which cannot be lived without an ethical norm. Both Naturalism and Vedanta recognize the need for ethics here on earth. This requirement is implicitly borrowed from the biblical worldview. The naturalist and the Vedantin live under ethical norms, however defined. However, they fail to provide an absolute standard for goodness since they deny the true standard in their alternatives to the Christian God, whether in materialism or in Brahman.

Moral goodness. Vedanta posits the worship of Isvara and acting in accord with karma and dharma. This command lacks value, especially for the enlightened one who claims to be one with Brahman, but must be constrained to live under an artificial and inferior law. Some try to justify moral actions by reducing them to identity among selves and non-attachment.[24] This attempt fails because Vedanta cannot provide a strong underlying definition of good in an undifferentiated reality. For Brahman, no values exist. In Maya, good can only be arbitrarily defined. Christianity, by contrast, proclaims a holy God who demands holiness in his creation that relates to him. The characteristic goodness of God translates into the "ought" for goodness in his people, who live in relation to their creator. Vedanta assumes this "ought" without a basis in Brahman, their ultimate reality.

Apologetic ethics. The Christian cannot speak of goodness without God as his referent. He also cannot speak of God in any abstract sense, because it is in relation to

---

[23]Frame, *Apologetics for the Glory of God,* 30.

[24]J. N. Mohanty, "The Idea of the Good in Indian Thought," in *A Companion to World Philosophies,* ed. Eliot Deutsch and Ron Bontekoe (Malden, MA: Blackwell Publishers, 1997), 292, 299-300. Mohanty notes how knowledge causes desire, which progresses to volition, motor effort, and finally action. Hindu instructions require a transcendence of moral distinctions to be an instrument of God's purpose. Mohanty looks into the relation of desire and duty: "we still wonder if the form of 'non-attachment' is only prefixed to the already available dharma. Are there any contents (that is, any actions) that are just incompatible with the form of 'non-attachment'? Many writers have sought to deduce some moral rules or virtues – such as love, non-killing and toleration – from the vedantic thesis of fundamental identity among selves, and would argue that certain actions, which by their very nature entail egoistic and selfish desires and destructive emotions such as lust and anger, preclude non-attachment" (ibid., 300).

God that he exists and acts morally. This ethic translates into apologetics as well. The most fundamental Christian truth is the existence of a loving and holy God. Analogically, if the existence or character of one's father was questioned by a stranger, a son naturally responds with high confidence in the fact of his father's existence, even if presently absent at the scene. The son's ability to convince the stranger may seem jeopardized by his assurance, but the son can start from no other base. He will showcase his evidence from a position of commitment to his belief. Assuming a neutral position on this subject, would deny his fundamental faithfulness to his father.[25] Vedanta presumes neutrality in its theological engagements, but the existence of a creator God precludes that option.

Alternatively, a Nazi's son may be unaware of his father's war records. Until he understands his father's role, he cannot but speak from the position of a loving son. He may even consider the witness who testified against his father, a traitor. Yet the witness's son will see the accusation differently. Such is the encounter between the sons of God and the sons of the devil – hard as this may seem. The challenge here is not to vilify the Nazi's son, but to extend grace and patience to one whose current allegiance needs to be broken for new alliances.[26] The Vedantin true to his system will see apologetical ethics differently, since there is no ultimate objective verity in the framework of time and space. The Christian places God's demand of ethical thinking in conformity to God and his character, even in the apologetical encounter.

Honesty. Honesty is a good ethical example – why must a Vedantin be honest if it will diminish his duty as a warrior or king? This was Yudhishthira's concern and still challenges the modern Vedantin. No claims of universal governance can satisfy what lacks in the wholesomeness of the individual following truth. Vedanta's ultimate being, Brahman, holds to no standards of goodness and honesty for either individual or universal ethics. This is no different from the Naturalistic lack of an ultimate standard.

Love. Love is crucial to life. Philosophical Naturalism struggles to reduce love to a functional object. Vedanta tries in its ultimate form to dissolve love into a desire-less state. Yet love is important in Vedantin devotion to Isvara. Vedanta ethics of love are fictional as relationships and qualifications are a by-product of Maya and thus without lasting value. The most basic of human values and emotions becomes a utilitarian tool for materialistic or spiritual advancement in each worldview. Christianity, however grounds love in the character of God. God is love. God's image in man grants him the ability to love God and his fellow-man. Jesus calls love the greatest commandment. God restores the ability of sinful man to love, by giving him the Holy Spirit, by whom we can love in purity and truth. Vedanta's attempts at love are short-circuited by its underlying philosophy. Arjuna's love for Krishna cannot be sustained when his actual nature is

---

[25]Lesslie Newbigin, *Truth to Tell: The Gospel as Public Truth* (Geneva: WCC Publications, 1991), 33-35. "The missionary action of the Church is the exegesis of the gospel." Using Polyani, Newbigin says, "All knowing is the knowing of a fallible human subject who may be wrong but who can know more by personally committing himself to what he already knows. All knowing is a personal commitment" (ibid., 35). See also Paul K. Moser, "Reorienting Religious Epistemology: Cognitive Grace, Filial Knowledge, and Gethsemane Struggle," in *For Faith and Clarity: Philosophical Contributions to Christian Theology*, ed. James K. Bielby (Grand Rapids: Baker Academic, 2006), 75, 79, 81.

[26]Greg L. Bahnsen, *Van Til's Apologetic: Readings and Analysis* (Phillipsburg, NJ: P&R Publishing, 1998), 461. William Edgar, *Reasons of the Heart: Recovering Christian Persuasion* (Grand Rapids: Baker Book House, 1997), 69-73.

revealed to him. Despite Sankara's injunction to love God, this fictional ethic has no energizing force in the final analysis for Brahman, just as it also fails for Naturalism.

Vedanta, Gnosticism, and New Age

Gnosticism also fails to provide for an earthly ethic with the spiritual life always trumping the mundane life lived daily. The Christian arguments made against the consequences of a faulty gnostic ethic are numerous, beginning with the apostle John.[27]

Theodicy. Christianity deals with evil, by responding to the source of evil and the right action of Christians. Vedanta, like Gnosticism, relates evil to ignorance. It claims that this ignorance assigns value to physical life over the spiritual union with the Brahman. Vedantins are not as concerned with goodness as with the denial of both good and bad ethics. Metaphysically, if there is neither the world nor Maya, evil cannot exist.

> Evil is the paradigmatic issue from which the notion of Isvara (Lord) and creation are to be discerned (regarding karma). In order to extricate the Lord from the tangles of evil, Sankara is willing to argue that Isvara is not the sole force or factor in creation . . . . The evil that one encounters has no beginning except to say that it is traced to individuality . . . [which] leads us back to maya . . . . Duality obscures knowledge of the self (atman) and that is certainly problematic for the Advaitin . . . . This beginningless superimposition is correlated with ignorance and this, Sankara says, is "the cause of all evil."[28]

Social norms. Justice is severely questioned when wicked Duryodhana attains heaven by following his ethical duty mandated by karma while the more righteous family of Yudhishthira suffers in hell. This seems to provide a graded system, which is not uniformly just. Even given the less-than-final nature of this state, this travesty is a consequence of having no absolute standard of good upon which the Hindu ethic is built. Rather this system is built upon a social structure of duty and responsibility, which is invoked for action on the basis of one's station in life, rather than on the basis of truth, goodness, equity, and justice. Such relativism finds no place in the Christian worldview.

Desire. Krishna's famous mandate to work without seeking the fruit of one's labor fails to give the right direction to honor God. The lack of desire, which is seen as a virtue in Vedanta, becomes its Achilles heel since it grants no true motive for good

---

[27]Among the many texts on holy living is 1 John 2:9-11 which says, "Whoever says he is in the light and hates his brother is still in darkness. Whoever loves his brother abides in the light, and in him there is no cause for stumbling. But whoever hates his brother is in the darkness and walks in the darkness, and does not know where he is going, because the darkness has blinded his eyes." 1 John 2:4-6 gives the broader mandate to obey God and follow after Jesus, "Whoever says 'I know him' but does not keep his commandments is a liar, and the truth is not in him, but whoever keeps his word, in him truly the love of God is perfected. By this we may know that we are in him: whoever says he abides in him ought to walk in the same way in which he walked."

[28]Stephen Kaplan, "Three Levels of Evil in Advaita Vedanta and a Holographic Analogy," in *A Companion to World Philosophies*, ed. Eliot Deutsch and Ron Bontekoe (Malden, MA: Blackwell Publishers, 1997), 116. Good and evil find an amoral definition here. Kaplan further notes: "This definition stresses the notion that evil is the responsibility of the individual – the individual's free act. Here also, it is not the responsibility of Isvara, the Lord" (ibid., 129).

action. Vedanta cannot provide the motive because Brahman lacks the ability to elevate good. Krishna's own actions lack moral necessity. Being enlightened, he has no internal imperative, but claims to act for those who would imitate him. This god is apparently constrained by the destruction of the world that would ensue if he would not act right. Yet in Krishna's action one finds no basis of moral goodness. His brute assertion to follow one's dharma is based on the devotional attraction one supposedly finds in Krishna as Isvara. Neither the character of Krishna nor the quality of the unqualified Brahman provides a genuine devotional affinity, like Jesus who dies for sinners.

Gods. It is no trivial matter that the Hindu gods stumble on common norms of ethical conduct. They fail because there is no ultimate standard upon which to evaluate right and wrong. The Gita talks extensively about right and wrong, while it is incapable of living by the norms that it claims to be necessary for the enlightened. The laws that are created fail to satisfy what is requisite for goodness. Ultimately Vedanta appeals to the spiritual nature of man by promising an illusory union with Brahman. The temporal moral injunctions create an artificial stricture upon a society that has failed to progress in the direction forecast by its religion. The Hindu society has moved in ethical directions to the extent that it has moved away from the false allurement of Vedanta, in its reform movements. Millions in Hinduism are still under the rank illusion that their rituals, like the Maha Kumbhamela held in 2013, will wash their sins and grant them liberation.

Ethical Failure
Vedanta has created an unlivable idealism. For practical living, especially in the realm of ethics, it has vested its virtues on Isvara and drawn out laws that govern the universe. From the Vedic tradition, the laws of karma and dharma find little justification in their originators such as Varuna and Mitra. These laws struggle to straddle freedom and determinism and can provide no definitive basis for their ethics.

For actual living, Vedanta has tied the ethical norms upon a fictional basis. Any system that lacks a genuine and true basis of goodness, but is purely pragmatic or based on non-absolute measures, cannot continue to ethically exhort its followers to adhere to its standards. Advaita has cut itself at its roots by denying any absolute good. Its attempt to invoke a temporal basis in Isvara is borrowed from the Christian worldview, but it fails to cohere with its broader assertions on Brahman. In essence, Advaita is self-professedly not good and cannot define an absolute, universal goodness.

Conclusion
The Christian worldview examination of Vedanta finds it markedly wanting in the philosophical categories of metaphysics, epistemology, and ethics.

Metaphysically, Vedanta has no firm basis upon which to justify our existence, as Christianity does in the eternal, personal, absolute God. Epistemologically, Vedanta cannot account for reason and knowledge in humans or our understanding of the divine. An incommunicable Brahman contrasts poorly with the eternal Word of God who communicates of himself through natural and special revelation and supremely in the person of Jesus Christ. Ethically, there is only fictional goodness in Vedanta whose absolute Brahman has no qualifications to justify good over evil, but radically reduces wickedness to ignorance. In contrast the Christian worldview relies on the goodness and holiness of God as the standard by which each Christian is called to live a life of goodness here on earth. He anticipates an eternity where sin and evil no longer exist, while their complements of obedience and goodness will endure forever.

The Hindu philosophical system has deep roots in the Indian tradition and has been precisely fine-tuned through logical acumen of brilliant men, relying on their scriptures and their presuppositions. It is humbling to see the heights that these towering intellectual giants reach and yet how in light of Christian revelation, they are fatally flawed on key foundational verities. This must give simple and frail Christians great zeal to present the pure and simple gospel to those who have built a towering edifice to the skies building themselves a name which will, in the end, not endure.

The Christian apologist attempted to find the logical flaws in Sankara's philosophical system from the inside out rather than just from the outside in. It is easy to critique any system from the outside, only to be rebuffed due to differing presuppositions. The best manner to critique Advaita was to examine the rich tapestry of an intricately woven network of coherence and consistency. At one end of this large and seemingly unassailable system was the loose thread of Maya. Its counterpart on the experiential side was a radical idealism which implicitly delegated the world of sense to a secondary status. Maya took a lot of responsibility for the non-ultimate status of the world, the relationship of Maya to Brahman, and the relation of Atman to the ego. Therefore this system was approached along the logical flaws of Maya. One of these flaws consisted in Maya's explanation of evil through the analogy of the cow-dung providing a stable environment for scorpions. The fact that scorpions thrive in the cow-dung does not require anything from the cow-dung. However, this is a dependency relation with a epistemological error rather than an ontological flaw. Maya is the Achilles heel of Advaita. The other Vedantins who do not prescribe to Advaita successfully attacked this error, by proposing alternate systems corresponding more realistically to this world of sense and experience.

Vedanta cannot resolve its philosophical conundrums within its religious worldview since they are directly tied to its foundational presuppositions that form the core of the Vedanta worldview. This worldview cannot be corrected, but must be given up. However, in Christian apologetics to Vedanta, each items represented can be further developed. The Christian apologist has many threads to follow up in each of the listed items, while developing new lines of thought that have not been explored thus far.

In the next chapter, the personal aspect of Worldview apologetics will be engaged. This individual aspect will provide another viewpoint with which to look at Vedanta. It will call upon the Vedantin to recognize the danger of the Advaitin worldview and to flee for safety to the God of Christianity.

CHAPTER 8
PERSONAL APOLOGETICS

The Christian Worldview apologetic presented the Christian proof, critiqued Advaita Vedanta, and responded to charges against Christianity. It reviewed the philosophical problems with Vedanta from the Christian perspective. This apologetic encounter, while honoring Christ at one level, still lacks the evangelistic force to complete the engagement. The academic interaction can seem platonic and disinterested, lacking the urgency and imperative theological force of Christian apologetics. This chapter engages with that missing element of apologetics. The Hindu needs to be engaged not only in his mind, but also in his heart. Personal apologetics extends the interaction from the domain of the theoretical Vedanta belief system to that of practical life. It personally challenges the individual Hindu to confront the paucity of Vedanta in his daily life, which in turn directly impacts his eternal life.

The Worldview apologetic method thus far dealt with information obtained by parsing data in an evidential manner. It also reasoned through the logical issues of Vedanta in a classical manner. The apologetic was specifically framed in the reformed method relying heavily on scriptural data and its injunctions. Having covered these crucial dimensions of apologetics, now finally, the capstone of the encounter is placed with a Fideistic appeal to the Hindu, having qualified its limitations.

The personal tone of apologetics is vital when addressing individuals as opposed to organizations or systems. The propositional content and intellectual strain of apologetics can tend to make apologetics more technical than personal. Apologetics cannot be divorced from evangelism, since it is not purely academic at a conceptual level. Instead, the individual's state before God and his perilous danger should motivate the Christian in his personal apologetic that is faithful to God, honest to himself, and acting out of the best intent toward the Hindu.[1]

Kierkegaard and the Will

Worldviews are deeply rooted in each individual. Shaking one's commitment to his worldview needs targeting the will, besides engaging one's mind. Soren Kierkegaard's perspective on the human spheres of life engages this stubborn human will.

---

[1]Cornelius Van Til, *The Defense of the Faith* (Phillipsburg, NJ: Presbyterian and Reformed Publishing Co., 1967), 319-27.

The radical nature of convictions requires a leap across worldviews. In Christian terms, the will of the Hindu must be inclined to submit to God and commit his entire life to God. Whether he is complacent or concerned with his current state, Kierkegaard's views on the will are helpful to approach the Hindu in his Aesthetic, Ethical, or often Religious way of life.[2] Kierkegaard has written much that is unhelpful to the Christian witness, especially in his fidesitic critique of reason, to oppose the Hegelian system. This book will be limited to draw mainly from Kierkegaard's stages of life. His Aesthetic, Ethical, and Religiousness A stages represent the unbelieving worldviews, while his Religiousness B represents the Christian state of existence. Kierkegaard classifies these spheres:

> The aesthetic sphere is that of immediacy, the ethical is that of requirement (and this requirement is so infinite that the individual always goes bankrupt), the religious sphere is that of fulfillment.[3]

The unbeliever's actual state is examined to identify his areas of receptivity. Kierkegaard intends to drive his readers from inauthentic to authentic selfhood, by providing an environment for "self-examination and self-judgment."[4]

Religiousness A would be claimed by the Vedantin, who values progress in moving toward Brahman. While this may be the stated ideal of the worldview, the actual subjective state of the individual can occupy the aesthetic or ethical in varying degrees. Thus, the personal apologetic engagement will exhort the individual to discover the impossibility of practically living the unrealistic ideal of Vedanta.

Each of Kierkegaard's worldviews is now existentially engaged, to provide a challenge to move the Vedantin to a biblical worldview. This is done in the context of obdurate or placating Hindus, who resist the gospel in their stubbornness or syncretism.

Aesthetic Worldview

The aesthetic worldview revolves around maximizing the individual's selfish pleasures. It begins with an immediate gratification of desires, just as a baby thinks only of itself or a seducer tries to maximize his conquests. It progresses through intellectual reflection to avoid the ennui of mere pleasure seeking. The aesthete avoids pain by living for desires, whether in simple enjoyment or through seeking detachment.[5] He progresses

---

[2]Mark C. Taylor, "Natural Selfhood and Ethical Selfhood in Kierkegaard," in *The Humor of Kierkegaard*, ed. Harold Bloom (Philadelphia: Chelsea House Publishers, 1989), 178-89. Louis Pojman, *Kierkegaard's Philosophy of Religion* (San Francisco: International Scholars Publications, 1999), 29-33. Pojman's classifications helpfully systematize Kierkegaard's works.

[3]Soren Kierkegaard, *Stages on Life's Way*, ed. and trans. Howard V. Hong and Edna H. Hong (Princeton: Princeton University Press, 1988), 430. Kierkegaard notes: "The metaphysical is an abstraction, there is no man who exists metaphysically. The ethical sphere is only a transitional sphere . . . . [Religious fulfillment is] not such a fulfillment as when one fills a can or a bag with gold, for repentance has made infinite room, and hence the religious contradiction: at the same time to lie upon seventy thousand fathoms of water and yet to be joyful" (ibid., 430).

[4]Taylor, "Natural Selfhood and Ethical Selfhood in Kierkegaard," 172. Kierkegaard helps to refocus the attention from pure cerebration to examine the lived life. His indirect communication is very effective in reflecting the parabolic words of Jesus to awaken the unbeliever from his entrenched system. His pithy and provocative language aids the apologist to approach the unbeliever in very personal terms.

[5]See also, Peter Vardy, *An Introduction to Kierkegaard* (Peabody, MA: Hendrickson Publishers, 2008), 43: "Three forms of the aesthetic stage all see enjoyment, or at least prevention of pain for the self, as the main aim of life."

from sensual to refined selfish pleasure.[6] This self-absorption should not be confused with one's self-identity. Consumed with himself, he lacks true identity.

Sought for its own sake, pleasure goes stale and boredom sets in "It is a herculean task to insure continuous sensuous titillation and even the more refined pleasures seem to lose their excitement, turn grey and tasteless after a time."[7] The "aesthete desperately seeks to flee the dullness and disillusionment of his failed life in a thousand ways."[8] Just as crops are rotated to maintain the soil, pleasures are rotated to enliven desires. The logic of evading boredom through rotation is to seek some level of "self-sufficiency and control." Thus the aesthete flees constraints as his imagination takes over reality. The use of the arbitrary retains this freedom by introducing random surprise.[9] Sadly, the frenzied rotation only postpones the inevitable boredom. Imagination permits falling in love with the "idea" of a woman, as a spectator and manipulator of life, rather than actually loving his spouse. In failing to appropriate life as intended, despair in this false gratification nudges the aesthete closer to death and suicide.[10] Authentic living must necessarily give up this aesthetic worldview.[11]

Vedantins in the aesthetic worldview are least consistent, since Advaita calls on individuals to eschew physical, sensual pleasures for the selfless joys of union with Brahman. The idealistic Advaitin aspires for this impossible ideal, while suffering the temptations common to man. Thus it is quite likely that even the most fervent Advaitin should inhabit the aesthetic world to some degree. The Vedantin worldview delegates this inconsistency to Maya and the ignorance of the self. Depending on where in the aesthetic spectrum the individual is, the Christian can present the gospel-centered apologetic in a personal manner to challenge the commitment of the Vedantin. This aesthetic Vedantin can either be obdurate or placating in his resistance.

Hindu individuals can range from obdurate, headstrong individuals at one end to placating, syncretistic individuals at the other end. An obdurate aesthetic Vedantin is stuck in his worldview through the sophisticated rotation of pleasures to avoid boredom. A placating aesthetic Vedantin is mindlessly living a sensual life dreaming of an ideal that he anticipates several lifetimes away. The Christian Worldview apologetic can expose the futility of both these positions.

---

[6]Pojman, *Kierkegaard's Philosophy of Religion*, 44-47. Pojman notes: "The individual lives for pleasure whether sensual or refined . . . generally characterized by a self-indulgent lack of regard for others" (ibid., 47).

[7]Ibid., 47. Aesthetic persons gradually differentiate and rank pleasures, with the difficulty of maintaining the state of continuous pleasure. With pleasure follows pain, ennui, and listlessness.

[8]Ibid. One specializes and substitutes intensity for extensity. He enjoys subtle delights, forgets and remembers selectively like the Epicureans. It is doubtful whether many aesthetes ever reach this state of refinement. Yet even here the way to fulfillment is foreclosed.

[9]Stephen C. Evans, *Kierkegaard: An Introduction* (Cambridge: Cambridge University Press, 2009), 79. Some would watch a show from the middle or read a book a third of the way in, just to introduce this random surprise.

[10]Donald D. Palmer, *Kierkegaard for Beginners* (New York: Writers and Readers Publishing, 1996), 87. Kierkegaard notes: "There are well-known insects that die in the moment of fecundation. So it is with all joy; life's supreme and richest moment of pleasure is coupled with death" (ibid.); and "Fill your life with cunning little surprises that . . . keep you from being swamped by life's tedium. Nevertheless, the more frenzied is the pursuit of the rotation method, the more despairing the aesthete becomes, and the closer he comes to suicide" (ibid.).

[11]Pojman, *Kierkegaard's Philosophy of Religion*, 29-33. Pojman's classifications here and throughout are helpful to systematize Kierkegaard's works.

Placating Hindus. The general tone of apologetics is intended to be cordial as individuals care and respect for one another. The Christian needs isolate the placating individual's desire to please the Christian from the urgent need to tend to the state of his complacent soul, which must be confronted with the gospel.

The placating aesthetic Hindu is a spontaneous hedonist seeking pleasure. Besides the obvious conflict between the theoretical aspiration of platonic Vedanta and a practical life that revels in sensual pleasure, this individual needs to have his ephemeral satisfactions measured against the impossibility of ever achieving his stated Vedanta goals. This approach closes out his alternatives until only the Christian path is available. The Vedanta position can be shown to be impossible from those very paths that the Hindu trusts – neither knowledge nor works nor devotion can transform the individual stuck in his uninhibited sins. The gospel is presented in stark contrast to the Vedanta worldview, as one where the work is done by God. The individual is transformed with a new heart that hates his selfish pleasures and loves God instead. The exclusive claims of Christianity are shown as the only viable truth to address the specific individual's need.[12]

Confronting the placating aesthetic with his actual state rather than what he peripherally agrees with, can be difficult. The syncretistic Hindu has many means to affirm the Christian claim without valuing it as unique or having any forceful claim upon himself. Vedanta does provide these options and a possibility for laxity that placating individuals can avail to avoid social pressure. The Christian evangelist can point out how the individual's actions belie his admission of assent. This conflict places the individual under the judgment of God's Word, when presenting the gospel as the arrow to pierce the armor of indifference. Since immediacy holds center-stage for the aesthetic Hindu, where everything is in the moment, the urgent need to submit to the gospel cannot be underemphasized to the placating Hindu.

Obdurate Hindus. Unlike the placating Hindu, the obdurate aesthetic Hindu has reflected and refined the path to pleasure, prolonging it to avoid the pain and ennui that inevitably follows. The ideal addicts here are intellectuals, satisfied with complex problems. Sophistication may seem a step up, but instead it hopelessly digs the aesthete further down. The Vedanta worldview is such a fascinating puzzle that can engage and occupy the pursuits of this individual in an unending maze.

Frustration with simple pleasures generates more complex and refined goals. Refined aesthetes are self-hardened in their deliberate hedonism. "The person in [this] demonic stage is self-aware, thoughtful and firmly in control of life. Nothing from outside can penetrate the iron-hard protective wall."[13] The obdurate aesthetic Hindu has invested much in his pursuit of pleasure, whether sensual, intellectual, or otherwise, that his will has toughened in his course. The boredom one experiences is a form of despair, which positions the person to rightly resolve it in the satisfaction found in Christ.[14]

---

[12]Greg, L. Bahnsen, *Presuppositional Apologetics: Stated and Defended*, ed. Joel McDurmon (Nacodoches, TX: American Vision Press, 2008), 116.

[13]Vardy, *An Introduction to Kierkegaard*, 43. Vardy further notes "Beyond this, however, is the person who has seen the bankruptcy of all forms of temporal enjoyment but who refuses to relinquish the aesthetic stage and persists in a way of living that he can control. Such individuals sink into their own despair and will not let go of it" (ibid.).

[14]Palmer, *Kierkegaard for Beginners*, 79-87. The refined aesthete's spirituality is an illusion, even realizing that pursuit of pleasure becomes boring.

Christians may appear mean toward the Hindu when they disregard the Hindu or dishonor him in their tone or manner of speech. However, obdurate Hindus need not find only sweet words from the Christian. Jesus and Paul used tough words with those adamant in their falsehood. Strong language, from irony to hyperbole, is not excluded in apologetics. The intention ought to honor God and aid the individual, rather than simply mock the individual for an audience. Considering the dangers of such speech, it is wise for one in full control of his passions to use any emotional entreaty prudently.[15]

The propositional refutation of refined aestheticism seeks to awaken the deluded one from the purposeless despair that awaits him. From his position of obduracy, no man can dislodge the aesthete. However, the gospel claims of Jesus speak directly to those seeking satisfaction with the world, as the parable of the rich man illustrates.[16]

The Christian can expect insults for his audacity to question the Vedantin. He can also expect to be refuted by the superiority of the Vedantin worldview even in sophisticated hedonism. The apologetic mandate requires the Christian to unwaveringly present the clear and pointed gospel so that the danger of the aesthetic Hindu is not minimized before the wrath of a holy God.

This concludes personal apologetics with the obdurate and placating Hindus not dissimilar from personal evangelism. Kierkegaard's tools help address the entrenched will. Each individual Vedanta Hindu monist with his peculiarity requires the Fideistic approach to direct the focus on these elements that would address his actual state.[17]

Ethical Worldview

The ethical worldview is a progression from the aesthetic one. The individual leaps into this worldview, which is dominated by duty, somewhat arbitrarily. It begins by choosing the good outside of one's own desires, to live for a broader purpose beyond oneself. In doing so, the individual becomes a true self and instantiates universals in his own life. Ultimately, however, the individual faces the inadequacies of the ethical by being unable to satisfy the demands of duty.[18]

The Hindu can identify quite well with the ethical state since karma or works form a vital role for Vedantins. Whether dictated by dharma or the rituals prescribed by the social norms, these ethics map well to the Advaitin dictum. Even the enlightened Vedantin is obligated in some form to conform to ethical standards. This moral man does not give free rein to his own passions and desires, but surrenders his life to the broader moral prerogative. His will submits to this law, aware that both his life and his society benefit by this law's rule. A consistent ethical Vedantin considers this ethical state as

---

[15]Evans, *Kierkegaard,* 70-76.

[16]In Luke 12:16-23, Jesus confronts the complacent rich man by shocking him from his view of material prosperity for many years. Jesus projects the ultimate value of the soul and its pitiful state which needs remedy. "And he told them a parable, saying, 'The land of a rich man produced plentifully, and he thought to himself, 'What shall I do, for I have nowhere to store my crops?' And he said, 'I will do this: I will tear down my barns and build larger ones, and there I will store all my grain and my goods. And I will say to my soul, Soul, you have ample goods laid up for many years; relax, eat, drink, be merry.' But God said to him, 'Fool! This night your soul is required of you, and the things you have prepared, whose will they be?' So is the one who lays up treasure for himself and is not rich toward God.' And he said to his disciples, 'Therefore I tell you, do not be anxious about your life, what you will eat, nor about your body, what you will put on. For life is more than food, and the body more than clothing.'"

[17]Pojman, *Kierkegaard's Philosophy of Religion,* 29-33.

[18]Ibid.,29-33.

temporary but necessary in this existence before union with Brahman. An inconsistent ethical Vedantin relies on moral works, hoping for knowledge and devotion in his future.

Placating Hindus. At the lower end of the ethical spectrum are those satisfied with conforming to the social and religious expectations of Hinduism. They find purpose in their existence by valuing a higher standard that is beyond themselves. By trusting in karma, they are freed from the simplistic pleasures and boredom of life. For them the Christian alternative is not as much unjustified as unnecessary, since they have a norm that will eventually lead them to the final goal, probably better than the Christian path.

The Christian attempts to show the practical folly of these works, along with the inability of the individual to fulfill it. Vedantic works range from religious rituals to diverse social stratification mandated by their scriptures. The more austere denials and the works of detachment remain the ideal that Hindus aspire for, often in their older age when they renounce family and normal desires in order to perfect their work. Irrespective of where they are, the lack of an absolute standard for these works highlights the ephemeral nature of these karmic works within the Vedantic system. Also, the actual failure of the individual to conform to his own standards can be brought up to set the basis of practical Christian holiness. Rather than purifying oneself to attain perfection, works show the inability of the individual to please God. The holiness of God and the depravity of man can be the wedge to sharply disengage the placating individual from his complacency. The failure in the Hindu standard and in the individual's ability to meet it, can be starkly marked against the absolute standard of God and their perilous state.

Obdurate Hindus. At the higher end of the ethical spectrum are Hindus who do recognize their inability to satisfy the ethical demands of their own law and their inner conscience. In acknowledging a universal law, the binding nature of the law forces the individual to examine every act for a judicial verdict, causing guilt.[19] Heightened moral sensitivity acerbates the ethicists' guilt of "innate selfishness, weakness of will, ulterior motives, vanity, and even a certain perversity."[20] The guilty soul realizes his inability to attain the perfect moral law, now necessitating a leap to a higher level.[21] This individual can seek easement by theistically referring his duty to the Hindu gods. This individual must either resolve his guilt or remain sinfully worshiping the law as an idol. In the latter case, the obdurate ethical Hindu can suppress this guilt by trusting in the Hindu gods, compounded by an indefinite number of lifecycles to hope for salvation.

---

[19]Palmer, *Kierkegaard for Beginners*, 103-05. Palmer further states: "In 'the leap' one has truly chosen oneself. His roles will no longer be fragmented, they will cohere since one's moral commitment will be expressed in each role. One must still live in a society with one's roles still socially dictated but the self will freely express even within the deterministic social system. Any of the roles incompatible with one's moral commitment will be discarded. Every future choice will be an occasion for self-judgment. Every future situation will be a moral one. The individual will judge herself in each situation and in each moment as either 'Guilty/Not Guilty'" (ibid., 105).

[20]Ibid., 53. Palmer notes: "Only by an infinite relationship to God could the doubt be calmed, only by an infinite free relationship to God could his anxiety be transformed into joy. God is always in the right, in an infinitely free relationship to God . . . he recognizes that he himself is always in the wrong."

[21]Ibid., 52. He who fails to leap into the religious stage stagnates spiritually, becomes a legalist as the law becomes an idol and the good is not sought with a pure heart. Again Palmer says, "A leap to this higher level presses upon this guilty soul . . . he cannot attain the perfection that the moral law demands."

The Christian can engage the guilt that the Hindu already experiences. Just as a doctor addresses the pain, the gospel addresses the problem of sin. For this universal need, the resolution for guilt is presented in the finished work of Jesus Christ as the genuine solution for sin. It is vital to contrast the absolute standard of holiness in God against the tainted efforts of the individual. It is also crucial to refer to the true revelation of God's law, in contrast to any human construal of the law. The Vedantin needs to be confronted on his idolatry in worshiping falsehood and for committing his life to a damning error. The ethical error can thus be confronted both with the internal conscience and the external Scriptures, as both correspond remarkably to impress the dangers facing the ethical Vedantin in a state of guilt.

Religiousness A Worldview

Religiousness A worldview is dominated by subjectivity. An intense inward introspection develops a self-knowledge that exceeds ethical norms. It tends God-ward through the dictates of natural religion. As an individual, the person recognizes the need for a primitive faith. This phase is the most that any unregenerate individual can attain and still ends with guilt and a crisis. It is only through Christian revelation, grace, and faith that the true believer enters Religiousness B which is dominated by paradox and makes him a witness or martyr for truth.[22]

Natural religion provides an "innate" knowledge of God which satisfies more than mere morals. The ethical person used God-awareness as his source of morality. He self-confidently hoped to achieve unique subjective selfhood before God. The religious person however, fathoms his brokenness and relies on God. He depends on God rather than his action to become whole again.[23] This relationship is in paradox. The religious person grasps both sin and awe before God's "utter" holiness and transcendence. In relation to God, his aesthetic and ethical needs are subsumed.

Only when the individual recognizes that there seems no alternative to despair and that all finite ends terminate in disappointment is it possible to relate him- or herself to God. Effectively, a person may be driven to God when all other alternatives fail – almost willy-nilly.[24]

The Vedantin relies on grace for trust in God rather than himself. Satisfaction in God depends on one's thirst for God. Without a need, the solution does not last. Ethicists and aesthetes profess belief in an inadequate God, since their need is insufficient for the God-solution.[25] Vedanta has bhakti or devotion as the central means of loving

---

[22]Pojman, *Kierkegaard's Philosophy of Religion*, 29-33.

[23]Evans, *Kierkegaard*, 116-23. Evans further notes: "The religious individual in the more distinctive sense is someone who has made discoveries about the difficulties of becoming an integral self, someone who is no longer confident in the God-relation as a goal to be achieved through action. Rather, the religious person sees herself as in some way broken, and finds in the God-relationship grounds to hope that the self can be made whole again" (ibid., 123).

[24]Vardy, *An Introduction to Kierkegaard*, 56. It is only a possibility to consider the religious worldview seriously.

[25]Pojman, *Kierkegaard's Philosophy of Religion*, 57. Pojman says: "Every individual has an ethical-religious task of developing his own individuality towards his highest *telos* . . . . The ethical is subsumed under the religious" (ibid.). Leo Stan, "A Reconsideration of Kierkegaard's Understanding of the Human Other: The Hidden Ethics of Soteriology," *Journal of Religious Ethics* 38 (2010): 349-70. Stan notes: "Kierkegaard enables us to discern why an ethical theory, when not supplanted by a salvation-

God. Gynana or knowledge of Brahman takes its place alongside devotion as the supreme means of Advaitin religion. These heighten the need for Isvara in an enduring sense.

This religious action is beyond full rational clarity since Brahman is beyond qualification. Unlike the ethical which is compatible with rational justification, the religious mystically provides inner certainty inarticulate by rational principles.[26] Faith is like divine madness as one passionately "commits" firmly to the object of belief. This inner movement is assumed to be self-correcting, since no idol can command continued genuine passion, since it cannot fully satisfy. Kierkegaard claims that he will discover the error of his choice due to the reason of his intense energy. This result is not necessarily valid since depraved minds can settle for demons over the divine, due to the deception of sin that settles for what is pleasing to the corrupt conscience. For Vedantins, this is precisely the conundrum of Religiousness A. Both devotion to the Hindu gods and knowledge of the supreme Brahman provide idols that appear elevated in relation to the aesthetic and ethical lifestyle. By marking this as his terminus, the Hindu fails to honor the true God. His devotion and knowledge remain as stumbling blocks until the veil is taken away and his will bows down before God.

Placating Hindus. Bhakti or devotion lends itself agreeably to the placating religious Hindu. Vedantins recognize devotion to Isvara in any god-form as a means to salvation. Yet devotion shares this honor with knowledge or finds a place under it in Advaita. Thus this devotional path is necessarily tinged with some inadequacy for most Advaitins. This path is the most ecumenical since the Hindu gods encompass a vast array of divinities including Jesus. Thus the Vedantin committed to Krishna can trust him for salvation, while seamlessly accepting another viable path of devotion through Jesus.

The Christian impresses the error of worshiping Krishna in light of who God really is, as presented earlier. It can also contest the satisfaction in worshipping a false god – through the ethical aberrations of Krishna's life, his inconsistent words, and the false matrix of Hinduism in which he subsists. This polemic can extend easily to the other gods of Hinduism. Making this personal, the placating Hindu can be shown the radical difference between Jesus and any personal god of Hinduism that he worships. Against the holiness of Jesus, the danger of idolatry should be elevated to warn this individual of its consequences. In rejecting Jesus, he needs to realize that he is not in an alternate path of devotion, but on a broad path that leads to destruction.

Obdurate Hindus. As the supreme path, gynana or knowledge lends itself above devotion to the obdurate religious Hindu, who is the most consistent advaitin. The personal challenge here is primarily one of pride. Vedantins committed to the path of knowledge trust in Brahman as the Supreme Being and staunchly attempt enlightenment

---

oriented psychology and an unswerving affirmation of divine transcendence, betrays its foundational goals and praiseworthy intentions" (ibid., 370).

[26]Jonathan Malesic, "A Secret Both Sinister and Salvific: Secrecy and Normativity in Light of Kierkegaard's *Fear and Trembling*," *Journal of the American Academy of Religion* 74 (2006): 446-68. Malesic notes: "Secrets are sinister. They harm and exploit and arrogantly refuse all criticism. But for Kierkegaard, humans' ability to keep secrets indicates an interior depth to the person who is the site of the religious sphere. On his account, religious individuals practice exceptionalism because religion—the sphere not only of the relation to God, but also of the relation to oneself in inwardness—*is* the exceptional in human life" (ibid., 465).

with Brahman. They see all other paths as inferior and do not count the Christian worldview as an alternative. These can be confronted with the sin of pride in contrast to God before whom no one can claim greatness. The state of the individual as opposed to his beliefs is used to examine the actual position of the individual.

Even the most radical obdurate religious Hindu is still tinged with the aesthetic and ethical lifestyle, given human nature. These sins can be repressed or ignored in this idealistic worldview. The Christian can bring the theoretical plane of thought down to the practical ground of living. This is done in the overt actions and in the thoughts that frame these sins. Inconsistencies can be examined to show how the Advaitin worldview is not only unlivable, but also incapable of meeting the most basic of human problems of dealing with sin. The issue of ignorance through Maya can be juxtaposed with the ignorance that stems from a hardened heart.[27] Personal evangelism confronts both the object of the religious Hindu and the impossibility of avoiding sin in life.

Religiousness B Worldview

Kierkegaard calls for a genuine conversion to Religiousness B, the Christian stage of paradoxes. No innate knowledge discovers the Christian incarnation, "except as God's grace reveals such a truth and illuminates the mind at the same time to believe it as true."[28] Contrary to natural religion, God approaches man and not vice-versa. Even sincere people cannot reach this sphere of transcendence except by divine revelation. This stark landscape is described by Abraham's frustrating inscrutability in offering up Isaac. On one hand, Abraham's certainty and strength is incomprehensible to us. On the other, his horrifying act is like criminal insanity. In a double movement of infinite "resignation" and "faith" Abraham loses all and in that very process he gains all.[29]

Gaining a new self loses the old. The second leap of faith can be horrific to the Hindu, since he falls away not just from his old self, but also from humanity. Seclusion is a very real stigma for the social Hindu. Abraham sacrifices both Isaac and himself. This state cannot harmonize with the previous worldviews but breaks away from all, including ethical standards apart from God. "Christianity not only offends the intellect, but is also an offence to secular standards and values . . . opposing the values of society."[30]

Religious immediacy takes up the opposing resignation and guilt to a higher degree. The painful dying to self of religious life is essentially a life of suffering. The promise of Christ to grant suffering takes what is unpleasant and through the power of God, enables the convert to enjoy this new life of joys and trails.

---

[27]Eph 4:18 addresses this ignorance: "They are darkened in their understanding, alienated from the life of God because of the ignorance that is in them, due to their hardness of heart."

[28]Pojman, *Kierkegaard's Philosophy of Religion*, 57. See also, Soren Kierkegaard, *Eighteen Upbuilding Discourses*, ed. and trans. Howard V. Hong, and Edna H. Hong (Princeton: Princeton University Press, 1990), 303.

[29]Palmer, *Kierkegaard for Beginners*, 109-16. Palmer explains: "The 'dread' is 'a sympathetic antipathy and an antipathetic sympathy.' Abraham's case is negative where he gives up Isaac, and positive where he gets Isaac back. The paradox is that each of these elements occurs at the same time in the same act. In this pain one gains his self. The knight of infinite resignation renounces everything. He loses his ethical self and is infinitely resigned to the loss" (ibid., 116).

[30]Pojman, *Kierkegaard's Philosophy of Religion*, 57. Soren Kierkegaard, *Fear and Trembling and Repetition*, ed. and trans. Howard V. Hong and Edna H. Hong (Princeton: Princeton University Press, 1991), 70.

Religious existence contains a kind of positivity, a new pathos, a higher form of "immediacy." However, this positivity is distinguished from the passion of the aesthetic life by the way it is conditioned by the negative.[31]

The religious individual lives with the paradox that the aesthete and ethicist cannot.[32] The religious person resigns from allegiance to any universal norm, thereby defying ethical standards, in exchange for that which God demands of him. Abraham's absurd motivation to simultaneously lose and gain Isaac makes him appear insane. The religious person does not find isolation severe, since only those lacking experience with God as their benefactor balk at the absurd. The act of infinite resignation is private and existential, not a justified dictum or a socially comprehended pact. To infinitely resign and to infinitely hope for Isaac at the same time is absurd.[33] The Christian gives up his earthly life for the heavenly, knowing that he still lives life in its abundance here on earth. By dying to himself, he attains eternal life, through his relationship with God.

Salvation

Kierkegaard sees salvation as crossing an impassable divide by an existential act of the will. Dialectics aids the path toward the object of faith. "Dialectics itself does not see the absolute, but it leads as it were, the individual up to it."[34] Salvation comes

---

[31] Evans, *Kierkegaard*, 124. Evans further notes: "Revelation is recognizable by mystery, blessedness by suffering, faith's certainty by uncertainty, easiness by difficulty, truth by absurdity; if this is not held fast, then the aesthetic and the religious run together in a common confusion'" (ibid., 124). Evans clarifies this allegiance: "Resignation defines an individual's 'absolute relation to the absolute and a relative relation to the relative.' A person unwilling to give up relative good for the absolute shows that he is not absolutely committed. 'Resignation' initially describes the religious life" (ibid., 137).

[32] Martin J. De Nys, "Faith, Self-Transcendence, and Reflection," *International Journal for Philosophy of Religion* 51 (2002): 121-38. De Nys claims: "That without reference to the task of radical self-transcendence religious symbolism is empty, and that without reference to religious symbolism that task is at least in grave danger of being blind" (ibid., 138).

[33] Palmer, *Kierkegaard for Beginners*, 117-25. Abraham's action has no relation to ethics, morality, and law: "Abraham's whole action stands in no relation to the universal . . . . By his act he has overstepped the ethical entirely" (ibid., 117). He believed God's promise and that God would not require Isaac of him. This was absurd since it could not be humanly calculated what God would do. "He believed by virtue of the absurd; for all human reckoning had long since ceased to function" (ibid., 121). Abraham's belief is in two mutually exclusive ideas at the same time and he acts on these contradictory beliefs in the same project. Abraham is not simply incomprehensible but mad. Incomprehensibly by virtue of his insanity Abraham became the father of faith. The intangible dimension of Abraham's madness establishes an absolute relation to God. "Abraham was greater than all, great by reason of his power whose strength is impotence, great by reason of his wisdom whose strength is foolishness, great by virtue of his hope whose form is madness, great by reason of the love which is hatred of oneself" (ibid., 123). This is lonely: "One knight of faith can in no way help another knight of faith. Comradeship is unthinkable in this realm . . . . For only an individual, just as an individual, can become a knight of faith" (ibid., 125). Only God judges the knight's madness as divinely inspired or demoniacal as the two types of lunacy appear the same. Kierkegaard's knight of faith is in absolute isolation. Kierkegaard's severity drove more people out of the religious sphere than into it. But anyone who could be driven out of the religious sphere by rhetoric did not belong there initially. However, Kierkegaard's celebration of absurdity exceeds any apparent paradox in Scripture, even when his goal is only to destroy the confidence of Christendom in Hegelian rationalism.

[34] Ronald M. Green, *Kierkegaard and Kant: The Hidden Debt* (Albany: State University of New York, 1992), 121. Green further notes: "Dialectics is a benevolent helper, which discourses and assists in finding where the absolute object of faith and worship is – there where the difference between knowledge and ignorance collapses in absolute worship with a consciousness of ignorance, there where the

from without and not within, despite the strong role that the internal will plays. Christian dialectic differs from the Socratic one by its emphasis on God's action.[35]

Understanding the lost Hindu's state helps in witnessing to what he must gain. One such matter is the loss of the self. Despite the Vedantin desire to lose oneself in Brahman, the practical loss of the self is a quiet hazard, as the unbeliever can entirely lose oneself in activity without even noticing it. It is in the subsisted life that the person gains or loses his life, rather than in an idealistic world. We often learn best from those who suffered most in an area, and Christians can best articulate their loss of identity and its recovery. Kierkegaard calls new birth as complicated since discovering one's non-existence is no easy feat. The unborn does not imagine birth. Such is the nature of the evangelistic challenge.[36]

Kierkegaard's indirect speech, like Jesus' parables, shocks people to see truth anew. The Christian leverages analogical truths of commonplace reality to focus the unbeliever on critical verities. Focusing on fitness is folly as death will spoil the goal of health. So also, the unbeliever misunderstands life – in studying for the wrong exam, no infinite preparation can prepare the self to be a self.[37] The Vedantin goal of union with Brahman is flawed as no amount of reincarnation can achieve this false objective.

Kierkegaard's three stages are interrelated, representing ideals with crossovers and varying fits. Each stage incorporates the previous one, progressing by a decisive will in freedom.[38] Each worldview is summarily reviewed for Vedanta apologetics.

Aesthetic Hindus may pursue active home projects or family activities as wholesome goals. These actions can develop in sharp disjunction from life's broader purpose, variously stated in Vedanta or Christianity. Even when life may seem culturally balanced, it is devoid of true spirituality since it is carnal. The pursuit of pleasure, simple or refined, aims for the self-satisfaction for a soul which lacks true self-identity. This effort ends in boredom which manifests itself as despair.

Ethical Hindus recognize the need for moral living. Their law derives from social and religious customs normative in their time and place. They try to be law-abiding

---

resistance of an objective uncertainty tortures forth the passionate certainty of faith, there where the conflict of right and wrong collapses in absolute worship with absolute subjection" (ibid.).

[35]See also, Pojman, *Kierkegaard's Philosophy of Religion*, 94: "The Truth is not within man; rather, man is in error, closed to the truth. The Teacher is necessary to the process of discovering the truth; he must bring it from without and create the condition for man's receiving it. The Moment is decisive for discovering the truth. The Eternal must break into time at a definite point (the fullness of time) and the believer must receive the condition in a moment of contemporaneity with the Teacher."

[36]Soren Kierkegaard, *The Humor of Kierkegaard: An Anthology*, ed. Thomas C. Oden (Princeton: Princeton University Press, 2004), 83-87. The greatest hazard is losing one's self quietly. Also, being born is unthinkable for the unborn. This analogy holds for new birth also. See also Soren Kierkegaard, *Either/Or Part I*, ed. and trans. Howard V. Hong and Edna H. Hong (Princeton: Princeton University Press, 1991), 20: "The melancholy have the best sense of the comic, the opulent often the best sense of the rustic, the dissolute often the best sense of the moral, and the doubter often the best sense of the religious." See also Soren Kierkegaard, *Either/Or Part II*, ed. and trans. Howard V. Hong and Edna H. Hong (Princeton: Princeton University Press, 1991), 191: "The man who lived for his health was, to use one of your expressions, just as hale and hearty as ever when he died."

[37]Kierkegaard, *The Humor of Kierkegaard*, 288.

[38]Ibid., 43. Kierkegaard notes, "The spheres are thus related: immediacy; infinite commonsense; irony; ethics with irony as incognito; humor; religiousness with humor as incognito; and then finally the Christian religiousness recognizable by the paradoxical accentuation of existence, by the paradox, by the breach with immanence, and by the absurd" (ibid.).

citizens and govern their public and private lives through disparate sets of laws. This effort results in guilt which fails to achieve the universal goal.

Religious Hindus belong to generic Religiousness A through innate or false religion. When aware of their problem, they remain in its clutches. All the above unbelieving circumstances can mix and match in varying degrees, but their underlying presuppositions seek selfish pleasure, legal observance, or religious belief. These goals inhabit a matrix of struggle with desolation, culpability, and reaching a watershed.

Christians in Religiousness B order their lives under God. Their order is in a state where the divine mandate overcomes the rest of life.[39] That governance may seem imbalanced for the carnal, moral, or religious Hindu. The Christians is cognizant of this perspective when presenting the gospel to a world of despair, guilt, and crisis.

Conclusion

Kierkegaard is notorious for his celebration of fideism and the absurdity of the Christian faith. His potent statements lose some of their injury when viewed as a polemic against the context of Hegelian rationalism which held his foremost antipathy. However, even when sympathetically reading Kierkegaard, one must cautiously avoid the dangers inherent in radical existentialism that intends to awaken the slumbering soul, but can step deeper into subjectivity, untethered from objectivity, than is biblically warranted. In this qualified sense, the writings of Kierkegaard become an invaluable tool for the Worldview apologist to engage the personal aspects of apologetics in a fresh and dynamic way.

Kierkegaard demonstrated a vital need in existential living where the truth changes lives and grants individuality in God. Apologetics can thus harness the focus of the will – by leveraging the underlying assumptions in the three stages of life. God's truth is multifaceted and delivered in both parables and propositions. The gospel can break resistant wills inured to reason and fact.

Today's aesthetes, ethicists, and religious of Hinduism have their own subconscious worldviews not far removed from that which Kierkegaard powerfully portrays. Our world still seeks to indulge the individual with no lasting purpose for the self. Their despair is treated by psychologists or rotating pleasures. Any morals are clung to with desperation. While the pervasive guilt is nearly eradicated in our vocabulary, it finds expression in deviant behaviors. Christian apologists would be wise to recognize the worldviews of our own times and self-consciously articulate our own. In personally applying the gospel cure in biblical narratives, allegories, and statements on God's terms, Hindu eyes are confronted with the glory of true salvation. Having seen the thrust of personal apologetics, the primacy of the gospel in apologetics is next elucidated.

---

[39]Norman Lillegard, "Passion and Reason: Aristotelian Strategies in Kierkegaard's Ethics," *Journal of Religious Ethics* 30 (2002): 251-73. Lillegard notes: "Salience is a function of cares and desires (passions) and thus governs choice in much the way Aristotle supposes when he describes choice as deliberative desire. Since rationality requires salience it follows that rationality requires passion. Thus Kierkegaard is no more an irrationalist in ethics than is Aristotle, though he continues to be charged with irrationalism" (ibid., 273).

CHAPTER 9
GOSPEL-CENTERED APOLOGETICS

Worldview apologetics to Advaita Vedanta has traversed the cognitive and volitional elements, culminating in a gospel-center. As stated before, Worldview apologetics maintains a vigorous evangelistic thrust. The gospel forms the core of the apologetic encounter, in content as well as in methodology. No specific proof, offense, or defense of Christianity is done in isolation from that gospel drive. The gospel's primacy forms the focal point and also informs the diverse tendrils of effective apologetics.[1]

Kierkegaard's spheres of life illuminated the allegiance that each state of unbelief demands. Human depravity that influences one's heart, mind, and will requires the power of the gospel to release him from these entrapping worldviews.

The Christian biblical worldview of the wholesomeness of life under God counteracts all other world systems. It is not purely rational or emotional, but includes the will and anticipates a supernatural element that initiates the flight from unbelief. Evangelism is a vital component of the Christian worldview and guides human participation in God's mission. Apologetics goes beyond these intellectual and existential realms, to facilitate a genuine spiritual work under God for salvation.

The gospel is central to salvation and thus also central to apologetics.[2] This centrality is possible only when it permeates all of life. The apologetic begins with a biblical framework and transforms every element of our worldview. The gospel is central in our worldview, including these crucial facts: God is the essential, absolute, and personal reality. Jesus is Lord of all – our thought and action ought to submit to God's revelation.[3] God's Spirit enables us to see and live out the objective truth in the Bible.

---

[1]Greg L. Bahnsen, *Van Til's Apologetic: Readings and Analysis* (Phillipsburg, NJ: P&R Publishing, 1998), 461. See also, Walter Campbell Campbell-Jack, Gavin J. McGrath, and Stephen C. Evans, *New Dictionary of Christian Apologetics* (Downers Grove, IL: IVP, 2004), 40: "Reason here [in theological apologetics] does not stand over the gospel, deciding what to accept and what to reject, but rather assumes the gospel as its ultimate explanatory and interpretative framework with which to make sense of all other knowledge and experience. The biblical narrative provides the fiduciary framework, or explanatory hypothesis, for making sense of everything else."

[2]Krish Kandiah, "Lesslie Newbigin's Contribution to a Theology of Evangelism," *Transformation* 24 (2007): 51-59. Newbigin uses election in defending the revelation of Jesus to a specific people in a specific moment in space-time history. The gospel revelation becomes central to the theology of evangelism and apologetics.

[3]See also, Aaron E. Hinkley, "Kierkegaard's Ethics of Agape, the Secularization of the Public Square, and Bioethics," *Christian Bioethics* 17 (2011): 56: "In the revelation of Christ, we are given the

God's revelation must fill our reason, our emotions, our volitions, and our spirit in order to view the world rightly and to live in accord with truth.

Current Evangelistic Apologetics

Many apologetic methodologies seek to honor Christ by utilizing the gospel. However, one can fail to appreciate the breadth of the gospel that spans the entire Christian worldview and addresses all unbelief. Such limited scope can lead to narrow circular arguments for Christianity by engaging only some elements of the unbelieving worldview with the gospel. This approach can make the Christian appear narrow-minded or even incapable of understanding the full-orbed Vedanta viewpoint.[4]

Christians can weaken gospel-centered apologetics by failing to draw out the Christian theological implications, including the depravity of man, the limitations of reason, and the necessity of the gospel.[5] Worldview apologetics centered in the gospel helps advance the Good News in Hindu apologetic contexts as shown previously.

The Worldview apologetic with Vedanta employed the gospel in its various elements. The personal apologetic through Kierkegaard's spheres of life drove home the application of the gospel message.[6] The central gospel thrust for Kierkegaard comes from the depravity of sin and the multitude of ways in which the sinner ensconces himself in patterns that have a death grip on him. The radical nature of the new life in Christ is portrayed as a supernatural action of God.

The Worldview apologetic had a heavy propositional content on the gospel. In the proof section of the apologetic, the nature of God was brought out from the Scriptures and explained in a reasonable manner. God as the absolute Trinity brought out the Trinitarian gospel along with the rationale of communication within the eternal godhead.

The creation of the world was shown in its relation to God from the Scriptures and its logical necessity was drawn out to evince the power of God in the gospel. The nature of man as evidenced from the Scriptures was shown to correspond to what is observed today. Man's central problem was isolated to the issue of sin against God and the only solution was shown to be in the person and work of Jesus Christ. These primary aspects of the proof were central themes from the gospel, while supporting evidences included the design and moral arguments.

The above elements are often associated with the gospel exclusively. In some apologetic methods, these elements are kept until the end of the apologetic encounter

---

example whose life we are to imitate, not simply admire. The command of divine revelation in the person of God incarnate does not ask for mere intellectual assent to the conceptual content therein, but instead a likeness toward which one is to grow ever more like. They are universally applicable because they are the commandments of the lord and creator of the universe, not because any rational human person as such would be able to arrive at the content of these commands through philosophical thought and careful reflection."

[4]John M. Frame, *Apologetics for the Glory of God: An Introduction* (Phillipsburg, NJ: P&R Publishing, 1994), 10, 122. This deficiency of narrow circularity is being addressed by more recent Reformed apologists.

[5]Ibid., 87. See also Norman L. Geisler, "An Apologetic for Apologetics," in *Defending the Faith: Engaging the Culture*, ed. Bruce A. Little and Mark D. Liederbach (Nashville: B&H Publishing Group, 2011), 78-81.

[6]Mark 1:14-15 says, "Now after John was arrested, Jesus came into Galilee, proclaiming the gospel of God, and saying, 'The time is fulfilled, and the kingdom of God is at hand; repent and believe in the gospel.'" Jesus proclaims the Good News and calls people to repent and believe, as the apologist does.

after the other questions plaguing the unbeliever are first addressed. In one sense, such an approach is appropriate where one needs to be able to converse with the other individual in any encounter and in any context that does arise. However, it cannot remain there. Any issue that is raised must provide an occasion to broach the gospel in a broader sense. In the offense section of Vedanta, the unbeliever raised concerns with monism, the Christian response used the Creator-creature distinction to discuss the uniqueness of God, affirming the gospel in the nature of God and humans, which then provided the matrix in which redemption became necessary, culminating in the person and work of Jesus Christ. This gospel thread is not artificially introduced into a disconnected conversation. Rather, the appropriate elements of the biblical worldview were raised in such a fashion as to pull every conversational thread back to the center of the gospel. The conversation moved from disproving monism to validating the rich diversity of the reality in the gospel.

Likewise in the defense section, the historicity of the gospel events was emphasized in a manner that impressed the need for the unbeliever to trust in the truth rather than in mythological stories. The point of contact for the unbeliever was which event actually happened. The gospel was emphasized by noting the historical events of Jesus Christ's death and resurrection that are central to evangelism. These contrasted starkly with Vedanta. The apologetic moved from showing Vedanta's impossible position to how the Christian worldview is fully consistent.

Frame notes how the apologist sees himself as representing God as his ambassador. His evidences included the Scriptures along with other data recognized by the unbeliever. The unbelief of skepticism was addressed by presenting data supporting the scriptural truth. This was done from the position of one who trusts in the gospel. He presents it as bearing down upon the Hindu rather than just something that the unbeliever can dispassionately examine.

Frame calls for a predispositionalism of the heart, where the attitude of the apologist is more vital to a gospel-centered apologetic, even more than his specific words or actions. Thus, the key is to honor Christ as Lord in one's heart and speak freely with the Hindu. One fully utilizes God's means of the gospel in the conversation in order to honor God.[7]

Future of Evangelistic Apologetics

In this section, some vital aspects of apologetics are individually examined from the viewpoint of the gospel. In refining apologetic theory, the need of the hour is fine-tuning the gospel-centered apologetic engagement with unbelieving worldviews. As more sound arguments are built around the gospel and tear down Hindu strongholds of the mind, the Christian can continue to confidently witness to the power of God in the gospel in the ever-changing contexts of unbelief.

In what sense can the gospel be in the forefront of apologetics? Firstly, it must remain the significant data-point in the evidence pool of the apologetic encounter. Next, the reasoning that is applied must leverage this data in drawing conclusions that have a gospel focus in their application. Some areas of foci are further drawn out below.

---

[7]Frame, *Apologetics for the Glory of God*, 88.

Ethics

Observation gains cognition. Virtue regulates our attention relevant to our cognitive concerns. Just as good eyesight helps observe, ethical sensitivity connects the information with its need and relevance.[8] Such use of reason is ethical. As an epistemic component, observation can be misused and virtue also helps to use it correctly. Wittgenstein presupposes judgment when connecting words and reality.[9] Just as discernment filters data, so is ethics vital to knowledge. Kierkegaard shifted the focus from evidence to the knower's state. Virtue epistemology attends to the knower and the qualities of good knowers.[10] We know based on who we are. This denies, not the valid objectivity of the self, but the proud human aspiration for God-knowledge.[11]

The gospel not only provides the data of Christianity, but also the ethical virtue to interpret it. To align the unbeliever's thoughts to the gospel, the appropriate priority is given to this information. Thus, not only are the evidences for the resurrection multiplied, but they are applied toward the death and resurrection of the unbeliever and the crucial danger that the unbeliever faces when rejecting the Christian proposition. The ethics of rejecting the truth are taken further than just their level of appeal. Instead the nature of depravity is impressed to show why that data may not seem as attractive to him. Thus Worldview apologetics highlights the conflict of worldviews or presuppositions, aiming to elevate the gospel. This activity is not a post-apologetic task, but remains central within the apologetic encounter.

---

[8]Christopher Hookway, "Reasons for Belief, Reasoning, Virtues," *Philosophical Studies* 130 (2006): 47-70. He notes that reasons for belief require attending to and using epistemically relevant things; habits guide deliberation, inquiry, and applying the results. Observance is necessary but insufficient. Virtues are vital.

[9]John M. Frame, "Presuppositional Apologetics," in *Five views on Apologetics*, ed. Stanley N. Gundry and Steven B. Cowan (Grand Rapids: Zondervan, 2000), 211-13. The "unbeliever's problem is first ethical, and only secondarily intellectual. His intellectual problems stem from his ethical unwillingness to acknowledge the evidence. Unbelief distorts human thought" (ibid., 211). Also, "reasoning is part of life, and it is subject to ethical predication" (ibid., 213). It can be done righteously or sinfully. See also Terrance W. Klein, "Act and Potency in Wittgenstein?" *The Heythrop Journal* 47 (2006): 601-19. Human knowledge needs judgment to understand. The knowing subject commits the self to what is perceived, an act present and implicated in every perceived object. Marechal argued that human beings possess an inchoate awareness of Absolute Being, out of which they judge the adequacy of any provisional formulation of what exists. Wittgenstein showed words as parts of worlds and have no meaning apart from them.

[10]Jason A. Mahn, "Kierkegaard After Hauerwas," *Theology Today* 64 (2007): 172-85. Mahn notes, "Still, the return of the virtues among Christians, so long as it emphasizes the increasing naturalness or ease of faithfulness, risks domesticating the unbounded love of God through Jesus Christ" (ibid., 185). See also David K. Naugle, *Worldview: The History of a Concept* (Grand Rapids: Eerdmans, 2002), 310.

[11]Stephen C. Evans, *Kierkegaard: An Introduction* (Cambridge: Cambridge University Press, 2009), 164, 46-56. Evans notes: "Kierkegaard does not want to deny that the self is a substantial reality. A 'logical system is possible' but 'a system of existence is impossible' for an existing human person. We humans are not God, and thus cannot see the world from God's point of view. Thus, uncertainty is simply a part of the human condition and the classical foundationalist aspires to transcend that condition" (ibid., 164). Also: "The fact that neither the ethicist nor the aesthete can produce a logical proof or demonstration that makes his or her viewpoint objectively certain is not a reason to despair. We human beings find uncertainty painful, and we would like to escape it" (ibid., 46). "Modern epistemology has typically ignored the knower and focused only on questions about evidence. From Kierkegaard's perspective, this is an error; what we can know is conditioned by the kinds of people we are" (ibid., 56). See also J. P. Moreland, *The God Question: An Invitation to a Life of Meaning* (Eugene, OR: Harvest House Publishers, 2009), 153.

Assertion

The apologist reminds the unbeliever's predicament by presenting propositional truth. The content and cogent presentation of this truth forms the apologetic. Considering the unbelieving mind's natural resistance, given its ethical and spiritual bias, the gospel may be better communicated via assertion followed by a sound explanation. The alternative where the truth is explained in a manner acceptable to the unbeliever cannot get off the ground, far less present the gospel thrust adequately.[12] Alistair McGrath, like Van Til, shifts the focus from explaining the unbeliever's many neural short-circuits to explaining explicability itself. He favorably quotes Aquinas that one could not prove God's existence by argument. But one could identify reasons for an explanatory framework in observing order in the universe and other such factors that make complete sense given the already affirmed God of the Bible.[13]

Framework

The Worldview apologetic to Vedanta demonstrated a broad, reformed framework for apologetics. Ted Peters cautions against merely explaining details and recommends local explanations only within the broader explanation.[14] This approach displaces even noble and lofty human constructs from the apologetic center. Instead all such efforts are made subordinate to display the gospel's grand meta-narrative. In this framework, the gospel permeates all aspects of apologetics. It is better positioned to pierce the mind's darkness, to excise tumors of error, and to patch in knowledge gaps in the noetic framework of the unbeliever.

Within this context of the grand gospel display, lies the explicatory function of reason and supplementary evidence. The unbeliever's role switches from student or

---

[12]David Owens, "Testimony and Assertion," *Philosophical Studies* 130 (2006): 105. A number of writers have recently questioned if an assertion can transmit knowledge only as evidence for the truth of the proposition asserted. Instead they note that successful testimony works by getting the audience to believe what the speaker asserts while putting the responsibility of justifying that belief on the speaker.

[13]See also, Alister McGrath, "Paley Memorial Sermon," *Science & Christian Belief* 18 (2006): 187: "It is the intelligibility of the universe itself that requires explanation. It is not the gaps in our understanding of the world, as the very comprehensiveness of that understanding, which requires an explanation." McGrath's reasons for stating this are not pragmatic but rooted in and energized by Christian theology: "Belief in God possesses immense explanatory vitality. C. S. Lewis believed Christianity because in seeing it like the sun, he could see all else through it as this meaning resonated with reality. A naturalistic world-view presupposes its conclusions. The world's order and our capacity to discern this needs to be explained; it is also a fundamental assumption of the scientific method itself" (ibid.). This is directly valid for Vedanta. See also R. C. Sproul, *Defending Your Faith: An Introduction to Apologetics* (Wheaton, IL: Crossway Books, 2003), 18. Calvin noted the distinction between proof and persuasion. Proof is objective and persuasion is subjective. People who are hostile to certain ideas may have those ideas proven to them, but in their bias they refuse to be persuaded – even by the soundest of arguments.

[14]Ted Peters, "Christian God-Talk While Listening to Atheists, Pluralists, and Muslims," *A Journal of Theology* 46 (2007): 84, 98. The atheists have no place in the world for God. God is missing from the equations; God does not aid with explaining specific natural phenomena; thus, no God exists. Must Christian apologists go to the equations and add the divine? Peters does not recommend this. Rather, the role of the concept of God in our explanations is more comprehensive, drawing on scientific knowledge of the physical world and knowledge from special revelation in Jesus Christ. Scientific explanations are methodologically reductionistic to look for proximate physical causes when making an explanation, excluding divine creation and providence. This is fine, if the reduction remains within the research domain. But the theologian offers a comprehensive explanation based on theology. This is just as valid against Vedanta. See also John Coates, "Chesterton's New Style in Apologetics," *Renascence* (2003): 236.

prosecuting attorney to defendant on a dock. Here his charges are cogently explained using the acuity of reason, but the apologetic primarily presents the indictment using the now established law of the land in the framework. Even as the defendant lives by other rules – he is no longer unaware of the gospel law or the guilt in his arraignment.

Aquinas argues that the human mind has limited competence to discover the divine ground of all things, but the higher sphere of truth is impenetrable to man. For him, God's presence is demonstrated, not proved, using reason while biblical authority is used for truths beyond reason.[15] Worldviews frame this apologetic state as

> a commitment, a fundamental orientation of the heart, that can be expressed as a story or in a set of presuppositions (assumptions which may be true, partially true or entirely false) which we hold (consciously or subconsciously, consistently or inconsistently) about the basic constitution of reality, and that provides the foundation on which we live and move and have our being.[16]

Ronald Nash sees presuppositions as axioms governing a theorem. Natural theology reminds the obvious state of affairs in the gospel framework, even if unable to prove the self-evident to the unbeliever.[17] The historic frameworks developed in a semi-theistic locale of a largely Christian world have an altered function in today's non-theistic and anti-theistic contexts. Apologetics is executed now in an active atmosphere of false religion, naturalism, pluralism, and relativism. The gospel framework is best suited for all the changing environs of the future, as it can engage every unbelieving worldview even when the specific topics of the debate change.

Logic

The unbeliever can use logic to raise apparent contradictions in the Scriptures like God being both one and triune. The Christian understands the unbeliever's difficulty, along with limitations of the same logic. Logic can explicate the apparent contradictions, but it cannot illuminate the mysteries of God without revelation. The Christian locates the basis of reason in the rationality of God. The unbeliever uses the tools of logic with no base, while Van Til recommends an analogical thinking from God.[18] Van Til sees the unbeliever, as the autonomous authority, using reason in a monistic manner. The interpretive divergence springs from the drastically different points of reference of the believer from those of the unbeliever.[19]

---

[15]Avery Dulles, *A History of Apologetics* (San Francisco: Ignatius Press, 1999), 113-22. Revealed truth is in harmony as revelation and natural truths coexist. Church dogma corresponds to human need.

[16]James W. Sire, *The Universe Next Door: A Basic Worldview Catalog* (Downers Grove, IL: InterVarsity Press, 2004), 17. False worldviews are best confronted with right ones before filling in the gaps.

[17]Ronald H. Nash, *Faith and Reason: Searching for a Rational Faith* (Grand Rapids: Zondervan, 1988), 28, 102. See also R.C. Sproul, John Gerstner, and Arthur Lindsley, *Classical Apologetics: A Rational Defense of the Christian Faith and a Critique of Presuppositional Apologetics* (Grand Rapids: Zondervan Publishing House, 1984), 47, 245-46.

[18]John M. Frame, *Cornelius Van Til: An Analysis of His Thought* (Phillipsburg, NJ: P&R Publishing, 1995), 152-54. See also Cornelius Van Til, *The Intellectual Challenge of the Gospel* (Phillipsburg, NJ: Lewis J. Grotenhuis, 1953), 9: The "non-Christian scientist discovers truth . . . not because of, but in spite of, his own theory of being and of knowledge."

[19]Cornelius Van Til, *The Defense of the Faith* (Phillipsburg, NJ: Presbyterian and Reformed

Thus the gospel provides the base from which logic proceeds, by positing the existence of reason in God. The gospel also forms the goal of the logical argument, by returning the conversation back to this mysterious God, now revealed by Scriptures – so that the unbeliever is not left merely with a logical argument to puzzle over, but a fully orbed gospel mandate which the discussion demands.

To critique standalone logic, Kierkegaard's attack of Hegel's reasoning can extend to all human systems of reasoning, including faulty Christians ones, that demand our complete allegiance.[20] He strongly emphasizes making truths real rather than abstract in individual lives.[21] However, objective truth is also necessary today where pragmatism and postmodernism are rampant. The gospel extends from the objective reasons to the subjective dimensions.[22] The gospel's powerful logic takes the historic events of Jesus Christ to bear upon the meta-narrative of God's redemption that must be appropriated by each person.

Biblical Warrant

Biblical warrant precedes pragmatism. The Bible presents God with evidences rather than prove him. It also represents the depths of his character. The truth of God's being and his attributes come from both natural revelation and the gospel narrative woven from Genesis to Revelation. Natural theology expands natural revelation for the believer to glorify God. To convince the lay of the biblical land to an outlaw whose own edicts are intellectually, emotionally, and volitionally seared into his spiritually dead being, is like teaching a plant to think. The plant turns to the light that shines on it. Explaining the operations and reasoning behind the light makes little difference to the plant. Humans are not plants, but the epistemic faculty of a depraved mind fails to grasp the spiritual truth.

Todd Furman, who is no Christian, claims that natural theology fails to convince him as a self-proclaimed, unbiased investigator. No facts are "brute" facts to be evaluated neutrally, but all are interpreted on the basis of presuppositions.[23] Furman castigates the eager-believer for offering categorically inappropriate evidence, begging

---

Publishing Co., 1967), 212, 218.

[20]Jamie Turnbull, "Kierkegaard on Emotion: A Critique of Furtak's *Wisdom in Love*," *Religious Studies* 46 (2010): 489-508. Turnbull notes: "Kierkegaard is concerned to make the case that religious love cannot be understood as a variety of cognitive phenomena, precisely to prevent it from being naturalized to Hegelian terms" (ibid., 508).

[21]Tamara Monet Marks, "Kierkegaard's 'New Argument' for Immortality," *Journal for Religious Ethics* 38 (2010): 143-86. Marks notes: "Kierkegaard's innovative argument for immortality introduced a new concern – that the resurrection is a cause for both joy and fear. With his emphasis on immortality as a task, a test in this life, *and* a fact in eternity, Kierkegaard desired to put an end to mere demonstrations and erroneous conceptions of it. He intended his argument to motivate one toward living a life in the belief that eternity is one's final goal" (ibid., 186).

[22]Murray A. Rae, "Kierkegaard and the Historians," *International Journal for Philosophy of Religion* 37 (1995): 87-102. Rae says: "Clearly the requirement to imitate requires a body of reliable historical knowledge concerning the character of Jesus' life" (ibid., 102). Kierkegaard had a high regard but did not emphasize the historicity and authenticity of the scriptures. See also Mark Brumley, *How Not to Share your Faith: The Seven Deadly Sins of Catholic Apologetics and Evangelization* (San Diego: Catholic Answers, 2002), 30.

[23]Kenneth D. Boa and Robert M. Bowman Jr., *Faith Has Its Reasons: Integrative Approaches to Defending the Christian Faith* (Colorado: Paternoster, 2005), 260-62.

the question, or concluding more than the argument allows.[24] Christian arguments are not necessarily faulty, but fail to appeal to an unbelieving mind. The premises of an unbelieving worldview intentionally exclude knowledge of God, along with the deductive movement from the phenomenal to the noumenal categories.

Kant sees natural theology as transcendental theology, faulting it as flawed for trying to prove God's existence and attributes for all people. While Christians disagree with his reasoning to arrive at the false conclusion – it does illustrate fallen man's unwillingness and inability to find the right conclusions from the same data points. Not many can debate Kant successfully to disprove him on his turf.[25] Kant raised a false knowledge barrier between the world as it appears to us and as it really is. He intended for reason to make way to faith in attaining to knowledge. The unbeliever's knowledge remains incomplete without regeneration, given the constraint of his depraved will.[26] Likewise, Kierkegaard did not endorse the traditional proofs for God's existence:

> He regarded them as spiritually pointless, and, in any case, it was rather the ethical and psychological correlates of religious (or nonreligious) life that drew his attention.[27]

The unbeliever rejects the believer's arguments although they are right and presented in detail. The gospel centered apologetic connects natural theology as a key element between creation and the epistemic faculty of man. It reminds the unbeliever's suppression of truth that causes the apparent failure of natural theology, thereby maintaining the primacy of the gospel as the power of God to save him. The biblical warrant thus models how the apologist can maintain the gospel as the foundation of Worldview apologetics.[28]

---

[24]Todd M. Furman, "In Praise of Hume: What's Right about Hume's Attacks on Natural Theology," in *In Defense of Natural Theology: A Post-Humean Asessment*, ed. James F. Sennett and Douglas Groothuis (Downers Grove, IL: InterVarsity Press, 2005), 42-43. This failure is despite Sennett's modest claims for natural theology, far short of arguing for theism, but "that a being (or beings) with a given characteristic exists (or has existed)" (ibid., 85).

[25]Frederick Copleston, *A History of Philosophy,* vol. 6, *Modern Philosophy,* pt. 2, *Kant* (Garden City, NY: Image Books, 1960), 46, 77, 93. Walter Campbell Campbell-Jack, Gavin J. McGrath, and Stephen C. Evans, *New Dictionary of Christian Apologetics* (Downers Grove, IL: IVP, 2004), 716.

[26]Ronald H. Nash, *Life's Ultimate Questions: An Introduction to Philosophy* (Grand Rapids: Zondervan, 1999), 265. Louis Markos, *Apologetics for the Twenty-First Century* (Wheaton, IL: Crossway, 2010), 105.

[27]Ronald M. Green, *Kierkegaard and Kant: The Hidden Debt* (Albany: State University of New York, 1992), 124. The religious thought relates to Kant's dismantling of traditional theology. Rational proofs of God's existence hardly interested him. Green says, "Neither was he an anti-rationalist, however, and for this reason it was important for him to base his own fresh and distinctive approach on a justified repudiation of the style of religious thinking that preceded him" (ibid.). See also Rodney Stark, *For the Glory of the God* (Princeton: Princeton University Press, 2003), 149.

[28]This emphasis is brought out well in Bryan Billard Sims, "Evangelical Worldview Analysis: A Critical Assessment and Proposal" (Ph.D. diss., Southern Baptist Theological Seminary, 2006). See also K. Scott Oliphint, "Cornelius Van Til and the Reformation of Christian Apologetics," in *Revelation and Reason: New essays in Reformed apologetics*, ed. K. Scott Oliphint and Lane G. Tipton (Phillipsburg, NJ: P&R Publishing, 2007), 302. Reformed theology consistently applies Bible teaching in apologetic methodology.

Bigotry

Gospel presuppositions may cause Christians to appear biased to the unbeliever. In daily speech, explicit hard-headed bias on fundamental issues leads to bigotry and rarely wins over people. Can such a method be employed in the sacred task of apologetics and evangelism? While Christians can wield the gospel as a heavy-handed tool, theological exclusivism must not shape sinful social attitudes or deflect the godliness demanded of believers. The Christian must be godly in modeling the gospel even when presenting it to the unbeliever in gentleness and respect.[29] The bigotry blame changes when the person is converted and is able to see aright.

When God changes the heart in regeneration, the mysterious leap from the secular to the Christian worldview becomes understandable.[30] The heart already loves God's world even as it struggles to let go of its past love.[31] Kierkegaard's apologetic focus addresses those who cannot yet experientially comprehend the mystery of a new biblical worldview. Balancing a right handling of cognitive knowledge and applying it in the appropriate affective contexts of individuals' lives is a vital skill for the contemporary apologist, replacing bigotry with love. The gospel lends itself to both, and is relevant to the individual state of affairs, which desperately needs a remedy.

Two Camps

Believers and unbelievers are the only two camps in the gospel perspective. From a human perspective, strict adherents of both camps are clearly distinguishable – the regenerate demonstrably live for Jesus and the convinced faithful of other religions, including Vedanta, are the unregenerate. From God's perspective the latter group is rebellious, as are many who span the broad spectrum between the two camps. Humanly speaking, all non-believers are ontologically and epistemically opposed to the gospel, but not all realize it. So the task of engaging the unbeliever who may be antagonistic, skeptical, inquisitive, or even sympathetic does require different approaches to engage with the same gospel. This was demonstrated in personal apologetics that confronted the will of the placating and obdurate Hindu. But underlying each approach is a conscious understanding of what element of the gospel the unbeliever needs to hear and how this must be presented in order to honor God and hope for the salvation of the unbeliever.

---

[29]Stephen M. Merino, "Religious Diversity in a 'Christian Nation': The Effects of Theological Exclusivity and Interreligious Contact on the Acceptance of Religious Diversity," *Journal for the Scientific Study of Religion* 49 (2010): 234-35. Theologically exclusive beliefs may cause poorly viewing those outside. God's rejection of non-Christian faiths may legitimate social exclusion of non-Christians. In addition to the primary role of personal beliefs, personal experiences with diversity may also play a role in shaping attitudes toward non-Christians. See also Michael W. Payne, "Philosophy among the Ruins: The Twentieth Century and Beyond," in *Revolutions in Worldview*, ed. Andrew Hoffecker (Phillipsburg, NJ: P&R Publishing, 2007), 355.

[30]Travis Tucker, "Kierkegaard's Purity of Heart and the 'Sunday-Monday' Gap," *Theology Today* 67 (2010): 24-35. Tucker notes: "The confessional perspective [regularly before God] aids the worker by developing and requiring at least three traits: personal unity, quietness, and self-knowledge [and ethical lifestyle that honors God on Monday]" (ibid., 35).

[31]Walter Kaufmann, "Kierkegaard," *Theology Today* 67 (2010): 24-35. Kaufmann notes: "More than any other writer, SK confronts us with the question: What does it mean to be a Christian? . . . . He presses us for a decision, one way or the other . . . . He sees that religion without intensity as a contradiction in terms" (ibid., 35).

Authenticity

Personal apologetics aims both directly and indirectly at the unbeliever's volition. It applies reason reflectively at cognition and will.[32] Authentic selfhood in faith contrasts with inauthentic selfhood in sin.[33] For example, concrete love for individuals challenges an abstract love for an idea, showing the actual state of man to be phony. Likewise, God alone is necessary.

For Kierkegaard, the experience of God has universal rational validity since truth is subjectivity. Humans exist contingently. Faith connects a contingent, inauthentic, and divided man to God. This experiential faith lacks theoretical certainties. The Christian believes by not knowing about God, but by knowing him. Subjectivity can waver, but it does not disbelieve. Faith can fear and tremble in the face of God and life, but does it without despair.[34] This is especially so for the ethical suspension under divine order, as God's revelation protects Christians from sinful, self-interpreted ethical suspensions, even if Kierkegaard himself is not as neat as some attempts to tidy him.[35]

Faith sharply transitions our mode of thinking. Faith's religious movement is beyond the self's will – it resigns but dares not on its own.[36] Only God can grant it confidence. Kierkegaard draws upon this authentic life in apologetics, which is a crucial element of the gospel. Those who come to Christ have life and have it abundantly. The yoke of Christ is not burdensome but easy. The promise of Christ is freedom in truth. Gospel-centered apologetics wisely targets the depraved, autonomous will with wisdom in addition to addressing its cognitive demands. As Kierkegaard puts it, only the gospel lovingly challenges that inauthentic autonomy to facilitate faith in God.[37]

---

[32]Evans, *Kierkegaard*, 24-30. Double reflection – "Genuine subjective understanding requires that a person first grasp the relevant concepts (first reflection), but then go on and think through what it would mean to apply those concepts to the person's own life (second reflection)" (ibid., 30).

[33]Samuel Loncar, "From Jena to Copenhagen: Kierkegaard's Relations to German Idealism and the Critique of Autonomy in The Sickness Unto Death," *Religious Studies* 47 (2011): 201-16. Loncar states: "Seen at least partly as an attack on autonomy, Kierkegaard's theory of the self may be as relevant now as it was when he developed it" (ibid., 216).

[34]Simon D. Podmore, "Kierkegaard as Physician of the Soul: On Self-Forgiveness and Despair," *Journal of Psychology and Theology* 37 (2009): 174-85. Podmore notes: "The infinite qualitative difference between self-forgiveness and divine forgiveness (between human impossibility and the sacred possibility of acceptance) asserts that the self should accept the forgiveness which, by ensuing from the divine *Other*, exceeds and transcends the self's introspective capacities for self-diagnosis and even despair" (ibid., 185).

[35]Zachary R. Manis, "Kierkegaard and Evans on the Problem of Abraham," *Journal of Religious Ethics* 39 (2011): 488: "If I have interpreted Kierkegaard correctly, his view implies that even though the scenario I have called "the problem of Abraham" is a possible state of affairs, God ensures that no one in the actual world ever (1) faces this scenario, (2) sincerely seeks God's true will in the matter, and yet (3) falls into grave moral error, nonetheless, because of a failure to discern God's will correctly. I do not pretend to have provided compelling evidence that this is Kierkegaard's own view."

[36]Lev Shestov, *Kierkegaard and the Existential Philosophy*, trans. Elinor Hewitt (Athens: Ohio University Press, 1969), 194-204, 75-84. Kierkegaard says, "I cannot accomplish the movement of faith; I cannot close my eyes and fling myself without a glance into the abyss of the Absurd" (ibid., 204). Shestov notes: "The obstacle between Kierkegaard and faith was not evil will. On the contrary, his entire will, of the sort to be found only in man – a will both good and evil – sought faith with an infinitely passionate intensity, but it did not arrive at faith and went no further than resignation. To realize the ideal of resignation is within the power of the man, but he does not find in his soul the capacity for the final act of daring." (ibid., 84).

[37]Mark L. McCreary, "Deceptive Love: Kierkegaard on Mystification and Deceiving into the Truth," *Journal of Religious Ethics* 39 (2011): 25-47. McCreary says, "Just as Jesus sought to help people

Individual Gospel

For the Worldview apologist who is theologically Reformed, every person needs to be given the gospel, beginning wherever the person may be at. Sometimes it begins with the emphasis on the holy creator God. Sometimes it begins with man in his current state of sin. Sometimes it begins with the person and work of Jesus. Sometimes it just begins with the person recognizing his need for the savior, to repent and believe. The point of engagement for the individual can be as diverse as each person and the state of his soul at the time of meeting. Wherever the engagement begins, it must encompass the entire gospel worldview for the unbeliever to understand and to be challenged to submit to God. The gospel does address all states of life, so that no one can claim that his particular situation is somehow beyond the Good News. The apologist must be able to bring the specific truth to bear upon the unbeliever. As seen with the obdurate religious Hindu, true knowledge of God is contrasted with the idolatry of Vedanta, while pressing the matter further into the issues of pride and sin, to which the unbeliever is blind.

At the other end, Kierkegaard claims that "truth is subjectivity."[38] His statement interprets well in a context of endemic objective truth with rampant infidelity. With the separation of thought and being in existential life, the relation between subjectivity and objectivity is not limited to epistemology, but extends to psychology, society, culture and religion.[39] Worldview apologetics must press the life-effects of belief and its consequences to the individual for meaning in life, even as this was done to the aesthetic Vedantin, with the gospel content.

Rigor

The Worldview apologist does not hide behind the framework presented with the gospel. He must rather rigorously engage with the various logical arguments and an array of evidences that support the biblical worldview within the context of the gospel presentation. Not every apologist can be an expert on every method to explain every available auxiliary support. The believer who knows the basics of the gospel is already a qualified apologist in keeping with the biblical mandate from 1 Peter 3:15.

Christians who develop their apologetics further can engage the philosophers of the world to bring every thought captive by clearly drawing out the folly of unbelief from the gospel base. Van Til exposed the philosophical problems underlying areas like

---

receive and respond to God's love, so also our love ought to aim at helping others love God" (ibid., 47). See also Benno van den Toren, "Challenges and Possibilities of Inter-religious and Cross-cultural Apologetic Persuasion," *Evangelical Quarterly* 82 (2010): 61-62. The worldview falls in place with Christ at the center.

[38] Robert Bretall, *A Kierkegaard Anthology* (Princeton: Princeton University Press, 1946), 210.

[39] See also, Mark C. Taylor, "Natural Selfhood and Ethical Selfhood in Kierkegaard," in *The Humor of Kierkegaard*, ed. Harold Bloom (Philadelphia: Chelsea House Publishers, 1989), 171-72: "The systematic idea is the subject-object, the oneness of thought and being. Existence, on the other hand, is their separation. It does not by any means follow that existence is thoughtless; but it has brought about, and brings about a separation between subject and object, thought and being." See also Matthew Gerhard, "Kierkegaard on Truth," *Religious Studies* 38 (2002): 27-44. Gerhard notes: "Kierkegaard certainly does have an objective reference in his notion of truth. The relationship itself is entirely determined by certain objective facts about certain acts of God in history for the benefit of man. Kierkegaard's notion of truth as subjectivity is itself based upon what Kierkegaard claims to be an objective reference" (ibid., 44).

possibility to acknowledge God or to autonomously submit to chaos.[40] How does this apologetic element fit in the broader gospel framework? It is but one of many links that shows the flaws of the non-Christian worldview.

Christian claims are typically substantiated within its own framework. But this runs into William Lane Craig's conflict between "know and show."[41] The Christian's confidence comes from knowing the gospel to be true. His apologetic strength is proportionate to its ability to showcase the gospel to the unbeliever. As shown in Worldview apologetics to Vedanta, this is shown, not by adopting the unbeliever's references, but by exposing the other worldview's internal inconsistencies and emptiness at its foundations. It then explains how those discrepancies are reconciled in the gospel which alone can address the failed attempts of man in his autonomous worship of idols and himself. Therein is the future of gospel-centered Worldview apologetics. Such an enterprise would show all unbelieving worldviews to lack valid foundations. Their internal inconsistencies would then become demonstrably unlivable without an anchor. Thus it presents a strong opportunity to extol God and the means he provides in the gospel that can not only sustain itself, but also rescue the unbeliever from his folly.

Conclusion

Worldview apologetics presented in this book has spread the gamut on the various methodological aspects of apologetics. It has provided a gospel thrust in its evangelistic presentation by adding a focus on the individual will. The current apologetic leverage of the gospel and the scope for greater fidelity to the gospel in its various dimensions, provide hope for even more robust engagements with diverse worldviews.

The Worldview apologetic needs to substantiate its gospel claims and fill current gaps by vigorously integrating specific apologetic work from other approaches within its framework. It must continue to develop stronger arguments to justify its own framework and its ability to showcase how the opposing worldview is impossible to develop or live without borrowing from the Christian worldview. This broadens its line of attack and tightens the gospel presentation. It can learn from Boethius' engaging pagans with well-defined terms.[42] Timothy Keller exemplifies taking the theological language and adapting it to the language of the culture and the world. The challenge in this process is avoiding compromise in language or thought.

Every Christian apologist's ultimate purpose is for God to be glorified in evangelism. The Worldview apologist relies on the power of God in the gospel to save the unbeliever. The believer does well to proclaim Christ; to coherently explain the breadth of the gospel in all its theological out-workings is better; to further address the correspondence relation of the gospel to reality in its broader outworking is even better; to be able to show the folly of the opposition is best. However, every believer can and must begin with the gospel. From the newborn Christian to the most knowledgeable apologist, all need to rely front and center on the gospel.

---

[40]Bahnsen, *Van Til's Apologetic*, 281. His explanation for philosophical possibility resting in the nature of God, reflects the issues with the system of his time rather than current debates.

[41]William Lane Craig, *Reasonable Faith* (Wheaton, IL: Crossway, 2008), 51. His distinction is vital, but not as strong in a reformed theological setting.

[42]William Edgar and K. Scott Oliphint, *Christian Apologetics Past & Present: A Primary Source Reader* (Wheaton, IL: Crossway, 2009), 1: 315-19.

In a disillusioned world with crumbling edifices, the gospel is not naturally attractive to the lost. Believers must live out the gospel, proclaim it boldly, and love their neighbor as they love Jesus. They must speak the truth in love and trust the Lord to save.

Satyaputra rightly notes that God works even through limited evidence, just as he does through preaching and witnessing.[43] However, this does not diminish the various apologetic tools that the Christian has at his disposal. Even Pascal's wager, crass though it may seem, has its rightful place to culminate rather than be the apologetic base.[44]

Kierkegaard drew the temptation to sin down into the earthly sphere of individual responsibility, under God's sovereignty.[45] He said that we live according humanity's understanding of what it is to be a person. However, our capacity is too much rather than too little.[46] We need God to take away our own wisdom and for him to give us his life. What evangelism exists without that visceral call to fall before God, all arguments besides? When all is said and done, one thing remains – a plea to let God be our Lord through the clarion call of the gospel.[47]

---

[43] Agus Gunawan Satyaputra, "The Problem of Objectivity in History and the Use of Historical Evidence in Christian Apologetic," *Evangel 25 (2007)*: 79. Accepting the reliability of evidence does not make us Christians. Committing our lives rather than intellectual decisions is vital. Logic and evidence cannot force anyone into the kingdom. Evidence helps reach and challenge unbelievers by the Holy Spirit.

[44] Costica Bradatan, "Rhetoric of Faith and Patterns of Persuasion in Berkeley's Alciphron," *The Heythrop Journal* 47 (2006): 555. Humans accept logical, philosophical, historical, authoritative, evidential and utility support. This does not mean philosophical arguments are weak or inadequate; but there is an abundance of argument, of diverse nature and types of force, for accepting Christian theism.

[45] Simon D. Podmore, "The Lightning and the Earthquake: Kierkegaard on the Anfechtung of Luther," *The Heythrop Journal* 47 (2006): 570.

[46] Alvin Plantinga, *Warranted Christian Belief* (New York: Oxford University Press, 2000), 81. Bruce S. Thornton, *Plagues of the Mind: The New Epistemic of False Knowledge* (Wilmingdon, DE: ISI Books, 2004), 5. David R. Hall, *The Seven Pillories of Wisdom* (Macon, GA: Mercer University Press, 1990), 23. Nancy Pearcey, *Total Truth: Liberating Christianity from Its Cultural Captivity* (Wheaton, IL: Crossway, 2004), 217.

[47] Soren Kierkegaard, *For Self-Examination and Judge for Yourself,* ed. and trans. Howard V. Hong and Edna H. Hong (Princeton: Princeton University Press, 1990), 86-87.

CHAPTER 10
THE PAST, THE PRESENT, AND THE FUTURE

This book presented a practical Christian Worldview apologetic to Vedanta Hindus. It highlighted the framework, key methodological strengths, and the broad areas where it is applied in the context of Advaita. This book focused our apologetics in a biblically self-aware approach to honor God in our apologetics. In the process, it validated a strong defense of the Christian faith against Advaita Vedanta.

Worldview Apologetic

The Worldview apologetic followed the biblical mandate to honor Christ by boldly providing a reason for the faith with gentleness and respect. The reasons were provided in the proof, offense, and defense categories, while retaining theological, personal, and interpersonal fidelity. Calvin's views on faith and depravity were extensively used through the Worldview apologetic. While Kierkegaard and Frame were mainly used in the framework, several apologists were used to provide robust responses, including C. S. Lewis' Moral Argument. Thus, the Reformed apologetic was used as a framework in Worldview apologetics, with strong support from the Classical and Evidential methods. The positive elements of Fideism were specifically covered through Kierkegaard's personal apologetic. The success of the Worldview apologetic engagement was hinged on faithfulness to God.

The book applied the principles of Worldview apologetics to engage Advaita Vedanta with the biblical responses of historical Christianity. It took maximum advantage of a Reformed theological perspective in approaching the daunting philosophical challenges of Vedanta, since it had not yet been addressed sufficiently by Christian apologists of the Reformed persuasion. This book hoped to meet in some small part, what was lacking as an overall integrated Christian Worldview apologetic to Vedanta. It explored such an engagement and hopefully opened up more vistas for the evangelism of Vedanta Hindus.

In using Vedanta as a case study for Worldview apologetic, a detailed study of Vedanta was made, including its flavors of Advaita, Visistadvaita, and Dvaita. With sufficient details for each, Advaita was chosen as the primary Hindu worldview to engage in apologetics. The Worldview apologetic engaged with presuppositions and reasoned assertions of Advaita, using Vedanta's internal debates to bring out its areas of weakness.

The Worldview apologetic took specific care to avoid the extremes of conceding truth for rapprochement or drawing a harder line than necessary in refuting the errors of Advaita. The points of contact were not simply embraced for the apologetic engagement, although they were recognized and used to highlight the differences that inhere in them. For example, the issue of dependence of the world on Brahman was used to acknowledge dependence, but the discussion emphasized the nature of that dependence and the ontological difference between the worlds. This careful line was used in engaging the entire worldview from a Christian framework.

The Worldview apologetic used the proof, offense, and offense from John Frame. The proof section maintained the presentation of each worldview from within its own framework and definitions. This granted a comprehensive presentation of the Christian presuppositions and its consequent belief system. The Christian worldview was framed around the gospel and the proof was presented mainly to target areas of particular concern with the opposing worldview, ignoring those arguments common in other engagements, but irrelevant to the Vedantin. The Christian worldview was presented in its entirety around the gospel with supporting information to make cogent connections to the thought processes of the Vedantin.

The offense of each worldview picked key themes that were in opposition to the other worldview. It was presented within each framework, with Christianity making strong inroads into the deficiencies of the Vedantin worldview while highlighting the gospel strengths that pertain to the specific issues such as historicity. The Christian worldview then provided a defense to those areas of offense from Vedanta on subjects such as the nature of the personal God and theodicy. These difficult questions were engaged from a position of biblical fidelity augmented by philosophical acuity rather than vice-versa. This brought out the gospel thrust in a comprehensive Christian worldview. These exchanges were reviewed for the honesty and faithfulness of the apologist to maintain the biblical mandate in the encounter.

The Worldview apologetic was then examined through the philosophical lens of metaphysics, epistemology, and ethics. These categories gave a fresh perspective of the strengths of the Worldview apologetic to showcase the problems with Vedanta. The apologetic also compared Vedanta with the errors of philosophical naturalism and Gnosticism, to reuse prior Christian apologetic arguments with Vedanta.

Existential questions facing individuals today were approached in personal apologetics, as an indispensable element of the gospel proclamation. This book attempted an evangelistic apologetic that strove to be faithful to its biblical mandate while engaging and addressing the Vedanta Hindu with a thorough-going Christian worldview. Kierkegaard's spheres of life, leveraged in a gospel framework, personally engaged Vedantins in the broad spectrum of life, from aesthetic and ethical to the religious. In each category the specific problems with placating and obdurate Vedantins were engaged to expose the vulnerability of attempting to live the Vedanta worldview and the necessity of submitting to the gospel.

The Worldview apologetic concluded by highlighting how the entire exercise was centered in the gospel and focused the unbeliever toward the gospel in each engagement. It then went on to identify various aspects of apologetics that can be sharpened in its gospel focus, extending from ethics and logic to bigotry and rigor.

This book made a small step toward filling a gap by providing a Worldview apologetic toward Vedanta using the Reformed framework. It attempted an expansive engagement by laying out the broader framework of the apologetic. This engagement was necessarily limited in drawing out the specifics in greater detail.

Future Research

There are a few vital avenues of research that are incomplete in this book and available for exploration. The most obvious of these is the depth with which Vedanta was engaged. The current work took the broad outlines of Advaita as propounded by its famous expositor, Sankara. Modern Advaitins have more sophisticated positions on specific issues in Advaita. It is helpful to engage with some of today's more popular expositions of Vedanta. On the one hand, one can take on the Visistadvaita of Ramanuja due to its popularity with the Bhakti movement today. Alternatively, one could take on the Advaitin engagement that is popularized by Francis Clooney and Bradley Malkovsky. If exploring specific areas within Advaita, Richard De Smet's works are helpful to delve deeper into Advaita. The challenge here would be to maintain the context of the Worldview apologetic while diving deep into specific areas in Vedanta.[1] These can go down the path of mystical experience or philosophical issues relating to Maya or Atman. It can also respond to Christian attempts at syncretism by showing how biblical theology rejects certain consensuses that have developed in these areas, making it an apologetic against liberal Christianity, rather than Advaita per se.

The second area to explore is the broader mandate of Worldview apologetics. As shown through the stages of proof, offense, and defense, this engagement better represents the worldview conflict and engagement using all the tools available to the Christian apologist. Further work can be done in refining each of these stages further when engaging with any worldview.[2] For example, the offense section can be further broken down into a two-stage approach which takes the charges against the unbelieving worldview purely within that worldview before invoking a broader use of philosophy. It can then make a direct response for the corresponding elements in Christianity. Refining this framework can assist in a clearer presentation of key principles in each worldview.

The third area of improvement is in the domain of philosophy. The metaphysical, epistemological, and ethical evaluations of the worldviews can be broadened further to make them tent-pegs of the Worldview apologetic. This effort can not only sharpen the discourse, but eliminate loose threads early in the engagement as the conversation continues. This is specifically important to further develop in Vedanta where the baseline definitions need reevaluation in light of the radical differences in its philosophical assumptions.

The final area for engagement is probably the one that could use the most attention. This involves taking insights from Kierkegaard for personal apologetics and leveraging the gospel more strongly in Worldview apologetics. While the recommendations were listed already for Worldview apologetics, a broader effort to strengthen all existing methodologies using these tools can help make the task of

---

[1] This article provides a good avenue for further research: Bradley Malkovsky, "Advaita Vedanta and Christian Faith," *Journal of Ecumenical Studies*, 36 (1999).

[2] Nicholas Wolterstorff, *Reason Within the Bounds of Religion* (Grand Rapids: Eerdmans, 1976), 23, 42, 63, 67, 94-96, 102. Each Christian scholar is called "under the control of his authentic commitment to devise theories that lead to promising, interesting, fruitful, challenging lines of research" (ibid., 102). This is valid in scientific research as well as in apologetic study.

apologetics more focused on evangelism and take the apologetic encounters deeper both in the academic domain and in the individual witness to Jesus Christ.

Conclusion

This book hopes to move the Worldview apologetic along the above recommended paths, in order to glorify God and to aid the lost. It hopefully provided an incentive to develop the engagement with Hinduism further and to use a similar approach with other unbelieving worldviews.

APPENDIX
VEDANTA COMPARISON

A high level summary of the teachings of Sankara, Ramanuja, and Madhva:

Sankara
1. Source: Primarily scripture with a unifying system of thought found in his works.
2. Epistemology Maya: Progresses from revelation to reason to intuition, apprehending truth.
3. Living Life: Sorrow comes by clinging to the transient and enlightenment frees one from the suffering.
4. World and Maya: The world represents practical reality, but is the projection and substance of Maya.
5. Atman: This Self is made different from individual ego through Maya.
6. Brahman and God: The Absolute Brahman has no predication while the personal God is highly regarded in the phenomenal world and implied to be secondary.
7. Liberation from samsara: Man is purified through karma and bhakti to attain gynana.

Ramanuja
1. Source: All Vedantin scriptures along with some Tamil scriptures.
2. Epistemology: Perception, inference, and scriptures are valid. Language conveys veridical truth and the self as knower reflexively attains knowledge.
3. Living Life: Devotion is central as is understanding of a qualified Brahman.
4. World and Maya: The world is real and the Advaitin Maya is false. Avidya accounts for ignorance. Prakrti contains the three aspects that Sankara's Maya had. By attaining pure sattva, liberation is attained from the eternal effects of karma.
5. Atman: The Self is atomic, but has infinite existence and attribute consciousness.
6. Brahman and God: The Absolute has predication and is the same as God, relating to the world in the self-body relationship.
7. Liberation from samsara: Bhakti is the primary means of liberation. Meditation helps this effort, but occurs only after death, and the distinctions remain even post-mortem.

Madhva
1. Source: The scripture is considered authorless and the primary source.
2. Epistemology: Knowledge is through perception, inference, and scriptural testimony.
3. Living Life: Devotion is the supreme means of living life.
4. World and Maya: The world is eternal, and there is difference between God, Self, and matter. God's supreme Will rules the world.
5. Atman: There are infinite Selfs and each is different from the rest, operated upon by karma.
6. Brahman and God: The Absolute Brahman is the same as the personally supreme God, who rules the world absolutely and saves or damns selfs eternally in samsara or hell as he wills.
7. Liberation from samsara: Bhakti is vital, ultimately dependent on God's Will. This dependence continues even after liberation and the self is always inferior to God.

BIBLIOGRAPHY

Books

Aiyar, C. P. Ramaswami. *Fundamentals of Hindu Faith and Culture: A Collection of Essays and Addresses.* Madras: Ganesh & Co., 1959.

Albright, W. F. *Archeology, Historical Analogy, and Early Biblical Tradition.* Baton Rouge: Louisiana State University Press: 1966.

_____. *The Bible after Twenty Years of Archeology: 1932-1952.* Pittsburgh: Biblical Colloquium, 1954.

_____. *From the Stone Age to Christianity.* Baltimore: John Hopkins Press, 1940.

Ariarajah, S. Wesley. *Hindus and Christians: A Century of Protestant Ecumenical Thought.* Grand Rapids: William B. Eerdmans Publishing Company, 1991.

Bahnsen, Greg L. *Presuppositional Apologetics: Stated and Defended.* Edited by Joel McDurmon. Nacodoches, TX: American Vision Press, 2008.

_____. *Van Til's Apologetic: Readings and Analysis.* Phillipsburg, NJ: P&R Publishing, 1998.

Baxter, Richard. *The Practical Works of Richard Baxter.* London: James Duncan, 1830.

Beckwith, Francis J., William Lane Craig, and J. P. Moreland. *To Everyone an Answer: A Case for the Christian Worldview.* Downers Grove, IL: IVP, 2004.

Berkouwer, G. C. *Man: The Image of God.* Grand Rapids: Wm. B. Eerdmans Publishing Company, 1962.

The Bhagavad-Gita: Krishna's Counsel in Time of War. Translated by Barbara Stoler Miller. New York: Bantam Books, 1986.

Bielby, James K., ed. *For Faith and Clarity: Philosophical Contributions to Christian Theology.* Grand Rapids: Baker Academic, 2006.

Blackburn, Simon. *Oxford Dictionary of Philosophy.* Oxford: Oxford University Press, 2005.

Blomberg, Craig L. *The Historical Reliability of the Gospels.* 2nd ed. Downers Grove, IL: Apollos, 2007.

Boa, Kenneth D., and Robert M. Bowman, Jr. *Faith Has Its Reasons: Integrative Approaches to Defending the Christian Faith.* Colorado Springs: Paternoster, 2005.

Bretall, Robert. *A Kierkegaard Anthology.* Princeton: Princeton University Press, 1946.

Bruce, F. F. *The Books and the Parchments.* Grand Rapids: Fleming Revell, 1984.

_____. *Jesus and Christian Origins Outside the New Testament.* Grand Rapids: Eerdmans, 1974.

_____. *New Testament Documents: Are They Reliable?* Radford, VA: Wilder Publications, 2009.

_____. *New Testament History.* London: Thomas Nelson, 1969.

Brumley, Mark. *How Not to Share your Faith: The Seven Deadly Sins of Catholic Apologetics and Evangelization.* San Diego: Catholic Answers, 2002.

Campbell-Jack, Walter Campbell, Gavin J. McGrath, and Stephen C. Evans. *New Dictionary of Christian Apologetics.* Downers Grove, IL: IVP, 2004.

Casserley, J. V. Langmead. *Apologetics and Evangelism.* Philadelphia: The Westminster Press, 1962.

Chesterton, Gilbert Keith. *Orthodoxy.* London: John Lane Company, 1909.

Clark, Gordon Haddon. *The Biblical Doctrine of Man.* Jefferson, MD: The Trinity

Foundation, 1992.

Clooney, Francis Xavier. *Hindu God, Christian God: How Reason Helps Break Down the Boundaries between Religions.* New York: Oxford University Press, 2001.

Copan, Paul. *When God Goes to Starbucks: A Guide to Everyday Apologetics.* Grand Rapids: Baker Books, 2008.

Copan, Paul, and William Lane Craig, eds. *Passionate Conviction: Contemporary Discourses on Christian Apologetics.* Nashville: B&H Academic, 2007.

Copleston, Frederick. *A History of Philosophy.* Vol. 6, *Modern Philosophy.* Pt. 2, *Kant.* Garden City, NY: Image Books, 1960.

Countryman, William. *Biblical Authority or Biblical Tyranny? Scripture and the Christian Pilgrimage.* Philadelphia: Fortress Press, 1981.

Coward, Howard, ed. *Hindu-Christian Dialogue: Perspectives and Encounters.* Maryknoll, NY: Orbis Books, 1989.

Craig, William Lane. *Reasonable Faith: Christian Truth and Apologetics.* 3rd ed. Wheaton, IL: Crossway, 2008.

Cupitt, Don. *Mysticism after Modernity.* Malden, MA: Blackwell Publishers, 1998.

Daniel-Rops. *Israel and the Ancient World: A History of the Israelites from the Time of Abraham to the Birth of Christ.* London: Eyre & Spottiswoode, 1949.

Danielou, Alain. *A Brief History of India.* Rochester, VT: Inner Traditions, 2003.

Dawkins, Richard. *The God Delusion.* Boston: Houghton Mifflin Company, 2006.

Dembski, William A., and Michael R. Licona, eds. *Evidence for God: 50 Arguments for Faith from the Bible, History, Philosophy, and Science.* Grand Rapids: Baker Books, 2010.

Dembski, William A., and Jay Wesley Richards, eds. *Unapologetic Apologetics: Meeting the Challenges of Theological Studies.* Downers Grove, IL: InterVarsity Press, 2001.

Dembski, William A., and Thomas Schirrmacher, eds. *Tough-Minded Christianity: Honoring the Legacy of John Warwick Montgomery.* Nashville: B&H Academic, 2008.

Deutsch, Eliot, and Ron Bontekoe, eds. *A Companion to World Philosophies.* Malden, MA: Blackwell Publishers, 1997.

Devanandan, Paul David. *The Concept of Māyā: An Essay in Historical Survey of the Hindu Theory of the World, with Special Reference to the Vedanta.* London: Lutterworth Press, 1950.

Dulles, Avery. *A History of Apologetics.* San Francisco: Ignatius Press, 1999.

Edgar, William. *Reasons of the Heart: Recovering Christian Persuasion.* Grand Rapids: Baker Book House, 1997.

Edgar, William, and K. Scott Oliphint. *Christian Apologetics Past & Present: A Primary Source Reader.* Vol. 1. Wheaton, IL: Crossway, 2009.

Evans, Stephen C. *Kierkegaard: An Introduction.* Cambridge: Cambridge University Press, 2009.

————. *Philosophy of Religion: Thinking about Faith.* Downers Grove, IL: InterVarsity Press, 1985.

————. *Pocket Dictionary of Apologetics & Philosophy of Religion.* Downers Grove, IL: IVP, 2002.

Feinberg, John S. *No One Like Him: The Doctrine of God.* Wheaton, IL: Crossway

Books, 2001.

Feldmeier, Peter. *Encounters in Faith: Christianity in Interreligious Dialogue.* Winona, MN: Anselm Academic, 2011.

Finegan, Jack. *Light from the Ancient Past: The Archeological Background of the Hebrew-Christian Religion.* Princeton: Princeton University Press, 1951.

Frame, John M. *Apologetics for the Glory of God: An Introduction.* Phillipsburg, NJ: P&R Publishing, 1994.

_____. *Cornelius Van Til: An Analysis of His Thought.* Phillipsburg, NJ: P&R Publishing, 1995.

_____. *The Doctrine of God.* Phillipsburg, NJ: P&R Publishing, 2002.

_____. *The Doctrine of the Knowledge of God.* Phillipsburg, New Jersey: P&R Publishing, 1987.

_____. *Salvation Belongs to the Lord: An Introduction to Systematic Theology.* Phillipsburg, NJ: P&R Publishing, 2006.

Geisler, Norman. *Baker Encyclopedia of Christian Apologetics.* Grand Rapids: Baker Books, 1999.

Geisler, Norman, and William C. Roach. *Defending Inerrancy: Affirming the Accuracy of Scripture for a New Generation.* Grand Rapids: Baker Books, 2011.

Geisler, Norman, and Patrick Zukeran. *The Apologetics of Jesus: A Caring Approach to Dealing with Doubters.* Grand Rapids: Baker Books, 2009.

Goel, Sita Ram. *History of Hindu-Christian Encounters.* New Delhi: Voice of India, 1989.

Goldberg, Philip. *American Veda: From Emerson and the Beatles to Yoga and Meditation – How Indian Spirituality Changed the West.* New York: Harmony Books, 2010.

Gordon, Cyrus H., and Gary A. Rendsburg. *The Bible and the Ancient Near East.* New York: W. W. Norton & Company, 1997.

Grant, Michael. *Jesus: An Historian's Review of the Gospels.* New York: Macmillan, 1977.

Grant, Sara. *Sankaracarya's Concept of Relation.* Delhi: Motilal Banarsidass, 1999.

_____. *Towards an Alternative Theology: Confessions of a Non-Dualist Christian.* Bangalore, India: Asian Trading Corporation, 1987.

Green, Ronald M. *Kierkegaard and Kant – The Hidden Debt.* Albany: State University of New York, 1992.

Griffiths, Bede. *Vedanta and Christian Faith.* Los Angeles: The Dawn Horse Press, 1973.

Gupta, Mahendranath. *The Gospel of Sri Ramakrishna.* Translated by Swami Nikhilananda. New York: Ramakrishna-Vivekananda Center, 1942.

Habermas, Gary R. *The Historical Jesus: Ancient Evidence for the Life of Christ.* Joplin, MO: College Press, 1996.

Hall, David R. *The Seven Pillories of Wisdom.* Macon, GA: Mercer University Press, 1990.

Helm, Paul. *Faith and Understanding.* Grand Rapids: Eerdmans Publishing Company, 1997.

Hiriyanna, M. *Outlines of Indian Philosophy.* Delhi: Motilal Banarsidass Publishers, 2009.

Hoffecker, Andrew, ed. *Revolutions in Worldview*. Phillipsburg, NJ: P&R Publishing Company, 2007.

Hogg, Alfred George. *The Christian Message to the Hindu: Being the Duff Missionary Lectures For Nineteen Forty Five on the Challenge of the Gospel in India*. London: S.C.M. Press, 1947.

Holmes, Arthur F. *Contours of a World View*. Grand Rapids: Eerdmans Publishing Company, 1985.

Hooker, R. H. *Themes in Hinduism and Christianity: A Comparative Study*. Frankfurt: Verlag Peter Lang, 1989.

House, Wayne H., and Joseph M. Holden. *Charts of Apologetics and Christian Evidences*. Grand Rapids: Zondervan, 2006.

Joshi, P. V. *Introduction to Sankara's Advaitism*, Delhi: Motilal Banarsidass Publishers, 2006.

Kierkegaard, Soren. *Eighteen Upbuilding Discourses*. Edited and translated by Howard V. Hong and Edna H. Hong. Princeton: Princeton University Press, 1990.

_____. *Either/Or Part I*. Edited and translated by Howard V. Hong and Edna H. Hong. Princeton: Princeton University Press, 1991.

_____. *Either/Or Part II*. Edited and translated by Howard V. Hong and Edna H. Hong. Princeton: Princeton University Press, 1991.

_____. *Fear and Trembling and Repetition*. Edited and translated by Howard V. Hong and Edna H. Hong. Princeton: Princeton University Press, 1991.

_____. *For Self-Examination and Judge for Yourself*. Edited and translated by Howard V. Hong and Edna H. Hong. Princeton: Princeton University Press, 1990.

_____. *The Humor of Kierkegaard: An Anthology*. Edited by Thomas C. Oden. Princeton: Princeton University Press, 2004.

_____. *Stages on Life's Way*. Edited and translated by Howard V. Hong and Edna H. Hong. Princeton: Princeton University Press, 1988.

K. A. Kitchen. *Ancient Orient and Old Testament*. London: Tyndale Press, 1966.

_____. *The Bible in Its World: The Bible and Archaeology Today*. Eugene, OR: Wipf & Stock Publishers, 2004.

_____. *On the Reliability of the Old Testament*. Grand Rapids: Wm. B. Eerdmans Publishing Company, 2006.

Lewis, C. S. *The Abolition of Man*. New York: HarperCollins, 2001.

The Life of Swami Vivekananda by His Eastern and Western Disciples. Calcutta: Advaita Ashrama, 1955.

Lipner, Julius. *The Face of Truth: A Study of Meaning and Metaphysics in the Vedantic Theology of Ramanuja*. Albany: State University of New York Press, 1986.

_____, ed. *Truth, Religious Dialogue, and Dynamic Orthodoxy: Reflections on the Works of Brian Hebblethwaite*. London: SCM Press, 2005.

Little, Bruce A., and Mark D. Liederbach, eds. *Defending the Faith: Engaging the Culture*. Nashville: B&H Publishing Group, 2011.

Lott, Eric. *Vedantic Approaches to God*. New York: Barnes & Noble Books, 1980.

Malkovsky, Bradley J., ed. *New Perspectives on Advaita Vedanta: Essays in Commemoration of Professor Richard De Smet*. Boston: Brill, 2000.

_____. *The Role of Divine Grace in the Soteriology of Śankarācārya*. Boston: Brill, 2001.

Markham, Ian S. *Against Atheism: Why Dawkins, Hitchens, and Harris are Fundamentally Wrong.* Malden, MA: Wiley-Blackwell, 2010.

Markos, Louis. *Apologetics for the Twenty-First Century.* Wheaton, IL: Crossway, 2010.

McDowell, Josh. *The New Evidence that Demands a Verdict: Evidence I & II Fully Updated in One Volume to Answer Questions Challenging Christians in the 21st Century.* Nashville: Thomas Nelson Publishers, 1999.

McGrath, Alister E. *Intellectuals Don't Need God & Other Modern Myths: Building Bridges to Faith through Apologetics.* Grand Rapids: Zondervan Publishing House, 1993.

McIntosh, Mark A. *Mystical Theology.* Malden, MA: Blackwell Publishers, 1998.

McRay, John. *Archeology and the New Testament.* Grand Rapids: Baker Book House, 1991.

Meister, Chad V. *Building Belief: Constructing Faith from the Ground Up.* Grand Rapids: Baker Books, 2006.

Moreland, J. P. *The God Question: An Invitation to a Life of Meaning.* Eugene, OR: Harvest House Publishers, 2009.

Moreland, J. P., and William Lane Craig. *Philosophical Foundations of a Christian Worldview.* Downers Grove: IL, InterVarsity, 2003.

Morris, Thomas V. *Our Idea of God: An Introduction to Philosophical Theology.* Downers Grove, IL: InterVarsity Press, 1991.

Murty, K. Satchidananda. *Revelation and Reason in Advaita Vedānta.* Grand Rapids: Eerdmans, 1959.

Nash, Ronald H. *Faith and Reason: Searching for a Rational Faith.* Grand Rapids: Zondervan, 1988.

_____. *Life's Ultimate Questions: An Introduction to Philosophy.* Grand Rapids: Zondervan, 1999.

Naugle, David K. *Worldview: The History of a Concept.* Grand Rapids: Eerdmans, 2002.

Netland, Harold A. *Dissonant Voices: Religious Pluralism and the Question of Truth.* Grand Rapids: Eerdmans, 1991.

_____. *Encountering Religious Pluralism: The Challenge to Christian Faith & Mission.* Downers Grove, IL: Intervarsity Press, 2001.

Newbigin, Lesslie. *Truth to Tell: The Gospel as Public Truth.* Geneva: Eerdmans, 1991.

Nicholson, Hugh. *Comparative Theology and the Problem of Religious Rivalry.* Oxford: Oxford University Press, 2011.

Oliphint, K. Scott. *The Battle Belongs to the Lord: The Power of Scripture for Defending Our Faith.* Phillipsburg, NJ: P&R Publishing, 2003.

Olivelle, Patrick. *The Early Upanisads: Annotated Text and Translation.* Oxford: Oxford University Press, 1998.

Origen. *Origen On Prayer* [on-line]. Accessed 27 January 2013. Available from http://www.ccel.org/ccel/origen/prayer.v.html; Internet.

Padgett, Alan G., and Patrick R. Keifert, eds. *But is it All True? The Bible and the Question of Truth.* Grand Rapids: William B. Eerdmans Publishing Company, 2006.

Palmer, Donald D. *Kierkegaard for Beginners.* New York: Writers and Readers Publishing, 1996.

Parthasarathy, Indira. *Ramanujar: The Life and Ideas of Ramanuja.* Translated by T. Sriraman. New Delhi: Oxford University Press, 2008.

Pearcey, Nancy. *Total Truth: Liberating Christianity from Its Cultural Captivity.* Wheaton, IL: Crossway, 2004.

Phillips, Richard, ed. *Only One Way? Reaffirming the Exclusive Truth Claims of Christianity.* Wheaton, IL: Crossway Books, 2006.

Plantinga, Alvin. *Warranted Christian Belief.* New York: Oxford University Press, 2000.

Plantinga, Alvin, and Michael Tooley. *Knowledge of God.* Malden, MA: Blackwell Publishing, 2008.

Pojman, Louis. *Kierkegaard's Philosophy of Religion.* San Francisco: International Scholars Publications, 1999.

Potter, Karl H. *Presuppositions of India's Philosophies.* Englewood Cliffs, NJ: Prentice-Hall, 1963.

Price, Randall. *The Stones Cry Out: What Archeology Reveals About the Truth of the Bible.* Eugene, OR: Harvest House Publishers, 1997.

The Proceedings of the Conference on Biblical Inerrancy 1987. Nashville: Broadman Press, 1987.

Radhakrishnan, S., and Charles E. Moore, eds. *A Source Book in Indian Philosophy.* Princeton: Princeton University Press, 1957.

Raju, P.T. *The Philosophical Traditions of India.* London: George Allen & Unwin, 1971.
_____. *Structural Depths of Indian Thought.* Albany: State University of New York Press, 1985.

Ramm, Bernard. *Varieties of Christian Apologetics.* Grand Rapids: Baker Book House, 1982.

Ramsay, Richard B. *The Certainty of the Faith: Apologetics in an Uncertain World.* Phillipsburg, NJ: P&R Publishing, 2007.

Reid, J. K. S. *Christian Apologetics.* London: Hodder and Stoughton, 1969.

Robinson, John A. T. *Can We Trust the New Testament?* Grand Rapids: Eerdmans, 1977.

Sankaracharya. *A Thousand Teachings: In Two Parts: Prose and Poetry of Sri Sankaracharya.* Edited and translated by Swami Jagadananda. Madras: Sri Ramakrishna Math, 1949.

Schaeffer, Francis A. *The Francis A. Schaeffer Trilogy: The Three Essential Books in One Volume.* Westchester, IL: Crossway Books, 1990.

Sharma, Chandradhar. *A Critical Survey of Indian Philosophy.* London: Rider & Company, 1960.

Sherwin-White, A. N. *Roman Society and Roman Law in the New Testament.* Oxford: Clarendon Press, 1963.

Shestov, Lev. *Kierkegaard and the Existential Philosophy.* Translated by Elinor Hewitt. Athens: Ohio University Press, 1969.

Sheveland, John N. *Piety and Responsibility: Patterns of Unity in Karl Rahner, Karl Barth, and Vedanta Desika.* Burlington, VT: Ashgate, 2011.

Sinari, Ramakant A. *The Structure of Indian Thought.* Springfield, IL: C. Thomas Publisher, 1970.

Sire, James W. *A Little Primer on Humble Apologetics.* Downers Grove, IL: IVP Books, 2006.
_____. *The Universe Next Door: A Basic Worldview Catalog.* 4th ed. Downers Grove, IL: InterVarsity Press, 2004.

Sproul, R. C. *Defending Your Faith: An Introduction to Apologetics.* Wheaton, IL:

Crossway Books, 2003.

Sproul, R. C., John Gerstner, and Arthur Lindsley. *Classical Apologetics: A Rational Defense of the Christian Faith and a Critique of Presuppositional Apologetics.* Grand Rapids: Zondervan Publishing House, 1984.

Stackhouse, John G., Jr. *Humble Apologetics: Defending the Faith Today.* New York: Oxford University Press, 2002.

Stark, Rodney. *For the Glory of the God.* Princeton: Princeton University Press, 2003.

Stewart, Robert B., ed. *The Reliability of the New Testament: Bart D. Ehrman and Daniel B. Wallace in Dialogue.* Minneapolis: Fortress, 2011.

_____. *The Resurrection of Jesus: John Dominic Crossan and N. T. Wright in Dialogue.* Minneapolis: Fortress, 2006.

Strobel, Lee. *The Case for Christ: A Journalist's Personal Investigation of the Evidence for Jesus.* Grand Rapids: Zondervan, 1998.

Taliaferro, Charles. *Contemporary Philosophy of Religion.* Malden, MA: Blackwell Publishers, 2009.

Taylor, James E. *Introducing Apologetics: Cultivating Christian Commitment.* Grand Rapids: Baker Academic, 2006.

Thatamanil, John J. *The Immanent Divine: God, Creation, and the Human Predicament – An East-West Conversation.* Minneapolis: Fortress Press, 2006.

Thomas, I. D. E. *The Golden Treasury of Puritan Quotations.* Simpsonville, SC: Christian Classics Foundation, 1999.

Thornton, Bruce S. *Plagues of the Mind: The New Epistemic of False Knowledge.* Wilmingdon, DE: ISI Books, 2004.

Unger, Merrill R. *Archaeology and the Old Testament.* Grand Rapids: Zondervan Publishing, 1954.

Upanisads. Translated by Patrick Olivelle. Oxford: Oxford University Press, 1996.

Van Til, Cornelius. *A Christian Theory of Knowledge.* Philadelphia: Westminster Theological Seminary, 1975.

_____. *Christianity and Idealism.* Philadelphia: Westminster Theological Seminary, 1955.

_____. *The Defense of the Faith.* Phillipsburg, NJ: Presbyterian and Reformed Publishing Company, 1967.

_____. *The Intellectual Challenge of the Gospel.* Phillipsburg, NJ: Lewis J. Grotenhuis, 1953.

Vardy, Peter. *An Introduction to Kierkegaard.* Peabody, MA: Hendrickson Publishers, 2008.

Vivekananda, Swami. *The Complete Works of Swami Vivekananda.* Madras: Vedanta Press, 1947 [on-line]. Accessed 27 January 2013. Available from http://en.wikisource.org/wiki/The_Complete_Works_of_Swami_Vivekananda/Volume_4/Lectures_and_Discourses/Thoughts_on_the_Gita; Internet.

Walshe, Thomas Joseph. *The Principles of Christian Apologetics: An Exposition of the Intellectual Basis of the Christian Religion, Specially Written for Senior Students.* New York: Longmans, Green and Co., 1919.

Watts, Robert. *The New Apologetic or, The Down-grade in Criticism, Theology, and Science.* Edinburgh: T. & T. Clark, 1890.

Wolterstorff, Nicholas. *Reason Within the Bounds of Religion.* Grand Rapids: Eerdmans,

1976.

Wright, G.E. *The Bible and the Ancient Near East.* New York: Doubleday, 1961.
_____. *Biblical Archeology.* Philadelphia: Westminster Press, 1957.
Wright, N. T. *The Resurrection of the Son of God.* Minneapolis: Fortress Press, 2003.
Zaehner, R. C., ed. *Hindu Scriptures.* New York: Everyman's Library, 1972.
_____. *Hinduism.* Oxford: Oxford University Press, 1962.

Articles

Albright, W. F. "Archeology Confronts Biblical Criticism." *American Scholar* 7 (1938): 176-88.

Alston, Anthony J. "Samkara in East and West Today." In *New Perspectives on Advaita Vedanta: Essays in Commemoration of Professor Richard De Smet*, edited by Bradley J. Malkovsky, 84-108. Boston: Brill, 2000.

Alston, William. "Psychoanalytic Theory and Theistic Belief." In *Philosophy of Religion: An Anthology*, edited by Charles Taliaferro and Paul J. Griffiths, 123-40. Malden, MA: Blackwell Publishing, 2003.

Anthony, Francis-Vincent, Chris A. M. Hermans, and Carl Sterkens. "A Comparative Study of Mystical Experience among Christian, Muslim, and Hindu Students in Tamil Nadu, India." *Journal for the Scientific Study of Religion* 49 (2010): 264-77.

Avery, Dulles. "Mere Apologetics." *The Institute on Religion and Public Life* May (2004): 15-20.

Bauman, Whitney. "The Problem of a Transcendent God for the Well-Being of Continuous Creation." *A Journal of Theology* 46, no. 2 (2007): 120-27.

Bradatan, Costica. "Rhetoric of Faith and Patterns of Persuasion in Berkeley's Alciphron." *The Heythrop Journal* 47, no. 4 (2006): 544-61.

Buckley, James J. "Roger Haight's Mediating Christology." *Modern Theology* 23, no. 1 (2007): 108-11.

Bush, L. Russ. "Christ in the New Age." In *Passionate Conviction: Contemporary Discourses on Christian Apologetics*, edited by Paul Copan and William Lane Craig, 170-86. Nashville: B&H Academic, 2007.

Bussey, Peter J. "Physical Infinities: A Substitute for God?" *Science & Christian Belief* 18, no. 2 (2006): 133–50.

Chakrabarti, Arindam. "Rationality in Indian Philosophy." In *A Companion to World Philosophies*, edited by Eliot Deutsch and Ron Bontekoe, 259-78. Malden, MA: Blackwell Publishers, 1997.

Chatterjee, Amita. "Truth in Indian Philosophy." In *A Companion to World Philosophies*, edited by Eliot Deutsch and Ron Bontekoe, 334-48. Malden, MA: Blackwell Publishers, 1997.

Christian, Rose Anne. "Plantinga, Epistemic Permissiveness, and Metaphysical Pluralism." *Religious Studies* 28, no. 4 (1992): 568-69. Quoted in James Beilby, "Plantinga's Model of Warranted Christian Belief." In *Alvin Plantinga*, edited by Deane-Peter Baker, 125-65. Cambridge: Cambridge University Press, 2007.

"Christian Witness in a Multi-Religious World: Recommendations for Conduct: World Council of Churches Pontifical Council for Interreligious Dialogue World." *International Bulletin of Missionary Research* 35, no. 4 (2011): 194-96.

Clooney, Francis X. "Samkara's Theological Realism: The Meaning and Usefulness of

Gods (Devata) in the Uttara Mimamsa Sutra Bhasya." In *New Perspectives on Advaita Vedanta: Essays in Commemoration of Professor Richard De Smet*, edited by Bradley J. Malkovsky, 30-50. Boston: Brill, 2000.

_____. "Why the Veda has no Author: Language as Ritual in Early Mimamsa and Post-Modern Theology." *Journal of the American Academy of Religion* 55, no. 4 (1987): 659-84.

Coates, John. "Chesterton's New Style in Apologetics." *Renascence* (2003): 235-51.

Corduan, Winfried. "Corduan On Sudduth" [on-line]. Accessed 29 March 2013. Available from http://triablogue.blogspot.com/2012/01/corduan-on-sudduth.html; Internet.

_____. "Eastern Religions: Hinduism: Empty Diversion." *Areopagus Journal* May-June (2009): 13.

Cowan, Steven B. "Introduction." In *Five views on Apologetics*, edited by Stanley N. Gundry and Steven B. Cowan, 7-20. Grand Rapids: Zondervan, 2000.

Coward, Howard. "The Experience of Scripture in Hinduism and Christianity." In *Hindu-Christian Dialogue: Perspectives and Encounters*, edited by Howard Coward, 247. Maryknoll, NY: Orbis Books, 1989.

De Nys, Martin J. "Faith, Self-Transcendence, and Reflection." *International Journal for Philosophy of Religion* 51, no. 2 (2002): 121-38.

Deutsch, Eliot S. "Karma as a 'Convenient Fiction' in the Advaita Vedānta." *Philosophy East and West* 15, no. 1 (1965): 3-12.

Duquette, Jonathan, and K. Ramasubramanian. "Is Space Created? Reflections on Sankara's Philosophy and Philosophy of Physics." *Philosophy East & West* 60, no. 4 (2010): 517-33.

Fost, Frederick F. "Playful Illusions: The Making of Worlds in Advaita Vedanta." *Philosophy East and West* 48, no. 3 (1998): 387-405.

Foster, Paul. "Who Wrote 2 Thessalonians? A Fresh Look at an Old Problem." *Journal for the Study of the New Testament* 35 (2012): 150-75.

Frame, John M. "Presuppositional Apologetics." In *Five views on Apologetics*, edited by Stanley N. Gundry and Steven B. Cowan, 207-64. Grand Rapids: Zondervan, 2000.

Fremstedal, Roe. "Kierkegaard's Double Movement of Faith and Kant's Moral Faith." *Religious Studies* 48, no. 2 (2012): 199-220.

Furman, Todd M. "In Praise of Hume: What's Right About Hume's Attacks on Natural Theology." In *Defense of Natural Theology: A Post-Humean Asessment*, edited by James F. Sennett and Douglas Groothuis, 42-57. Downers Grove, IL: InterVarsity Press, 2005.

Geisler, Norman L. "An Apologetic for Apologetics." In *Defending the Faith: Engaging the Culture*, edited by Bruce A. Little and Mark D. Liederbach, 78-81. Nashville: B&H Publishing Group, 2011.

Gerhard, Matthew. "Kierkegaard on Truth." *Religious Studies* 38 (2002): 27-44.

Grant, Colin. "Why Should Theology Be Unnatural?" *Modern Theology* 23, no. 1 (2007): 91-106.

Grant, Sara. "Contemporary Relevance of Advaita." In *New Perspectives on Advaita Vedanta: Essays in Commemoration of Professor Richard De Smet*, edited by Bradley J. Malkovsky, 148-64. Boston: Brill, 2000.

Grass, Tim. "Scripture Alone: Is the Bible All We Need?" *Evangel* 25, no. 3 (2007): 66-

68.

Harrison, Peter. "The Bible and the Emergence of Modern Science." *Science & Christian Belief* 18, no. 2 (2006): 115-32.

Hartley, Donald E. "Essential Doctrines: The Implications of the Fall: Romans 5:12." *Areopagus Journal* March-April (2009): 16.

Hinkley, Aaron E. "Kierkegaard's Ethics of Agape, the Secularization of the Public Square, and Bioethics." *Christian Bioethics* 17, no. 1 (2011): 54-63.

Hookway, Christopher. "Reasons for Belief, Reasoning, Virtues." *Philosophical Studies* 130, no. 1 (2006): 47-70.

Horton, Michael S. "Consistently Reformed: The Inheritance and Legacy of Van Til's Apologetic." In *Revelation and Reason: New Essays in Reformed Apologetics*, edited by K. Scott Oliphint and Lane G. Tipton, 131-48. Phillipsburg, NJ: P&R Publishing, 2007.

Jeffner, Anders. "Truth and Religious Dialogue." In *Truth, Religious Dialogue, and Dynamic Orthodoxy: Reflections on the Works of Brian Hebblethwaite*, edited by Julius J. Lipner, 50. London: SCM Press, 2005.

Kandiah, Krish. "Lesslie Newbigin's Contribution to a Theology of Evangelism." *Transformation* 24, no. 1 (2007): 51-60.

Kaplan, Stephen. "Three Levels of Evil in Advaita Vedanta and a Holographic Analogy." In *A Companion to World Philosophies*, edited by Eliot Deutsch and Ron Bontekoe, 116-29. Malden, MA: Blackwell Publishers, 1997.

Kaufmann, Walter. "Kierkegaard." *Theology Today* 67 (2010): 182-211.

Kelly, Benjamin. "Deviant Ancient Histories: Dan Brown, Erich von Daniken and the Sociology of Historical Polemic." *Rethinking History* 12, no. 3 (2008): 361–82.

Klein, Terrance W. "Act and Potency in Wittgenstein?" *The Heythrop Journal* 47, no. 4 (2006): 601-19.

Lillegard, Norman. "Passion and Reason: Aristotelian Strategies in Kierkegaard's Ethics." *Journal of Religious Ethics* 30, no. 2 (2002): 251-73.

Loncar, Samuel. "From Jena to Copenhagen: Kierkegaard's Relations to German Idealism and the Critique of Autonomy in The Sickness Unto Death." *Religious Studies* 47 (2011): 201-16.

Mahn, Jason A. "Kierkegaard After Hauerwas." *Theology Today* 64 (2007): 172-85.

Malesic, Jonathan. "A Secret Both Sinister and Salvific: Secrecy and Normativity in Light of Kierkegaard's Fear and Trembling." *Journal of the American Academy of Religion* 74 (2006): 446-68.

Malkovsky, Bradley. "Advaita Vedanta and Christian Faith." *Journal of Ecumenical Studies* 36, nos. 3-4 (1999): 397-422.

_____. "Samkara on Divine Grace." In *New Perspectives on Advaita Vedanta: Essays in Commemoration of Professor Richard De Smet*, edited by Bradley J. Malkovsky, 70-83. Boston: Brill, 2000.

Manis, Zachary R. "Kierkegaard and Evans on the Problem of Abraham." *Journal of Religious Ethics* 39, no. 3 (2011): 474-92.

Marks, Tamara Monet. "Kierkegaard's 'New Argument' for Immortality." *Journal for Religious Ethics* 38, no. 1 (2010): 143-86.

Marshall, I. Howard. "Raised for Our Justification." In *Tough-Minded Christianity: Honoring the Legacy of John Warwick Montgomery*, edited by William Dembski and Thomas Schirrmacher, 245. Nashville: B&H Academic, 2008.

Mavrodes, George I. "Jerusalem and Athens Revisited." In *Faith and Rationality: Reason and Belief in God*, edited by Alvin Plantinga and Nicholas Wolterstorff, 192-218. Notre Dame, IN: University of Notre Dame Press, 1983.

McCreary, Mark L. "Deceptive Love: Kierkegaard on Mystification and Deceiving into the Truth." *Journal of Religious Ethics* 39, no. 1 (2011): 25-47.

McGrath, Alister. "Paley Memorial Sermon." *Science & Christian Belief* 18, no. 2 (2006): 181-87.

Mei, Todd S. "Heidegger and the Appropriation of Metaphysics." *The Heythrop Journal* 50 (2009): 257–70.

Merino, Stephen M. "Religious Diversity in a 'Christian Nation:' The Effects of Theological Exclusivity and Interreligious Contact on the Acceptance of Religious Diversity." *Journal for the Scientific Study of Religion* 49 (2010): 234-35.

Metzger, Bruce M. "Trends in the Textual Criticism of the Illiad, the Mahabharata, and the New Testament." *Journal of Biblical Literature* 65 (1946): 339-52.

Moeller, E. Wilhelm. "God and the Creation." In *History of the Christian Church*. Vol. 2, *Ante-Nicene Christianity A.D. 100-325*. Edited by Philip Schaff. Grand Rapids: B. Eerdmans Publishing, 1994 [on-line]. Accessed 10 January 2013. Available from http://www.ccel.org/ccel/schaff/hcc2.v.xiv.vi.html; http://www.ccel.org/ccel/schaff/hcc2.v.xiii.vi.html; Internet.

Mohanty, J. N. "A History of Indian Philosophy." In *A Companion to World Philosophies*, edited by Eliot Deutsch and Ron Bontekoe, 24-48. Malden, MA: Blackwell Publishers, 1997.

_____. "The Idea of the Good in Indian Thought." In *A Companion to World Philosophies*, edited by Eliot Deutsch and Ron Bontekoe, 290-303. Malden, MA: Blackwell Publishers, 1997.

Moser, Paul K. "Reorienting Religious Epistemology: Cognitive Grace, Filial Knowledge, and Gethsemane Struggle." In *For Faith and Clarity: Philosophical Contributions to Christian Theology*, edited by James K. Bielby, 75-81. Grand Rapids: Baker Academic, 2006.

Nicholson, Hugh. "Two Apologetic Moments in Sankara's Concept of Brahman." *The Journal of Religion* 87, no. 4 (2007): 528-54.

Oliphint, K. Scott. "Cornelius Van Til and the Reformation of Christian Apologetics." In *Revelation and Reason: New Essays in Reformed Apologetics*, edited by K. Scott Oliphint and Lane G. Tipton, 279-304. Phillipsburg, NJ: P&R Publishing, 2007.

Oviedo, Lluis. "Is Christian Theology Well Suited to Enter the Discussion between Science and Humanism?" *Zygon Journal of Religion and Science* 41, no. 4 (2006): 825-68.

Owens, David. "Testimony and Assertion." *Philosophical Studies* 130, no. 1 (2006): 105-29.

Payne, Michael W. "Philosophy among the Ruins: The Twentieth Century and Beyond." In *Revolutions in Worldview*, edited by Andrew Hoffecker, 318-35. Phillipsburg, NJ: P&R Publishing, 2007.

Peters, Ted. "Christian God-Talk While Listening to Atheists, Pluralists, and Muslims." *A Journal of Theology* 46, no. 2 (2007): 84-98.

Podmore, Simon D. "Kierkegaard as Physician of the Soul: On Self-Forgiveness and

Despair." *Journal of Psychology and Theology* 37, no. 3 (2009): 174-85.

_____. "The Lightning and the Earthquake: Kierkegaard on the Anfechtung of Luther." *The Heythrop Journal* 47, no. 4 (2006): 562-78.

Polkinghorne, John. "Where is Natural Theology Today?" *Science & Christian Belief* 18, no. 2 (2006): 169-79.

Poythress, Vern Sheridan. "Why Scientists Must Believe in God." *Journal of the Evangelical Society* 46 (2003) [on-line]. Accessed 27 January 2013. Available from http://www.frame-poythress.org/why-scientists-must-believe-in-god/; Internet.

Rae, Murray A. "Kierkegaard and the Historians." *International Journal for Philosophy of Religion* 37, no. 2 (1995): 87-102.

Reid, Louis Arnaud. "Correspondence and Coherence." *The Philosophical Review* 31, no. 1 (1922): 18-40.

Richie, Tony. "Hints from Heaven: Can C. S. Lewis Help Evangelicals Hear God in Other Religions?" *Evangelical Review of Theology* 32, no. 1 (2008): 38-55.

Saraswathi, T. S. "Hindu Worldview in the Development of Selfways: The 'Atman' as the Real Self." *New Directions for Child & Adolescent Development* 109 (2005): 43-50.

Satyaputra, Agus Gunawan. "The Problem of Objectivity in History and the Use of Historical Evidence in Christian Apologetic." *Evangel* 25, no. 3 (2007): 11-24.

Srivastava, Kalpana. "Human Nature: Indian Perspective Revisited." *Industrial Psychiatry* 19, no. 2 (2010): 77-81.

Stan, Leo. "A Reconsideration of Kierkegaard's Understanding of the Human Other: The Hidden Ethics of Soteriology." *Journal of Religious Ethics* 38, no. 2 (2010): 349-70.

Stoker, Valerie. "Conceiving the Canon in Dvaita Vedānta: Madhva's Doctrine of 'All Sacred Lore.'" *Numen* 51, no. 1 (2004): 47-44.

Sudduth, Michael. "Reformed Epistemology and Christian Apologetics." *Religious Studies* 39 (2003): 299-321.

Taylor, Mark C. "Natural Selfhood and Ethical Selfhood in Kierkegaard." In *Kierkegaard*, edited by Harold Bloom, 224-29. New York: Chelsea House Publishers, 1989.

Tucker, Travis. "Kierkegaard's Purity of Heart and the 'Sunday-Monday' Gap." *Theology Today* 67 (2010): 24-35.

Turnbull, Jamie. "Kierkegaard on Emotion: A Critique of Furtak's *Wisdom in Love.*" *Religious Studies* 46 (2010): 489-508.

Van den Toren, Benno. "Challenges and Possibilities of Inter-religious and Cross-cultural Apologetic Persuasion." *Evangelical Quarterly* 82, no. 1 (2010): 61-62.

Wade, Rick. "The History of Apologetics: Four 20th-Century Apologists: E. J. Carnell, Cornelius Van Til, Gordon Clark, Norman Geisler." *Areopagus Journal* (January-February 2008): 29-30.

Walton, Steve. "The Acts – of God? What is the 'Acts of the Apostles' All About?" *Evangelical Quarterly* 80, no. 4 (2008): 291–306.

Wright, G. E. "Archeology and Old Testament Studies." *Journal of Biblical Literature* 77 (1958): 39-51.

Williams, Travis B. "Suffering from a Critical Oversight: The Persecutions of 1 Peter within Modern Scholarship." *Currents in Biblical Research* 10, no. 2 (2012): 275-292.

Wilson, Jonathan R. "Stanley J. Grenz: Generous Faith and Faithful Engagement." *Modern Theology* 23, no. 1 (2007): 113-21.

Dissertation

Sims, Bryan Billard. "Evangelical Worldview Analysis: A Critical Assessment and Proposal." Ph.D. diss., Southern Baptist Theological Seminary, 2006.

Made in the USA
Middletown, DE
22 October 2023

41223117R00091